FORENSIC DETECTIVE

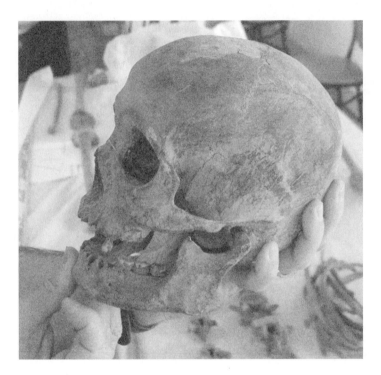

FORENSIC DETECTIVE

How I Cracked the World's Toughest Cases

ROBERT MANN, PH.D.,
AND MIRYAM EHRLICH WILLIAMSON

BALLANTINE BOOKS NEW YORK

Published in the United States by Ballantine Books, an imprint of The Random House
Publishing Group, a division of Random House, Inc., New York.

BALLANTINE and colophon are registered trademarks of Random House, Inc.

Frontispiece photo: Photo by Ken Dunn
Chapter opening photo: Courtesy of Bob Mann
ISBN 0-345-47941-6

Printed in the United States of America

Book design by Simon M. Sullivan

This book is dedicated to Drs. Bill Bass and Doug Owsley,
who lit the fuse for me.

—R.W.M.

CONTENTS

FOREWORD

HENRY LEE, PH.D.

Forensic Detective is a fascinating look at cases in forensic anthropology covering the twenty-year career of Dr. Robert Mann. Mann studied and honed his skills under the world-renowned forensic anthropologist Dr. William Bass at the University of Tennessee. Upon completion of his master's degree in anthropology and nearly a year at the Memphis morgue, he worked at the Smithsonian Institution and later at the Department of Defense's Central Identification Laboratory in Hawaii, where he is deputy scientific director. Mann is a true forensic scientist. He has spent thousands of hours in the laboratory analyzing human remains and developing techniques and national standards for human identification. He also has devoted much of his time to working in the field. He has assisted many law enforcement agencies around the world in the recovery and identification of human remains. Mann also leads search-and-recovery missions to some of the most dangerous and remote places in the world. In his own words and through his own eyes, he walks us through the mountains and jungles and takes us through the rivers and deltas. Along the way, he tells true tales and solves mysteries.

His knowledge, experience, and writing skills make him the perfect author for a book such as this one. *Forensic Detective* brings the reader into the world of forensic science—the grisly hands-on world of a forensic detective. He shares with us how a forensic anthropologist works from the past to identify a World War II sailor killed at Pearl Harbor, using the same methods he used when he examined Civil War sailors who died aboard the USS *Monitor* and CSS *Hunley*. He works with more recent evidence, helping identify victims' remains of the 9/11 tragedy and solving the mystery of an American kidnapped and murdered by a terrorist group in the Philippines in 2001. This book covers many interesting cases and depicts the solving of many mysteries. For example, who was the person buried at Arlington's Tomb of the Unknown Soldier and how did we prove it? Mann not only shares with readers the techniques and methods he uses in forensic anthropology, but also takes us through the principles and logic of criminal investigation.

On the surface, this book is a collection of true caseworks of Bob Mann. Each story reads like a great mystery novel. But beyond this, each case provides a glimpse into the workings of forensic anthropology. Real-life examples show how the history of life can be retold through the study of bones. This is a great contribution to our society. Dr. Mann provides the family members of the victims and us with the answers to those missing pieces of history. More important, this book is an excellent teaching tool for students, forensic scientists, criminal justice practitioners, and the general public.

PREFACE

The stories you are about to read are true. Some names have been changed to protect the innocent, but the stories themselves are real. They are drawn from the career of a high school dropout and 1960s hippie who went on to become a physical anthropologist at the Smithsonian Institution and then deputy scientific director at the largest forensic skeletal laboratory in the world. I'll take you on a journey through the jungles of Vietnam, Laos, and Cambodia; lead you through the quest to sort out and identify the remains of a serial killer's victims; and teach you how to read a person's life history by looking at his bones and teeth. You'll learn how to examine a crime scene through the eyes of a forensic anthropologist—a bone detective—as he confronts homicides, hangings, mummies, mysteries, and the search for American soldiers listed as missing in action (MIA). It's a fascinating journey, one filled with intrigue, suspense, and—when a puzzle is finally solved—elation.

The traditional view of anthropologists as bearded and bespectacled professors hunched over Egyptian sarcophagi in the Valley of the Kings is out of date. Sure, some of us are still bearded and bespectacled, and Egyptian studies still play an important role in anthropology, but the field has expanded into many surprising areas, including the identification of victims of serial killers and plane crashes. If forensic anthropology had existed as a discipline in 1888, scientists might well have contributed significant information on the victims of Jack the Ripper—maybe even determining the type of knife the killer used.

Though we might not have realized it, we have all seen forensic anthropology in action in newspapers and magazines. A new literary genre, the forensic novel, has emerged in the past decade. O. J. Simpson's 1995 murder trial and the 9/11 terrorist attack on the World Trade Center and the Pentagon fueled the public's fascination with things forensic to the extent that each week tens of millions of television viewers tune in to shows such as *CSI* and its spin-offs, as well as *Cold Case* and *Navy NCIS*. And Court TV has renewed its daily *Forensic Files* series to run through 2009.

Anthropologists have played key roles in identifying the person buried in the Tomb of the Vietnam Unknown Soldier and the remains of gunslingers Jesse James and Wild Bill Longley. We have also helped identify the victims of such notorious serial killers as Jeffrey Dahmer and, more recently, Kendall Francois, who ultimately confessed to the murder of eight women in Duchess County, New York. Anthropologists are also heavily involved with human rights issues in troubled regions such as Bosnia and Kosovo. In fact, forensic anthropologists might well be the scientists called in to identify the remains of Osama bin Laden if ever he's blown into small pieces. After all, that's our specialty: fragmentary human remains that have been bludgeoned, beaten, battered, and burned. A good forensic scientist could even identify a body run through a wood chipper. Unlike prosecutors, who occasionally get a homicide conviction without a body, anthropologists require a few bones or teeth—sometimes just one—to do their job.

The largest single employer of forensic anthropologists in the world is the U.S. military. The organization responsible for finding, recovering, and identifying our missing American service members has a proud history dating back to World War II. It began as the Central Identification Unit (CIU) in the 1940s, then became the JPRC (Joint Personnel Recovery Center) during the Vietnam War, CIL-THAI in Thailand after the Vietnam War, CILHI when it moved to Hawaii in 1976—the suffix denoting the location of the laboratory—and then JPAC (CIL) when it became a joint military organization in 2003. While there have been variations on the name and the location has changed several times, the mission has remained the same. Throughout this book, I'll refer to it as the CIL, because the scientific part of JPAC is still known that way.

The Central Identification Laboratory is based on the island of Oahu, near Pearl Harbor. Its staff of more than four hundred includes thirty forensic anthropologists. We work in teams to search for, recover, and identify members of the military services killed in battle or missing in action since as far back as the War of 1812. Forensic anthropologists have also been called upon as consultants in high-profile cases such as the search for Anastasia of the last Russian royal family and the Sam Sheppard murder case (made famous in the movie and television show *The Fugitive*), and to help identify victims of mass disasters, including the terrorist attacks on the World Trade Center's Twin Towers and the Pentagon, and the crash of United Flight 93 in Shanksville, Pennsylvania. We have also been called upon to testify against terrorists in the Philippines and to assist in the aftermath of the December 2004 tsunami.

The unusual combination of skills we forensic sleuths possess makes us integral in a wide range of cases in which authorities seek to find or identify bodies, particularly those who have been dead long enough to become skeletons. And we bone detectives can work a case from start to finish—we find buried bodies, identify them, and determine what killed them and how long they've been dead. As you read, I think you'll be amazed at how much a forensic anthropologist can tell about a person's life by examining even fragments of his bones. These skills, learned in the classroom and perfected in the field and the laboratory, are not replicated in any other medical or legal discipline. Often the last specialists to be called in to assist on a case, forensic anthropologists may well be society's last hope of finding a buried body or identifying a faceless skeleton.

Most professional disciplines, including those that deal with evidence, crime scene investigation, and the human body, have certification boards to ensure that each practitioner meets and maintains certain standards in his respective field. For example, when we go to the doctor, we feel reassured when we look at the professional certificates and degrees hanging on the office wall. There's the American Board of Surgeons for many physicians and the American Board of Forensic Odontology for dentists. For those of us who deal with human remains for the police, medical examiners, and the FBI, there's the American Board of Forensic Anthropology. Anyone wanting to sit for the board examination in forensic anthropology must have a Ph.D. in physical anthropology (the study of bones), and three years' experience with skeletal cases performed for law enforcement agencies. Best of all, there is a four-hour written test *and* a four-hour practical (hands-on) qualifying examination.

As with so many things in my life, I approached taking the board exam a little differently and a little later than most people; I didn't get my Ph.D. until I was fifty-one. I passed the board examination four years later, in 2005, while this book was being written.

I'm sure, though, that I was no different from my colleagues in that it took me months to prepare for the two-part examination, given in New Orleans in February 2005. The first thing I did was read every relevant book and journal article I could get my hands on—an undertaking that took me four months and abundant doses of Tylenol. Although I'd been doing skeletal cases in the laboratory and field for more than twenty years and had pretty much kept up my hands-on skills, I did a refresher by spending a week at the Smithsonian Institution. The hard work paid off, and I am the seventy-first person to become a diplomate of the American Board of Forensic Anthropology.

My colleagues often joke that sitting for our Ph.D. was *supposed* to be the last time we would ever have to take an exam. But in the forensic arena, one's credibility as an expert witness in court is enhanced by being a diplomate. Having earned the title means you've achieved the highest status in the field of forensic anthropology—and that, at last, you've really taken your final exam.

Since few people have the opportunity or the desire to examine human remains in their various stages of decomposition and incompleteness, I decided to write a book on some of the more interesting cases I've worked on over the past twenty-four years. This book will let you follow the detective work of grisly cases without ever having to put on surgical gloves and mask, grapple with the nausea inspired by the odor of decay, or even leave the comfort of your home. Each case is a snapshot of history that imparts information and techniques used to identify human remains. Above all, these are fascinating cases that reflect aspects of humanity—from heroism to homicidality—that few people have ever heard of or witnessed, much less experienced.

ACKNOWLEDGMENTS

My thanks go to Drs. Bill Bass, Doug Owsley, Doug Ubelaker (Smithsonian Institution), Hugh Berryman, P. Willey, and Richard Jantz for their encouragement, inspiration, and teaching when I was a student at the University of Tennessee.

I also thank my friends and colleagues at the University of Tennessee who formed the basis of my academic "circle of friends." When I was a new graduate student, Drs. Steve Symes and Bill Rodriguez, with whom I shared a laboratory and office, always included me in cases that came into the department, and stirred my interest in doing research at the Body Farm. I also thank Carol Lee Bass for her homegrown kindness and the Krebs family in Colorado for their many years of friendship and for helping me to stay grounded, despite the distance between their home and mine.

Others whom I have met and worked with along the way include Erica Bubniak and Dr. Murray Marks; Kari Sandness-Bruwelheide, and Craig Lahren; Drs. Lowell Levine, O. C. Smith, and M. Lee Goff; Dr. Mike Pietrusewsky and Wilson T. "Sully" Sullivan III. Thanks also go to the men and women of the Honolulu Medical Examiner's Office for allowing me not only to work on their cases, but also to include them in this book. Special thanks and gratitude go to the men and women of law enforcement in Hawaii; the men and women of the Federal Bureau of Investigation for involving me in several of their cases; the Johnson City Police Department; Dr. Barbara Wolf; Florida Pinellas County Sheriff's Department; Bath Township and Summit County law enforcement, coroner, and medical examiner; the Albany (New York) Police Department; Dr. Craig Mallak of the

Office of the Armed Forces Medical Examiner; Naval Criminal Investigative Services (NCIS) Hawaii Cold Case Squad; the Naval Investigative Service (NIS); State of Hawaii Department of the Attorney General, Investigations Division; Mr. Ray Emory for his dedication and research on the Hembree case (and others); Oahu Civil Defense Agency; Police Department, City of New York; Arson Investigator Johnny Robertson and the Washington County Sheriff's Department; and the Office of the Armed Forces Medical Examiner's Office, Okinawa. My sincere thanks go to all members of law enforcement and the medical community for their tireless efforts in solving these and other cases.

Others who played pivotal roles in these cases include District Attorney General Jerry Estes, Criminal Investigator Darrell Alley, Detective Steve Housley, and McMinn County Medical Examiner Dr. William Foree Jr.; Tennessee Bureau of Investigation and the men and women of the Knox County Police, and State Medical Examiner Dr. Jerry T. Francisco. Assistant Chief Ranger Jerry Hobbs, Park Ranger Robert Wightman, Shirley Allen, sister of Rosalyn Goodman, and the Blount County Medical Examiner's Office; Dr. C. Owen Lovejoy and Dr. Elizabeth Moore. Judge Lynn C. Slaby, Detective Richard W. Munsey, and Chief Investigator Joe Orlando; Senior Investigator Tommy Martin and the men and women of the New York State Police Department for their support and camaraderie, as well as for allowing use of the Kendall Francois photos; Dr. John Naughton of the National Marine Fisheries Service; and Bill Stirlen and family, who provided us with some of the history (a 1980 typed letter) behind the skull labeled "Butter Cup."

I also thank the soldiers, sailors, airmen, Marines, and civilians of the Joint Task Force—Full Accounting, the U.S. Army Central Identification Laboratory–Hawaii (CILHI), the Joint POW/MIA Accounting Command (JPAC), Stony Beach, and the Defense POW/Missing Personnel Office. These professionals put their lives on the line as they search for and recover America's missing service members in some of the most inhospitable areas of the world—"until they are home."

Although it's impossible for me to thank everyone who has contributed to my career at the CIL, or to solving the cases in this book, there are a few people deserving of special recognition. They are Drs. Tom Holland, Kim Schneider, Jimmie Schmidt, Bruce Anderson, Madeline Hinkes, and Johnie E. Webb Jr.; analysts Rick Huston, Robert "Bulldog" Maves, Dickie Hites, and H. Thorne Helgesen. Also deserving of recognition are the gifted scientists of the Armed Forces DNA Identification Laboratory in Rockville, Maryland, especially Dr. Brion Smith, and the men and women at Fort Lee, Virginia.

Exceptional recognition goes to the National League of Families of American Prisoners and Missing in Southeast Asia; and the many veterans' service organizations and family members who keep hope alive.

Special thanks to Tanis Hackmeyer and family. You afforded each of us a perspective on both the love and pain that accompanies the loss of a loved one. I also thank the Hembree family for graciously providing photographs of Thomas Hembree, as well as information on his life. Special thanks to all of the friends and family members of those depicted in this book.

I send my heartfelt apologies to anyone whose contribution to any of the cases in this book I have failed to recognize. After more than five decades on this wonderful planet, I have now accumulated enough sense to know that I am neither infallible nor a one-man show when it comes to solving these cases. The success of these cases was the work of many dedicated professionals. If I failed to thank you, or recognize you for your contributions to any of these cases, I do so now (and owe you a drink).

Special thanks go to Miryam Ehrlich Williamson for being such a talented writer, good listener, and literary companion.

My most humble thanks and all my love go to my wife, Vara, for her love and support and for always being there.

—R.W.M.

When I was in danger of drowning in detail, a major hazard in the writing of a complicated book, the members of my National Writers Union affinity group—Chris Rohmann, Steve Simurda, Maria Trombly, Jan Whitaker, Stanley Wiater, and Allen Woods—were my lifeline. For this I thank them.

I send thanks, too, to Giles Anderson, our agent, and Mark Tavani, our editor, for their enthusiastic encouragement. Mark gets an extra thank-you for his gentle edits and constructive suggestions. And Bob Mann, without whom this book could not exist, gets thanks and a virtual hug for being such a delight.

—M.E.W.

FORENSIC DETECTIVE

1. FRAGMENTARY EVIDENCE
JEFFREY DAHMER'S FIRST VICTIM

I should have gone to college and gone into real estate and got
myself an aquarium, that's what I should have done.
—JEFFREY DAHMER

When they pulled the car over at three in the morning on June 21, 1978, police in Bath Township, Ohio, thought they had a drunk driver on their hands. It was the summer solstice, the year's longest day and shortest night. The sky was already beginning to lighten when the police officers ordered the man behind the wheel, a blond, bespectacled teenager, out of the car and put him through a sobriety test. He passed. One policeman shined his flashlight in the car, spotlighting a pair of garbage bags in the backseat. "What's in the bags?" he asked.

The young man said the bags contained old garbage he'd forgotten to take to the dump. The police ticketed him for crossing the center line in the road and sent him on his way. "Scared the hell out of me," Jeffrey Dahmer later told an FBI interviewer.

Had the officers detected the odor of decaying flesh, Dahmer might not be known today as one of the most evil men who ever lived. Seducer, murderer, necrophiliac, cannibal—Dahmer was all of these things. Thirteen years later, on the cusp of his eighteenth murder, he would be found out and would willingly, almost eagerly, tell all.

"I couldn't believe it. I thought I was dreaming, so I went back home," Dahmer said of his encounter that June night when, according to pagan legend, a fair brother kills his darker brother, who descends to the underworld until the winter solstice, and then returns to slay the lighter brother. Dahmer played out half of the legend that night in 1978. Another man would complete the cycle sixteen years later.

Four days before his nineteenth birthday, Steven Hicks was hitchhiking to his girlfriend's house after a rock concert when Jeffrey Dahmer picked him up. The date was June 18, a few days after Dahmer's graduation from high school. Dahmer's parents were divorcing. Locked in a bitter custody battle over Jeffrey's younger brother, neither parent showed any interest in the older boy's future. His father had moved out of the family home in the upper-middle-class suburb of Akron, Ohio; his mother and younger brother were visiting relatives in Wisconsin. Jeffrey had the house to himself. Hicks, with brown hair and an engaging smile, accepted Dahmer's invitation to stop at the house for a few beers, expecting Dahmer would drive him to see his girlfriend afterward. But Dahmer intended nothing of the sort.

Interviewed by a special agent of the FBI on August 13, 1992, Dahmer spoke of a "pretty good, pretty average" relationship with his parents and brother. His father was a research chemist with a Ph.D. His mother had emotional difficulties; Dahmer told investigators he felt guilty for having been born, as his mother had told him she suffered a nervous breakdown after his birth. While he was growing up both parents apparently were so absorbed in their own marital difficulties that they left him pretty much to himself. Neither appears to have worried about young Jeff's fascination with dead animals, the way he brought them home, dissected them, removed their flesh, and preserved their skeletons. Heads of dead animals were impaled on sticks in the yard. Even if he wasn't doing it consciously, young Jeffrey was perfecting his grisly art. While he worked on dogs, cats, and rats, I wonder if he imagined that one day he would use these skills on human beings. By the time he was sixteen, Dahmer was having homosexual fantasies in which he envisioned having total control over others. He told his FBI interviewer of one dream in which he struck someone with a blackjack and had sex with the inert body. His thoughts troubled him, and in high school he turned to alcohol to numb himself.

Standing at the side of the road, his thumb extended, Hicks provided an opportunity Dahmer found irresistible. The two shared a twelve-pack of beer, but when Hicks asked for a ride to his girlfriend's house, Dahmer became furious. "I just didn't want him to leave," he later told detectives. As Hicks sat on a chair in the bedroom, Dahmer hit the young man on the back of his head twice with an eight-inch barbell, then strangled him. When he knew Hicks was dead, Dahmer cut the body open to examine it. A day or two later, he dragged the body to a crawl space under the house, cut it into small pieces, put it into garbage bags, and stuffed the bags into a drainage pipe in the backyard. Three days later, afraid that dogs attracted by the odor would dig up the remains, he loaded the bags into the car and had his encounter with the police.

Frightened by his narrow escape, Jeffrey drove home and set to work removing flesh from Hicks's bones. Then, using his father's sledgehammer and a large boulder at the side of the house, he smashed the bones and threw the fragments into the woods behind the house, turning first in one direction then another, as though he were scattering seeds.

Based on my own experience rendering bodies down to the bone, even after only a few days in the summer heat I'm sure the remains were difficult to work with. Despite the ugliness of it all, Dahmer could easily have smashed the bones and scattered them in half a day. Years later, when Dahmer was telling the police about his Milwaukee murders, he mentioned the Hicks episode as well, supplying only Hicks's first name and saying he had gotten rid of the remains so thoroughly that no one would ever find them.

He was wrong. You can smash a blue-and-white china plate into a hundred pieces, but you'll still be able to recognize that it's a broken blue-and-white plate. You can smash bones and strew them around, but you still haven't destroyed their value as evidence. What Dahmer did to Steven Hicks's bones was identical to what happens to bones when a jet plane crashes or, to a lesser degree, what happens to the human skull when a bullet passes through it. It's my job as a forensic anthropologist to piece bone fragments back together and identify to the highest possible degree of certainty whose bones they are. And that's what I did when Steven Hicks's bones arrived at the Smithsonian Institution in Washington, D.C., where I was working in the physical anthropology department's laboratory.

The long, dark corridor that leads from the elevator on the third floor of the Smithsonian Institution to the physical anthropology department's laboratory is lined with drawers, each containing human remains. The Smithsonian houses the bones of some thirty thousand individuals. Some have been identified, others have not. Most were collected by Smithsonian scientists during an era of exploration when laws governing exhumation were more relaxed than they are now. I remember listening to one anthropologist as he recounted nights spent traveling down rivers in the Yukon, searching for graves and burials. He would collect as many remains as he could and then hurry off before neighborhood dogs caught up with him. The Smithsonian has for many years served as an institution fostering research and knowledge about humankind, and part of that knowledge is about past generations and people from around the world. When I worked there, I felt like the proverbial kid in the candy store.

Unlike the first two floors of the Smithsonian, where the public is welcome to explore the results of the institution's work to increase knowledge of American history and heritage, the third floor is off limits. You have to apply at the security office with a very good reason for visiting what the news media often call "America's attic." Even with your security badge, a Smithsonian employee will turn the key in the elevator panel lock that opens the way to the third floor and accompany you to the lab, releasing you into the custody of the person you've come to see. Getting upstairs at the Smithsonian is difficult and carefully monitored for good reason. When the Federal Bureau of Investigation moved in across the street from the institution, in 1936, Smithsonian anthropologists began helping to solve crimes. The privacy of the third floor is necessary, not only to ensure the safety of the human remains and priceless artifacts housed there, but also to protect the integrity of the scientific processes practiced in the lab. Along the third floor's dark hallway on August 16, 1991, strode William A. Cox, coroner in Summit County, Ohio, carrying a carton containing remains he wanted us to analyze. Dr. Cox wanted to know if the bones he was bringing us belonged to Steven Hicks, murdered thirteen years earlier—and whether anyone else's bones were mixed in with Hicks's.

I'd come to the institution in 1988. To me it was hallowed ground, the former domain of Larry Angel, the man who first exposed me to forensic anthropology. I had gone on a field trip while I was an undergraduate at the College of William and Mary, and Dr. Angel had been there to give us an overview of the field. A smallish fellow, with muttonchop sideburns and a bow tie, christened by one magazine writer as Sherlock Bones, he'd run us through some of the things you could find out from examining a human bone. I was hooked. Dr. Angel, the personification of a "skeleton sleuth," occupied the physical anthropology lab at the Smithsonian for many years, although he didn't set the longevity record. That belonged to Dr. T. Dale Stewart, one of the lab's founding fathers, who came to work faithfully for sixty-six years.

When Dr. Angel died, the Smithsonian brought in Doug Owsley to take his place. I'd known Doug from the University of Tennessee, where I began my doctoral work; he brought me along with him to Washington. Typically, Smithsonian anthropologists are hired for their expertise in a particular area. For example, Owsley's research spans some three hundred years, specializing in Native Americans who lived on the Central Plains of the United States between the eighteenth and early twentieth centuries. He's also done considerable research on soldiers of the Civil War, remains found on Easter Island, Kennewick Man, and corpses buried in cast-iron coffins. He is a voracious examiner and collector of information. Doug brought me to the Smithsonian because of my eye for detail. The summer I met Doug, within moments of looking at some foot bones, I found cut marks suggesting that the bodies of some American Indians had been ritualistically taken apart at the joints and defleshed. This talent, which I consider a visual gift, came into play more than a decade later while I was working the Dahmer case.

Doug and I made a highly effective team. He's probably the brightest, most driven, and most gifted scientist with whom I've ever worked. Still, he remains humble, gentle, loyal, and a great listener. I learned to recognize when he was on the brink of solving a complex problem: his eyes would dart from side to side as though he was examining every angle, making him look like a professional chess player, lining up his moves to close in for the kill.

Those were great days for me. There was always something more to learn, and I was perpetually in awe of the fact that I was working at the Smithsonian. It was the pinnacle for any forensic anthropologist, and I was settled in at Dr. Angel's desk. In the drawer was a rubber stamp from the Jefferson Medical College in Philadelphia—a souvenir of his years there, no doubt. I keep that stamp in my desk at the Central Identification Laboratory in Hawaii, where I now work. It reminds me of the debt I owe to one of the founders of forensic anthropology.

Dr. Cox was well acquainted with the capabilities of the Smithsonian's physical anthropology lab. He had worked with Dr. Angel on a few cases at the institution. Earlier Angel had confirmed Cox's work identifying a navy man missing in action, done at the Central Identification Laboratory. Such review is standard procedure in forensic anthropology; one scientist does the analysis and another affirms that it has been done with sufficient precision. And here I am, more than twenty years later, working for the laboratory that got Angel and Cox together in the first place.

In my time at the Smithsonian, many cases had challenged me in the extreme. I'd excavated Civil War burials in the eastern United States, trying to reconstruct and interpret past historical events. I'd traveled to Easter Island in search of evidence to validate or refute long-told tales of cannibalism practiced there. Once, I dug in a local cemetery to figure out whether a buried casket had been broken into. Police suspected vandalism because of graffiti scratched into the headstone and melted wax suggesting some form of ritualized behavior. They feared members of a cult had stolen a human skull to use in their worship. If that were so, a search would have to be undertaken. It's very difficult to tell if someone has re-moved soil and then put it back to camouflage the act. Forensic anthropol-ogists are trained to look for subtle changes in the soil—marbling, for example, which suggests soil types have been mixed, and anomalies such as green leaves deep in the ground, since leaves turn brown if they've been buried for even a few days. As it turned out, I could tell from the undis-turbed soil on top of the casket that no one had gotten to it since it was buried nearly a century before.

Each undertaking I'd been involved in was unique, each was fascinat-ing, and each afforded me another opportunity to hone my forensic skills both in the field and in the laboratory. None, however, prepared me for what was about to come into the lab that August day. Dr. Cox's arrival marked the start of one of the most gripping cases I would encounter in my time at the Smithsonian's forensics lab.

The door to the lab is like something out of a Mickey Spillane mystery, all gray metal and frosted glass. Considering the gravity of what goes on there, you'd be surprised at how small the room is; it's only about twenty by twenty-five feet. The room is well lit, in stark contrast to the darkness of the hallway that leads to it. Banks of fluorescent lights hang from the high ceiling. Desk lamps can be moved from table to table so that scientists don't miss any subtleties in bone or tooth. Good lighting is essential when you're examining bones lest you miss something important, such as a small nick or a tiny hole through which a blood vessel passes. Reading the minutiae of bones is much like trying to read a faded date on a coin: you can probably make it out in full sunlight, but not sitting in your living room.

To make the room even brighter, lining the wall opposite the doorway are tall glass windows that look out onto a central courtyard that contains nothing you could call pretty. Some bone specimens and a human skele-ton hang in the near right-hand corner. The most outstanding feature of the courtyard is a structure that looks like a big trash can; that's the air-conditioning unit. The lab is generally comfortable throughout the year if the windows are kept shut and someone keeps an eye on the thermostat. I did, however, at times wear my white lab coat to keep warm in the winter.

Four gunmetal gray tables that looked like they were right out of a World War II movie occupied most of the floor space, topped with foam pads to protect the bones that were assembled on them. As you entered the room, in the left-hand corner you would see a sink, the drying area, and—at that time—my desk, with shelves behind it to hold remains waiting to be examined. A computer table and small photo stand were lined up along the right-hand wall. The white walls, high ceiling, and outdated decor made me think of a ward in the motion picture *One Flew Over the Cuckoo's Nest.*

The lab is actually three rooms. The main room held my desk and hosted most of the skeletal exams. Doug's office was off to the right, and another small office to the right housed interns and volunteers. We were known for examining many sets of remains at the same time. In order to preserve the integrity of the specimens—and maintain our own sanity—Doug and I imported an assembly line process we'd developed at the University of Tennessee in the late 1980s, borrowing an idea or two from Henry Ford. At the Smithsonian, an intern laid out the remains on plastic trays in approximate anatomical order and took an inventory of each bone and tooth; the tray then went to Doug, who examined the remains and estimated the deceased's race, sex, and age at death. I examined them for evidence of trauma and disease; another scientist measured all the bones; another examined and measured the teeth; yet another photographed everything; and the intern put it all back into the boxes.

When Dr. Cox entered the lab, Jeffrey Dahmer was on his way to becoming a household name. Less than a month earlier, on July 21, two Milwaukee police officers had discovered, almost by accident, Dahmer's collection of human body parts, some neatly preserved and others in various stages of decomposition, in apartment 213 at 924 North Twenty-fifth Street. (The building has since been demolished.) Over the next two weeks, Dahmer, then thirty-one, revealed details of seventeen episodes of murder and dismemberment. Between September 1987 and July 1991, he had killed sixteen young men. Steven Hicks, killed thirteen years earlier, was among them. Dahmer was working on his eighteenth killing when he was caught. Milwaukee police contacted officials in Summit County, Ohio, where Bath Township and the Dahmer home were located. Dr. Cox was the medical examiner in Summit County. With help from Ohio anthropologist Owen Lovejoy, he mapped out a grid in the Dahmers' 1.7-acre backyard at 4480 West Bath Road, turning it into an archaeological dig site. Following standard procedure, the search team sifted the top few inches of soil, bagging each item they found and identifying its location according to the grid. They found what they suspected were human and nonhuman remains, and some other artifacts—a dinner fork; a prescription label for Joyce Dahmer, Jeffrey's mother, dated 9-23-77; a marble; a rusty wristwatch; a shoehorn; and three coins, including a 1926 penny. It wasn't the least bit unusual to find such items in a backyard, especially one as overgrown and densely wooded as the Dahmers'. But other items were worth a raised eyebrow—among them a dog's femur nailed to a fence and a dog's skull impaled on a stick.

Like practically every other sentient American, Doug and I had heard about Dahmer's deeds on the nightly news. It wasn't a great surprise when Dr. Cox called and asked us to verify the identity of the bones. Doug accepted the case; Cox said he would personally deliver the remains to us in a few days, after Dr. Lovejoy, the anthropologist, conducted his examination. We went back to what we were doing; other skeletons awaiting analysis required our attention.

It was exciting to become involved in a case that was capturing so much public attention, and to learn the case's true details. Although I thought I was familiar with the case, news reports hadn't yet scratched the surface. I knew Dahmer was a serial killer, but I didn't know the particulars of what he had done. Details of his cannibalism, his tendency to preserve his victims' genitalia, and his habit of cleaning and painting skulls emerged in news reports while we were assembling Hicks's bones on a padded table in the physical anthropology lab.

Dr. Cox brought out bag after bag of evidence, each bearing a grid number that detailed where it had been found. Then he unpacked a diagram of the West Bath Road site that Dahmer himself had drawn. On it were the initials RWM with a circle around them. Those are my initials. When I saw them, the hair on the back of my neck stood up; it seemed like some kind of hideous omen. Although I knew I hadn't yet examined the remains, my initials were on the document that Dahmer drew. It seemed as though I had somehow already been involved with the case, that someone had foreseen my participation and named me without my knowledge.

The explanation, of course, was much simpler. RWM were also the initials of Bath Township Detective Richard W. Munsey, one of those who had interviewed Dahmer in Milwaukee. I got to meet Munsey, my initials double, when he came to the lab to pick up Hicks's remains after we were finished with them.

After Dr. Cox's briefing, Doug and I set out the remains on plastic trays and began sorting them: human bones and teeth in one pile, nonhuman bones in another, and a third pile for other items. It sounds much harder than it is to tell the difference between human and animal bones. There are differences in size and, sometimes, shape. A human femur (thighbone) is the same shape as a squirrel's, but the size is quite different. You can look at the humerus of a human being and those of five other creatures and know which one belonged to the human being. What we couldn't do was say for sure which nonhuman bones belonged to which animal. That job fell to Elizabeth Moore, one of the Smithsonian's experts on fauna. Dr. Moore identified the bones of a cow, sheep, pig, cat, opossum, woodchuck, and at least three dogs. The opossum and woodchuck were no surprise for a lot as wooded as the Dahmer property. As to the others, the likely explanation was that the boy Jeffrey had a penchant for bringing home dead animals. Sometimes neighbors found the corpses of frogs and cats impaled on sticks or staked to trees. Occasionally, a neighborhood dog would disappear. Apparently no one suspected Jeffrey of killing small animals, although his mother later said she knew he liked to use acid to remove the meat from dead animals.

Among the bones found in the Dahmers' yard was a small ring-shaped bone from the center of a slab of ham. The smooth saw marks on either side of the bone suggested that it had been sawed by a butcher at a local supermarket. Here was part of a Dahmer family dinner, eaten neither at the table nor while lying on the forest floor.

Although we thought we knew whose remains we were working on, we followed the scientific procedure of examining everything we had and using all the evidence available, just as we would have if we'd had no idea of the dead person's identity. The bone fragments ranged in size from one centimeter to five centimeters (just under four-tenths of an inch to two inches) in length. It was the most fragmented set of remains I'd ever worked on and, other than those at some plane crashes and explosion sites, the most fragmented skeleton on which I've worked to this day. When Dahmer smashed the bones they were fresh, somewhat flexible, and very thick. I don't know anyone strong enough to break a human femur or tibia with his bare hands, but Dahmer and his sledgehammer managed to break up almost every one of Hicks's bones and teeth. The few he didn't demolish eventually gave us the proof of identity for which we were looking.

First, we sorted each bone fragment according to which part of the body it came from—skull, jaw, arm, hand, spine, hip, leg, and foot. For a forensics specialist, telling the difference between a fragment of tibia and fragment of fibula is about as difficult as it is for a skilled woodworker to tell the difference between oak and cherry wood shavings. It's all about visual clues: there are distinct differences in texture, grain, and coloration. We placed them into small piles, one for each body part, to get an idea of how much had been recovered and how much of each bone we would be working with. We estimated we had less than 20 percent of the complete skeleton. Unless it's reduced to mere dust, any bone in the body can be glued back together if all of the bone fragments have been recovered and you know what you're doing. If the bones are unbroken, a forensic anthropologist can lay out all 206 bones of an adult skeleton in about fifteen minutes. It takes much longer, however, if they're in thousands of pieces due to some violent accident such as a plane crash—or an encounter with Jeffrey Dahmer's sledgehammer. This analysis took us the better part of a month;

Doug and I each worked on it an average of two or three hours a day. I found the work so absorbing that I'd get restless at home on weekends and come into the lab to put in a few hours. It certainly took me longer to undo what Dahmer had done to Hicks's remains than it took Dahmer to do it. It was as though two opposing experts had worked on the same case to achieve opposite results. Dahmer had set out to destroy the evidence, and I had set out to reconstruct it, thirteen years later. By the time we completed our analysis, we had identified six human teeth and sorted most of the fragments of bone by size and element—for example, the left femur or right tibia.

Once the identification and sorting were complete, we went on to reconstruct as much of each bone as possible. We had too little material to work with to be able to rebuild a single complete bone. Surely, animals had eaten some of the bones. A man hired to rake the Dahmers' yard in 1979 probably unknowingly discarded others. Given young Jeffrey's interest in animal carcasses, the family had no reason to believe the remains caught in the rake teeth were from anything but woods animals, so sending them to the dump was reasonable.

Most forensic anthropologists use good old Duco Cement and tape to reassemble bone fragments. I prefer to first use masking tape until I'm satisfied I have everything in the proper place. Reassembling bones is a bit like doing a jigsaw puzzle—a three-dimensional one, to be sure, but the process is much the same. You can do just so much of this at one time before you stop seeing the fine differences between edges of bone that make it possible to fit them together. After a while every shard of bone starts to look the same; your eyes play tricks on you. Then, an hour later, you may be having lunch when suddenly the image of two bones you saw earlier comes to mind and you go back to the lab and put them together.

Despite the extreme fragmentation, we could tell that the skeleton was that of a seventeen- to twenty-year-old male. Bones tell you someone's age at death; the bones of a child haven't finished growing and are made up of pieces loosely joined or incompletely formed. An adult femur is all one piece; that of a child is in five pieces. These five bones will fuse in the teen years. In addition, each bone has a cap on each end. Bone caps are loose while the person is growing; during puberty, when bone growth ends, the caps become fused onto the bones. Similarly, a child's skull is loosely held together to accommodate a growing brain. Once brain growth is complete, the skull bones become one.

Judging from the dry condition of the remains lying in front of us, as well as the lack of odor and bone grease, we knew the victim had been dead for several years. Although we couldn't find any evidence of what killed the man, we did notice several knife cuts in two ribs, one of the cervical vertebrae, the sternum at the center of the chest, and one on the left collarbone. All we could tell from these cuts was that they occurred at or near the time of the person's death. Cuts into bone have many of the same characteristics as cuts into wood. We can tell if the bone was moist or dry when the cut was made. If you cut into fresh bone, the cut edges will curl a bit; if it's dry, they won't. As it turned out, these cuts were a result of Dahmer's dismembering his victim after death. This case serves as a reminder to all anthropologists and medical examiners that a cut in bone doesn't necessarily mean the person was stabbed. It might suggest postmortem defleshing or dismemberment. A cut in bone, whether it occurred before or after death, is a crucial piece of information for investigators.

Putting the bones back together, although the most time-consuming part, is just preliminary to the real purpose of the exercise. Identification of the deceased, the reason the bones came to us in the first place, remains to be done. In nearly a month of reconstructing shattered bones and teeth, we found two critical pieces, one neck bone and one tooth, that we might positively identify as belonging to Hicks. To do this, we compared a dental X-ray of Hicks when he was alive with the size and shape of the roots of the recovered molar; the two matched nicely. We corroborated our findings by comparing another of Hicks's dental X-rays taken when he was getting braces in 1973 at age thirteen. As it happened, the X-ray—intended only to capture the boy's teeth and jaws—showed the bones of his neck, as well. We took our own X-ray of one of the cervical (neck) vertebrae recovered from Dahmer's yard, compared it with the 1973 X-ray, and found enough similarities to say they matched.

While we were working on the Hicks remains, details of Dahmer's later murders were emerging. He was caught when Tracy Edwards, a thirty-two-year-old man whom Dahmer had selected to be his eighteenth victim, escaped from apartment 213 wearing handcuffs Dahmer had put on him. Edwards flagged down police and told them Dahmer had threatened him with a knife. He led the officers to Dahmer's apartment; Dahmer let them in and went to his bedroom to get the key to the handcuffs. Attracted to the kitchen by the odor of rotting flesh in an otherwise tidy apartment, one of the officers opened the refrigerator and screamed when he found a human head inside. Police reported that Dahmer seemed almost relieved to have been found out. Through his own confession and evidence found at his apartment, the world soon learned that this good-looking, well-mannered man had killed, dismembered, and eaten parts of his seventeen male victims, two of whom were only fourteen years old.

Authorities found Polaroid photographs and drawings of Dahmer's dead and dying victims, and many body parts in various stages of decay. Besides the severed head in the refrigerator, police found in a bedroom file cabinet spray-painted skulls made to look like models, body parts being defleshed in a blue drum containing acid, two more skulls on a shelf in the hall closet, hands and genitalia in a cooking pot, and hearts in the freezer. Despite the hundreds of cases I've worked in my years as a forensic anthropologist, I still consider the photographs of Dahmer's victims as the most grotesque and disturbing ones I've ever seen. They portray the victims in awkward and humiliating poses, almost as animals killed and gutted.

To deflesh his victims, Dahmer mostly used a knife. Then, according to his confession, he boiled down what remained with Soilex, a commercial chemical that, in his words, turned the flesh into a "jelly-like substance." He then removed the remaining soft tissue by soaking the bones in a mild solution of bleach for a day or two before laying them out on newspaper or cloth to dry. The amazing part of this is that Dahmer followed steps almost identical to the ones that forensic anthropologists take when rendering bodies to skeletons. The only difference is that as students at the University of Tennessee (UT) we were taught to use Biz, another commercially available product that speeds up the process. Dahmer came eerily close to professional methods when he devised his own technique of liquefying and acidifying bodies. Perhaps it is fortunate that Dahmer had failed his introduction to anthropology class during his brief stint at Ohio State University, where alcoholism devastated his efforts to get a degree. With his fascination for bones, imagine how cunning he could have been if he'd become a forensic anthropologist and used his talents to dispose of the bodies. There would have been no way of stopping him.

I sometimes wonder: Had young Dahmer planned to dispose of his first victim's body on the day of the solstice, or was it mere coincidence? Only one person knows for sure, and he is forever silent.

Dahmer was tried in Milwaukee on fifteen counts of murder. He pleaded guilty but insane to all counts. The jury rejected the insanity plea, and he was sentenced to fifteen consecutive life terms plus ten years—936 years in all—without the possibility of parole. Then he was extradited to Ohio, where he pleaded guilty to Hicks's murder and received another life sentence. Sent back to Wisconsin, Dahmer entered the Columbia Correctional Institute in Portage, where he met his own brutal death on November 8, 1994, at the hands of an inmate who thought he was God, deepening the nexus with nature and the solstice. This time the dark brother killed the fair-haired one as the pagan myth predicts.

Some men's names live on for their good deeds, others for acts of unspeakable evil. In a 1999 *New York Post* poll seeking readers' opinions on the twenty-five most evil people of the millennium, Dahmer came in twelfth. Among those deemed more evil than he were Adolf Hitler, Joseph Stalin, Pol Pot, and Charles Manson. Dahmer was listed ahead of serial killers Ted Bundy, John Wayne Gacy, and Oklahoma City bomber Timothy McVeigh.

2. FROM THE CRADLE TO THE FUNERAL HOME

THE MAKING OF A FORENSIC ANTHROPOLOGIST

Real life seems to have no plots.

—IVY COMPTON-BURNETT

The first home I remember is the white two-story frame house at 1702 Watrous Avenue in Tampa, Florida. It stood beside a large white shale parking lot bordering Beezee's Drugstore. It was in an old but nice part of town, where homes were connected in the back by unpaved alleys. A few years ago I took my wife to see it. It looked much the same in reality as it did in my memory. Inside were wooden floors and a fireplace. There were shrubs all around, a detached garage out back, and a cracked sidewalk out front.

I remember climbing into an old Dempsey Dumpster on the drugstore parking lot looking for anything interesting. To a six-year-old boy "interesting" included a can of shaving cream, a wooden shoe tree, a discarded address book, and an empty tin of Sir Walter Raleigh pipe tobacco. I remember chasing chameleons and grasshoppers in the backyard, and once sitting down in a red ant mound and getting stung all over. I ran back home, and my grandmother had me strip off my clothes to get rid of the ants. A few months later I stumbled over a nest of yellow jackets at the nearby playground. I guess adventure wasn't all I got into.

Four of us lived there: my mother, my mother's parents, and me. I remember playing with matches in that little strip of land beside our house and setting fire to a couple of house shingles. My grandma hid me under the bed upstairs when the firemen came to investigate. I was about five years old. She told them I couldn't have started the fire because I was asleep upstairs. That was my grandma—always loyal, always protecting me.

I am the adopted son of Adele and Bill Mann. I can't remember my adoptive father living with us, but I could be mistaken. I think Adele and Bill separated soon after they adopted me, probably when I was four. I remember going to the hospital for minor surgery at around that age and my grandfather, not Bill Mann, carrying me home. I think about my adoptive father often, but I know very little about him. I know he was in the army, probably during World War II, and was shot in the legs. He suffered from his wounds later in life. He had a mustache and dark hair and was a handsome man; Clark Gable reminds me of him.

Grandpa, who claimed to have American Indian blood running in his veins, was retired from a job in the warehouse at McKesson & Robbins, forerunner of today's drug and health supplies conglomerates. Grandpa's hobby was repairing old golf clubs in the garage out back, home to scorpions in the corners, cobwebs in the rafters, and roach eggs resembling miniature canoes everywhere. Grandma, with her waist-length hair braided and coiled around her head like a sleeping snake, had worked in a machine-gun factory during World War II, but by the time I came along her hobby was bugging Grandpa. They rarely spoke unless they were bickering; that was how they showed their love, and even I knew it.

The house was cold in the winter and hot in the summer. The one ancient window air conditioner fought a losing battle with the summer heat. In winter my grandmother tried gamely to control the temperature by closing off rooms with sheets hung in doorways. It was less effective than unsightly, but Grandma was in her fifties and didn't care what anybody thought. When we were home we spent most of our time in the living room, sparsely furnished with a couch, two chairs, and a hand-carved coffee table that I broke in my teens by putting my feet on it. The room's one luxury was a spinet piano that I never learned to play.

My name at birth was Robert Dean Churchwell. I was three when the

Manns took me off my birth mother's hands in 1952. They changed my middle name to Walter, for my maternal grandfather, and gave me Bill's last name. I had six brothers and sisters in West Virginia, where I was born. For my mother, Mary Churchwell, a seventh child may have been the last straw. She put me up for adoption, and I've never seen or heard from my biological parents or siblings since then. I never thought to ask the adults in my life how a couple in Tampa adopted a child from West Virginia, and there's no one left alive to ask now.

Instead of a birth certificate all I have is an adoption paper giving my adoptive parents' names and listing me as Robert Walter Mann, with no mention of my biological parents. Late nights and early mornings, in the world of dreams and musings, I sometimes wonder who I am and how I ended up as someone else's child. On a certain level I think I can understand how it feels to lose a loved one without warning. The sudden disappearance leaves an emptiness in the heart that nothing and no one can fill.

Adele and Bill divorced when I was about five, and I stayed with my adoptive mother. We moved to our own house in Tampa, then to another house, then another, all in the same town. It was a bit like being a military brat, never staying in one place long enough to put down roots or make friends at school. My mom remarried and divorced again in my early teen years, and we moved back in with my grandparents, who found themselves raising a teenage boy while their daughter, my mother, worked to support the two of us. If my grandparents resented having to take on the responsibility of raising a difficult teenager when they had earned the right to kick back and relax, they never let on. I felt that they genuinely loved me, and I just about idolized my grandpa. Some weekends he took me fishing with him down at the Bayshore, a paved boulevard bordering downtown Tampa and Tampa Bay, mostly used these days by joggers.

Looking back at the photos of how I dressed to go fishing in the early fifties I'm reminded of *The Little Rascals;* maybe that's why I loved that show so much. The way I looked, acted, and dressed, I could easily have been one of them. I always wore baggy clothes and hated getting dirty. As long as she lived my mom loved telling people about the time I rode my tricycle off a six-foot-high platform at her carpenter shop in Tampa. She said that I got up, ignoring my bloody lip, dusted myself off, and, in a voice that sounded like Elmer Fudd, said, "Ooh, I got my pants dirty." Some of my fondest memories, however, are of my grandma calling me "Bobby Boy" and my grandfather calling me "Sport." Thinking about them still gets me teary eyed.

I was never around when someone in my family died. In 1970 I was in the navy, on a destroyer in the middle of the Mediterranean, when I received a radio message saying that my grandfather had died of cancer. My grandmother died during the first week after I arrived in Hawaii in 1992, and I was still there when my mother, Adele, died nearly a decade later. I find it ironic that I can deal with the deaths of others so easily, but not those of my own family. While I've attended dozens of funerals in the course of my work, I've never attended the funeral of anyone in my family.

Perhaps I was born with a curious mind. Maybe my insatiable appetite for exploring the unknown grew out of the loss of my first family. My attraction to forensic anthropology makes me wonder if I've been searching for my own roots in other people's bones. I have spent my entire life searching for something or someone, trying to unlock mysteries that, with my mother Adele's death, will probably go unanswered forever. In a way, my search for the identity of others through their skeletons is an aspect of my searching for myself.

I can't remember a time when I wasn't consumed with curiosity about what makes people tick. My first childhood foray into psychological research was to find out where dreams originate in the brain. Much of my interest came about as a result of a recurring dream of mine: I'm in the bathroom at some dingy house with a dirt road out front, perhaps in West Virginia, and I've put soap in a drinking glass that someone in my family drinks. The soapy water makes the person ill. While I know that, in reality, whoever drank the soapy water wouldn't have died, in my dream the person—I don't know who it is—does die. Everyone blames me for the act, and I'm ostracized by the rest of my family. Hence, I'm given away. I was drawn to psychology and dreams because I wanted to understand that dream. Did it depict an actual incident or does it reflect the randomness of a child's imagination? To me, it seems like a child's attempt to figure out what he did that made his parents give him away.

Perhaps it's no coincidence that I didn't utter my first word until I was three years old, and that even then I could hardly have been considered to be speaking. Adele told me that my first word was "dee dot," which somehow meant cookie. Although I don't remember much from my early childhood, Adele told me that before she adopted me I was abused by an uncle who was mentally retarded. There's no way for me to know if this is true or not, but she said I was tied to my bed and locked in a closet for extended periods of time. Perhaps that's why I was so slow to talk—and why I've struggled with claustrophobia all my life. Maybe this is what prompted my birth mother to put me up for adoption. But my wife, Vara (pronounced Wella in her native Thai language), has a different way of looking at it. She says that Mary must have loved me a lot, enough to want me to have a better life than what she could give me. The same for Adele, who must have loved me enough to want to step in and give me a better life. You can look at it either way.

By the time I was fifteen I'd read the works of Sigmund Freud, Carl Jung, and Karl Menninger and wished to walk in their footsteps. My studiousness at home was at odds with my behavior in school, though. There I was a fish far out of water. I majored in skipping classes, hanging out with friends, and not getting caught. Looking back, I can see that school left me feeling bored and restless. So intense was my alienation that I dropped out of high school during my senior year. By that time I'd been to ten different schools, including a navy military academy, as my mother and I moved from place to place in Tampa. I didn't go to military school because we were rich (we weren't), but because I had a knack for getting into trouble, and military school was my mom's way of providing me with both a father figure and some much-needed discipline.

Not entirely willing to close the door on a chance at learning something, I enrolled in night classes at another high school. On the first night, the guy sitting two seats in front of me made a comment about my long hair, and we got into a fight right then and there. The instructor, who was also a football coach at the school, said it might be a good idea if I didn't come to class anymore. The year was 1968, a time of social and political turmoil. I enlisted in the navy that fall and started boot camp in January 1969. My friends were being drafted, and killed, serving in Vietnam. Having gone to a navy military school for a while as a teen, I figured I was better off joining the navy than taking my chances and getting drafted into the army or Marines. The navy helped me get my GED, the rough equivalent of a high school diploma. I'd enlisted for four years, but I got out after three on a hardship discharge so I could help my mom run her restaurant. That was the beginning of a downward spiral of dead-end jobs, lying around drunk on beanbag chairs, traveling across the United States with my thumb, and hanging out with a pretty bad crowd in a commune.

My friends nicknamed me Ghost because I would sometimes disappear without any warning. One day, when I was working as a welder in Tampa, on my regular morning break I went out for a pack of cigarettes and decided to keep going. I'd learned just enough about welding to be dangerous, then got the urge to learn another trade. I did that a lot back then. On this particular trip I remember hitchhiking along an interstate out West when a trucker driving an eighteen-wheeler at about seventy miles per hour tossed a beer bottle at me. I wore my hair long, and I suspect he didn't like the way I looked.

On one of my trips in those days I hitched a ride with two people in a dilapidated Jeep. The driver's nickname was Nasty (I never knew his real name), and his girlfriend's name was Angel. I remember waking up in the backseat in the middle of the night to the sound of him beating her in the front seat. We made it as far as Tucson, where I pawned my guitar and stereo for food money. I think I got fifteen dollars for both. We used the money to buy cigarettes and food: sardines and rolls. After the car broke down and they sold it to a junk dealer for fifty dollars, we hung out in the mountains around Tucson, sleeping out in the open and on the sand for a few days.

Out of food, out of money, and out of luck, I left them to their craziness and made my way to San Francisco by hopping trains and thumbing rides. I'd heard about Golden Gate Park, which was where I finally ended up, inspired by Scott McKenzie's hit song "San Francisco (Be Sure to Wear

Some Flowers in Your Hair)." That was one of the times I dropped what I was doing and left town—"ghosted"—because of some romantic song that got me thinking there was something out there, somewhere, for me, if I could just find it. A few days in San Francisco and I was heading back east on the first train I could jump. I made it to El Paso, where I caught a train going east, and ended up in Alabama. There I borrowed ten dollars from some guy for bus fare. Being the smart guy that I was, I used the money to buy cigarettes and used my thumb to hitchhike back to Tampa. I showed up at my friend John's door saying, "Hi, how ya been?" I spent the next few weeks on his couch. He's still my best friend.

By the time I was twenty-seven I had been married and divorced twice and had worked at about thirty different jobs. I was a dishwasher in one restaurant, a busboy in another, and a pizza cook in a third. I picked up trash on one parking lot, painted stripes on another, worked in a paint warehouse, and became a house painter; and no, I don't especially like parking lots or painting. I repaired cash registers; was a salesman in two different hardware stores; had a brief and menial job in a funeral home; and was a "counter" at a tropical fish farm, where I caught fish from man-made lakes, counted and put them in bags, and shipped them to pet shops all over the United States. I drove a truck carrying acids and chemicals; installed fiberglass insulation in new houses; and was a security guard at Busch Gardens in Williamsburg, Virginia. In my more creative moments I embroidered rainbows and flowers on my backpack while waiting to hitch a ride on the next train, car, or eighteen-wheeler to wherever it would take me.

Looking back, I see clearly that I was searching for something, someplace where I'd fit in and be happy. I slept under bridges and trestles, and bummed spare change from people in the cities through which I passed. I learned the difference between a hobo and a bum the hard way. (A bum hustles spare change; a hobo gets from place to place any way he can, looking for work.)

I was sitting under a trestle somewhere in Texas, waiting to hop on the next train, when I referred to one of the guys sitting a few feet away from me as a bum. He stood up, walked over to me, and punched me in the side of the head, saying, "I'm no fucking bum. I don't bum for money." We got into a brief scrap before he went back to his spot on the ground. Not knowing if he had a gun or a knife on him, retaliating wasn't the smartest thing I'd ever done in my life. His aroma left no doubt that he hadn't bathed in days or even weeks and that he was a true-blue alcoholic. A few hours later, I watched as this man struggled to climb aboard one of the empty and open boxcars. The "bulls" (railroad police) sometimes let us climb on the old boxcars if the doors were open, but they didn't want us on the new boxcars because the hobos often used them as toilets. After I was sure that he was settled, I climbed into the car behind his. My head still hurt from the first blow, and I didn't think I could survive being in his company on a rolling train. For hours I could hear him, even over the roar of the tracks, yelling and screaming to himself, to an imaginary person, or in his sleep.

Life on the road taught me I had to become creative if I was to survive. For example, I'd walk into a diner without a cent in my pocket and order a "hobo float"—a toothpick and a free glass of water—then use the water to wash down saltine crackers, which were put out for paying customers who ordered soup, but which I'd filched while the waitress's back was turned. One of my finest moments came when I woke up drunk on a beach in Tampa, surrounded by a litter of empty beer cans, as a hundred people waited for the police to remove me so that their Easter Sunday mass could begin.

I came down with both hepatitis A and B while I was living in a commune in Tampa. Debbie, the girl I was dating at the time, asked me what was wrong; the whites of my eyes were yellow. I had been trying to ignore the fact that my fingernails were also yellow, my urine looked like Coca-Cola, and I was as weak as a baby. I went to our family doctor, who diagnosed me. I asked him not to tell my mom, but he called her anyway. That night my mom's friend came to the commune and told me that I could stay at my mom's house. It had just been renovated but was empty. I agreed and spent the next three weeks hanging out there alone, aside from the occasional friend who stopped by to visit. After three weeks in bed, during which I practiced my guitar and wrote songs almost continuously, I joined the navy for another two years, hoping it would help me get my act together. I knew I had to get my life straightened out or I'd end up dead.

My mom used to tell me, "The one thing that no one can take away from you is your education." That advice finally sank in, and when I left the navy for the second time in 1976, I enrolled in Tidewater Community College, in Portsmouth, Virginia, earning an associate's degree in education two years later. On a whim I applied to the College of William and Mary; to my great surprise, I was accepted. During my four years there I discovered anthropology and, almost by accident, my fascination with bones. I moved on to the University of Tennessee. I got my bachelor's degree in anthropology there in 1985 and my master's degree two years later, took a job as assistant morgue director at the University of Tennessee Medical School in Memphis, then moved on to the Smithsonian Institution in 1988, where I stayed for four years.

It was at the University of Tennessee where I developed an interest in the subject that eventually, in 2001, led me to earn my doctoral degree in physical anthropology at the University of Hawaii. The subject of my dissertation was Stafne's defects of the human mandible (the lower jawbone). The term, named for Dr. Edward Stafne, a dentist who studied them in the early 1940s, describes a bony hollow that forms along the tongue side of the mandible, just below the molars. These crater-shaped spaces range in size from the diameter of a pencil tip to that of a dime. They are painless, cause no symptoms, and are usually found on X-rays during routine dental examinations. Between 80 and 85 percent of these show up in middle-age white men—the youngest person on record with the defect was an eleven-year-old boy in Sweden—but they're probably present in every group around the world. Although they're common, no one really knows how or why they form. But with my training as an anthropologist, I know that things happen for a reason.

I was lying in my dorm bed at the University of Tennessee, reading the *Knoxville News Sentinel*, when I saw an ad for a "schoolboy" posted by a funeral home located a few miles from the campus. Although the job paid minimum wage, the flexible hours were inviting. I was in my fourth year as an undergraduate student and didn't have a job or any money coming in. I won't say I was desperate, but I immediately liked the idea of being able to eat for the next couple of years.

Running downstairs, hoping to beat everyone else to the punch, I fed a quarter into the lobby phone and dialed the funeral home. A kindly sounding lady with an exceptionally strong southern accent answered my questions and asked a few of her own. My previous experience at a funeral home in Florida in the early 1970s seemed to give me an edge over the other applicants. Weaver Funeral Home was looking for someone to live there, go on "death calls" every other night and weekend, and answer the phone after hours. Mrs. Weaver invited me out for an interview, and I got the job that day. The job paid a hundred dollars a week; the Weavers would provide me with a small bedroom and kitchen privileges for a hundred dollars a month. The catch was that I wouldn't be able to cook until visiting hours were over and mourners were gone—at around nine o'clock at night. I saw it as an opportunity to earn a decent living doing work that wouldn't be too difficult. I would work for the Weavers for nearly four years, and I'd feel pretty much for that whole time like one of the family.

I moved out of my dorm room two days later and into my room at the Weavers'. Owned by Frank Weaver and his son, Gary, it was a beautifully maintained and landscaped property, and one of the most respected funeral homes in Knoxville. Nowhere did it smell of death, decay, or embalming fluid. It employed a handful of funeral directors, two full-time embalmers, and three students from the university. I would soon find that the job involved going on hundreds of death calls in the middle of the night, some requiring a four-hour drive each way. Sometimes, the only things that kept me awake at the wheel of the lonely hearse were a blaring radio and an ample supply of Marlboros.

I picked up bodies throughout the state from morgues, nursing homes, mobile homes, high-rise apartments, and hospital beds—anywhere that someone had died or undergone an autopsy. It wasn't at all unusual to get a call to pick up a three-hundred-pound man at two in the morning. The switchboard routed the after-hours calls to one of the funeral directors who, like the student employees, worked on revolving schedules. They took the biographical information on the deceased person, found out where the body was to be picked up, and sent one or two of us out on the pickup run.

For practical reasons, two of us always picked up a body if a person died at home. We didn't want family members to see us struggling to pick up or roll a body onto the wheeled gurney. And our biggest fear was that they'd see us drop the body. The hardest part of the job was when I'd have to get a three-hundred- or four-hundred-pound man off an autopsy table or stainless steel refrigerator tray and onto a gurney by myself. Bodies have a tendency to stiffen, spill fluids when you roll them on their sides, and "sigh" when you lift them by their arms. Despite stories you may have heard of people coming back to life after having been mistaken for dead, you can trust me on this: corpses don't move on their own.

One of my most difficult pickups was a 350-pound man who died in the back bedroom of his single-wide mobile home. The two of us who went on the call had to gently "bounce" the man from his king-size bed in the cramped bedroom onto a sheet on the floor. Once we got him on the floor we dragged him down the narrow hall into the living room, where we struggled mightily to lift him onto the gurney and out the front door. At the time I weighed only 135 pounds, so I don't mind telling you I thought I was going to break my back lifting the guy.

The elderly man who died in his third-floor apartment was a whole different story. A friend found him dead on the kitchen floor on a Sunday and, as the medical examiner didn't make house calls on the weekends, one of the sheriff's deputies acted as the coroner. I've always found it odd that someone with little or no medical training can examine a body and, if they see no evidence of foul play, order the body removed and embalmed without being autopsied, but such was the system in Tennessee in those days. The three flights of stairs leading down to the parking lot were very narrow and required us to lift the man's body over our heads to get him over the stair rail. Although he was strapped onto the gurney, we almost lost him over the side. Can you imagine trying to explain that to the family?

But even those weren't the worst cases I ever had to deal with. The award for the nastiest body would have to go to one that was bloated, filled with maggots, and stank to high heaven. I remember one Saturday when paramedics called asking if someone at the funeral home would mind helping them remove a body from a house. Although the paramedics and other rescue workers had respirators to keep out the stench, they would rather someone else go in and remove the body. The deceased was apparently sitting on his couch watching television and eating popcorn when he died. Because I dealt with decomposing bodies as part of my undergraduate work at the university, the call went straight to me. I knew the smell wouldn't bother me and seized the opportunity to see something new. I jumped into my truck and made my way to the man's house. When I arrived at the scene I surmised that the poor guy inside must have been a recluse; his windows were covered with black curtains. No light in, no light out.

I put on coveralls to keep the smell off my street clothes. I turned down an offered respirator; I was confident that I could handle any smell or sight I might encounter. I grabbed a body bag and a gurney and pushed my way through the crowd of onlooking police, firemen, and paramedics. I'd done a lot of death calls and often interacted with law enforcement and rescue personnel. Almost invariably, someone would enter the house with me and lead me to the body. This time was different. No one offered to accompany me.

I opened the rickety screen door and pushed the inner door. A blast of heat and stench wrapped itself around me like a wool blanket. Cautiously, I stepped through the doorway. Off to my left I saw a rather rotund man sitting on the couch. Investigators were right about one thing: he had died while watching television. It was still on. But the popcorn they thought he had been eating when he died was actually a combination of vomit and maggots caught in the creases of his distended stomach, mouth, eyes, ears, and lap. The poor guy had probably been dead four or five days in the thick of summer. His tongue, swollen and protruding from his mouth like a baby emerging from the womb, was a grim reminder of death's indignity.

I made my way over to one of the windows in the darkened room and, reaching up to open the curtains, found he had none. What I had thought were black curtains were actually flies crowding the window, trying to escape. I pushed out the screen and gave them their freedom. Once the flies were out of the room a couple of rescue workers came in and helped me get the man onto the gurney. His history of heart disease obviated the need for an autopsy. Back at the funeral home we put him in a clean body bag, doused him with gasoline to kill the maggots, and sealed the body bag zipper with silicone to keep the smell of both the gasoline and decay inside until after the services. The stench was so bad that the casket remained closed during the funeral.

Most of the cases I dealt with while I lived and worked with the Weavers were far less exciting. Some people think I'm weird to have found any pleasure or enjoyment living at a funeral home. For many people the whole thing conjures up images of bodies lying like zombies in open caskets and family members crying their eyes out. But funeral homes provide an essential service in our society, helping mourners sort out the details of honoring a loved one's life and giving the remains a respectful disposal. While I admit to thoughts of ghosts floating down the hall toward me in the dead of night as I contemplated taking the job, nothing like that ever happened, and I never had such a thought once I took the job. I was never scared, not even once in those four years. In fact, I thought of the dead merely as friends who had gone on before me. I do believe in ghosts, but not as anything except friendly and protective—though I will say I'm glad I've never had the pleasure of meeting one.

What I remember most about the Weaver Funeral Home are the people I worked with. They included Robbie, with his boyish looks; Ethel Monday, with her warm smile and encouraging words for me as a student; and Frank Jr., short of stature but not of wit. Buss Satterfield, at six feet three, towered over me. He wore a large Mason's ring on his left hand and impressed me as someone I wouldn't want to scrap with, but we soon became close friends. Warren, balding, quiet, and a chain smoker, spent his free time reading BMW parts catalogs and could quote the current price of any BMW car part if you asked him. It took me a couple of weeks to learn to relax around him, but now I look back on him almost as a brother. Who would think that otherwise normal people would willingly work and live in a place where people are taken when they die, drained of their life fluids, plugged with cotton and superglue, made to look like they're alive, and dressed in their Sunday finest? Together we spent many a night in front of the television doing what we did best—smoking and joking. It was a time in my life when I had few responsibilities and a thimbleful of money, some good friends, and an insider's view of what really happens to the dead. There was a lot of life at the Weaver Funeral Home.

3. THE BODY FARM

All human things are subject to decay
And, when fate summons, monarchs must obey.
—JOHN DRYDEN, *Mac Flecknoe II:1*

Suppose you were walking through the woods and you came upon a chain-link fence surrounding a yard in which human bodies were lying around in various stages of decay. What would you think? What would you do? My guess is that you'd think you'd stumbled on some kind of ghoulish ritual or a serial killer's lair. I'll bet you'd cover your mouth and nose with whatever you had handy—a handkerchief, a bandanna, the hem of your coat—trying to keep the stench out of your nose. Then, depending on how spooked you were by the sight and smell, you'd either walk up to the fence and peer in or you'd take off running.

If you've ever caught the scent of decaying flesh, you haven't forgotten it. The thickly sweet odor of decay is almost overwhelming, especially on a hot day, even to someone accustomed to it. It makes you salivate, and your mouth takes on the sour, metallic taste you'd get from sucking on a copper penny. People sometimes try to use another scent to mask the stench. When I was a new graduate student and I had to work on corpses, I tried to mask the odor with skin lotion that I applied to the inside of my mask, but it didn't work. The result was worse than its failure to work; I came to associate the pleasant scent of the lotion with the awful odor of death. And olfactory memory is said to be the strongest of all sensual memories. From then on, I couldn't smell the lotion without smelling death. My most desperate—and funniest—effort to mask the smell was putting spearmint Lifesavers between my surgical mask and my skin. The day was hot and humid; by the time I took off the mask, my face was covered with small white circles where the pieces of candy had melted. I couldn't eat Lifesavers again for months. Not only are attempts at obliterating the odor ineffective, most people in the field consider it wimpy. They may not laugh at you to your face, but they probably will behind your back.

Some autopsy suites try to eliminate the odor with aerosol canisters on the walls that emit a puff of spray, much like the deodorizers some people use in their bathrooms. But the truth is that there's nothing that can successfully mask the smell of "decomp" coming from a "floater," which is our term for a decomposing body, even one that was never near water. The scent is amazingly strong, sticky, and persistent. It stays in a room for days or weeks. Every so often, a story surfaces about a person who has committed suicide in a car and isn't found for days. Later, someone tries to clean up the inside of the car to sell it, but without success. The odor of death attaches itself to everything even slightly porous; it wraps itself around you like a malodorous blanket and makes no secret of where you've been.

One time at a McDonald's in Louisiana, the manager asked a group of which I was a part to eat outside so the other customers could enjoy their lunch. We had just worked on a floater in a small room at Louisiana State University. Not having learned from my mistake, I would repeat it at another fast-food restaurant a few years later while working at the Anthropology Research Facility (ARF) at the University of Tennessee, in Knoxville. Immortalized as the Body Farm in Patricia Cornwell's bestselling novel of the same name, the facility's mission was, and is, to study human decay. In 1983, after three years spent studying anthropology at the College of William and Mary in historic Williamsburg, Virginia, I'd transferred to Tennessee hoping to meet and study under Dr. Bill Bass, the man who in 1971 wrote the bible on human bones. *Human Osteology: A Labora-*

tory and Field Manual remains the book forensic anthropologists always want within their reach. I'd used it as a textbook at the college and developed a powerful desire to meet the man and learn from him in person.

Bill Bass founded the ARF after one of his cases revealed with great clarity how little forensic science knew about human decay after death. Although we who worked at the Body Farm took care to treat with total respect the corpses given to us for research, we were an irreverent lot, perhaps in an effort to shield ourselves from the reality of death. One of our inside jokes was to put the first letter of Dr. Bass's surname in front of the three-letter designation, turning ARF into BARF—a fitting acronym, especially on the kind of muggy summer day typical of Knoxville. Over time, though, the nickname BARF has fallen into disuse and nearly everyone refers to the facility as the Body Farm. Contrary to what the name suggests, though, bodies don't grow there; instead, weeds, flies, and maggots do—in abundance.

The Body Farm is the only facility of its kind: fresh or recently dead bodies are laid out on the ground, buried at various depths, immersed in water, wrapped in plastic, or put into automobiles to allow us to monitor the effects on decay of a variety of environmental variables. It's a school for the living taught by the dead, and the subject is important to many people other than scientists who study decay. Police investigators, prosecutors, defense lawyers, and bereaved families all have compelling reasons to know the interval between the time someone died under unusual circumstances and the time the body was discovered. As much as any other bit of data associated with a mysterious death, the time since death can be crucial in determining exactly what has transpired. Medical examiners (who used to be called coroners) are most often physicians with a specialty in pathology, and they can usually determine the time since death of someone who has died within the past twenty-four to forty-eight hours. But once decomposition begins, a different kind of expertise is needed. That's where the lessons learned at the Body Farm come into play.

By the time I enrolled at William and Mary, after two years at a community college, my academic aspirations had changed from biology to anthropology. The field has four subdisciplines: archaeology and physical, cultural, and linguistic anthropology. I wanted to take courses in all of them before making a choice, but in my third year my focus began to sharpen, thanks to a man who looked more like Santa Claus than a scientist.

One afternoon while working as a student volunteer for the Virginia Research Center for Archaeology, I came across Bill Buchanan, a long-haired, bearded archaeologist from Arkansas. Buchanan served as my laboratory supervisor as I painstakingly numbered thousands of pieces of broken pottery, as well as the occasional arrowhead. At one point, probably to ease my boredom, he showed me some bones and asked, "Can you tell me if these are human or not? And if they're not human, what animal are they from?"

I looked at the bones, having no earthly idea what kind of animal they were from, and gave the answer he must have expected. To my amazement, he proceeded to identify each bone by name and tell me the side of the body from which it came. He said the bones once belonged to a turkey, and a young one at that. "See here," he said enthusiastically, "you hold this bone up like this, point this curved portion of the shaft toward you and these two rounded condyles down, and you can see that it's a right femur. The growth caps aren't fused, so it's an immature bird." It was as simple as that. My respect for Bill Buchanan immediately shot up a thousand points. I now had a new idol.

I'd never thought of turkey bones as anything but what was left on the platter when Thanksgiving dinner was finished. Bill Buchanan opened my eyes to the way in which life events and activities are recorded in bones and teeth. In human beings, they reflect our age, race, sex, and dietary habits. They testify to many of the diseases that we either survive or die from: childhood illnesses, sexually transmitted diseases, broken bones, dental disease. Our skeletons also reveal whether or not we were physically strong in life and point to such activities as sewing, archery, and habitual squatting. Bones really do speak, if we're willing to listen.

I soaked up every bit of information Bill Buchanan offered. He showed me that the healed break in a bone can be used to identify a person, and that the bones of a person who is malnourished will not be as dense as those of someone living on a proper diet. Malnutrition can also lead to bowed legs and diseased teeth. From the day Bill Buchanan tried to relieve my boredom with a handful of turkey bones, I was intrigued with the framework that supports our flesh and protects our organs.

The next semester I signed up for a course in osteoarchaeology, the only class on bones at William and Mary, and my career in human osteology began to take shape. I wanted to learn everything I could about anthropology, so I stayed on a bit longer than some of my friends and took most of the anthropology classes the college offered. Equipped with all the knowledge I could absorb at William and Mary, in 1983 I set out for Knoxville, Dr. Bass, and a plot of land known as the Body Farm.

Bill Bass established the Body Farm in 1972 with two purposes in mind: to solve a problem and to contribute to scientific knowledge. The problem belonged to local police and medical examiners—what to do with unidentified and unclaimed bodies when they were no longer needed as evidence. The Body Farm would provide a place for these corpses, relieving already-strained budgets of the cost of burial. Access to these remains afforded Dr. Bass and his students the ideal opportunity to collect data on how long it takes for the human body to become a skeleton—information that can be crucial in solving crimes and bringing criminals to justice.

The Body Farm is located in a heavily wooded area, not far from the Alcoa Highway, several hundred yards behind the University of Tennessee Hospital. The area was once remote, but hospital expansion and the construction of a large parking lot, which now abuts it on two sides, have made it visible—and, when the wind is in the right direction, detectable by odor—to hospital workers sitting at the institution's picnic tables.

Now, you'd think that people would stay as far away as possible from a cage the size of a large closet that holds putrid corpses, but they don't. In fact, the facility has had to install a surveillance camera to deter spectators and intruders. Although winter seemed to see the fewest pranksters, certain seasons prompted strange behavior. Police had to be especially vigilant around Halloween when intrepid rascals would reach through the chain-link fence with sticks, trying to drag one of the bodies close enough to touch it. A few years after I left the facility, the university, funded in part by the author Patricia Cornwell, enlarged the ARF by several acres and topped its surrounding fence with barbed wire and razor wire—the same arrangement used to keep prisoners away from the rest of the world—to protect the dignity of decomposing corpses and the integrity of the experiments under way.

The research information obtained from the Body Farm has, over the years, proved invaluable repeatedly in establishing how much time has passed since a person's death. Before the Body Farm, the only way police and medical examiners could estimate the time since death of a corpse found after two or three days was either by the temperature of the body (taken rectally) or a SWAG, the acronym for a "scientific wild-ass guess." The Body Farm provides the medical and legal communities with precise information based on field studies. The results of these studies have been used in court to support or refute testimony as to when or how long ago a witness saw or spoke with the victim before his or her death. Over the years the Body Farm has become the Harvard of the three Ds—death, decay, and decomposition.

Bill Bass is a generous man, always willing to share his knowledge, even with a novice like me. That's an uncommon trait among high-profile tenured professors. Even before I applied to the University of Tennessee, I thought of him as the Walter Cronkite of forensic anthropology. When I got there, I headed for the anthropology department, which was housed in the bowels of the UT football stadium. Fighting back a shiver of trepidation, I hoped to meet with Dr. Bass himself, but didn't really expect that to happen. Annette Blackbourne, his secretary, asked me to wait. "Dr. Bass is on the phone to the police," she told me, with what sounded to my West Virginia–born ears like a strong Tennessee accent. Before long, the man himself came out of his office and, with a two-handed shake, greeted me, saying, "Well, hello, and what can I do for you?" in the distinctively high-pitched voice I would come to know so well. "I'm a new student and I want to major in forensic anthropology," I said, hoping that he wouldn't say I could not. We sat at his small conference table to discuss what my forensic anthropology major would consist of. I told him about my scholastic background, warts and all, and the classes I'd taken. He suggested the classes I should take at UT. I was impressed by his generosity; he had dropped what he was doing just to talk with me. Despite his busy schedule, his awards and certificates, Dr. Bass remains a genuinely kind person.

Having analyzed some sixty Native American skeletons as an undergraduate at William and Mary, I thought I could impress him with what was to me a hefty senior thesis. Until then I'd never met anyone who had spent a lifetime excavating hundreds of human burials in the Great Plains or identifying hundreds of homicide victims, so I really had no way of knowing if fifty-six skeletons was a lot or not. I would later learn it was not. I handed my thesis to Dr. Bass just as his wife, Ann, walked in and sat down beside me. Dr. Ann Bass was a nutritionist who specialized in living American Indians in the Southeast. She was a charming and personable woman who, very sadly, later died of cancer. Being surrounded by two Drs. Bass made me self-conscious. A voice in my head warned me not to say anything stupid. But I had just enough self-confidence to know that, given time, I would. Dr. Bill took my senior thesis without so much as reading the title. He laid it on the table in front of him like a used dinner napkin and through a beaming smile said, "Well, anyone can write a thesis, young man. But do you know your bones? That's what I want to know."

I squirmed in my chair a bit as I replied, "Yes, sir," my military days coming out in me.

"Well, why don't we go downstairs to the lab and see how you do on a bone quiz?"

I felt my face redden and my palms get sweaty as he led me downstairs and sat me at one of the lab tables. I hadn't picked up a human bone in nearly two years. He asked the lab curator to bring over the ten bones he'd used in his osteology class quiz the week before.

Dr. Bass wanted more than just an identification of the small pieces of bone, he wanted me to tell him as much as I could about each of them. Whatever confidence I'd possessed walking into his office melted like a spring snowflake. Still, I identified each of the bones he handed me. "This is a left humerus. This is the right femur of a child," and so forth, until I'd named all ten bones. Each time I finished with a bone he'd reply, "Good, good. You're doing a fine job, Bob." But inside I kept wondering when the zinger would come—the mystery bone that stumped me. It never did. I correctly identified the bones and both Drs. Bass congratulated me. We went back upstairs to his office and talked more about forensic anthropology. Then they invited me to join them for lunch.

Not long after that, Dr. Bass drove me out to the Body Farm in his blue Chevrolet pickup. I soon learned that every three years he traded in his truck and bought another of the same make, model, color, and interior. Only the year changed. We pulled off the main road behind the University of Tennessee Hospital and drove a short distance down the narrow dirt lane leading to a fenced-in area. I felt slightly spooked, knowing that just ahead was a cage holding four or five human bodies. I'd grown accustomed to looking at human bones, but the idea of being in the presence of decomposing corpses struck me as unsettling. Dr. Bass climbed out of his truck and unlocked the gate that kept out inquisitive people and other large animals. The facility itself was no bigger than most American backyards. It contained a smaller area enclosed by a chain-link fence, just large enough to hold a German shepherd. I felt like the most important person on campus, having Dr. Bass take the time to give me a private tour of the Body Farm. He showed me where bodies had been or were still buried and told me all the things I needed to know if I intended to be useful at the facility. At the time, the Body Farm was off in the woods with nothing near it—no houses, no gas stations, no pubs. Over the years, its size and surroundings have evolved, but its purpose remains the same.

Being what educators call a nontraditional student—that is, one considerably older than the rest of the student body—has some advantages, one of which is a greater knowledge of how the world works. Knowing the value of being in the right place at the right time, for instance, I volunteered to serve on the department's Forensic Investigation Team and was proud of my green mechanic's-style jumpsuit and the baseball cap with the team name and a skull embroidered across the front. This uniform was a real badge of distinction. Of course, we suited up only when we worked a crime scene or a floater was found. We never knew when a case was going to come in, or when we might be called out. I hung out at the anthropology department, waiting for an opportunity to be useful.

Dr. Bass could hardly fail to notice my presence at all hours of the day and night. He discerned, correctly, that I was a determined student, focused on absorbing every shred of knowledge about the human skeleton that my brain could hold. But it took a while for me to recognize that he understood my devotion to the subject.

My first semester was particularly difficult. I was living in one of the dorms on campus, although I was a good deal older than the other students. I'd just moved to Tennessee from Virginia and didn't have a single friend except my guitar. Since I'd already had a class on human bones at William and Mary, I signed up for Dr. Bass's graduate forensic anthropology class, but I took it for undergraduate credit. I soon started thinking that I wasn't doing well and that he didn't like me. It seemed to me that he always singled out other students in the class for praise and usually ignored me. I thought seriously of dropping out, but I didn't. Later, Dr. Bass would tell me he was impressed with my skills in forensic anthropology almost immediately and thought he needed to devote his attention to students who needed more guidance and help. I simply misread the situation, and it almost cost me my career. Just before I got my bachelor's degree in 1985, Bass suggested that I apply for his forensic assistant position the following year. I applied and was selected. I held that position until 1987, when I left the University of Tennessee with my master's in anthropology.

Although forensic assistant to Dr. Bass was something of a prestigious position, one of the more mundane parts of my job was changing the lightbulbs in the anthropology department. And though I was mortified at the time, I can now smile when I remember the morning Dr. Bass came to my office and asked me to come with him. We walked halfway down the main hall before he stopped and asked me what I saw. I drew a blank and told him so. Without a word, he fetched a ladder and a fluorescent light-bulb from a nearby closet and returned to the spot where we had stopped. Only then did I realize that I had walked down the hall that morning oblivious to the fact that one of the lightbulbs had burned out and needed to be replaced. Despite my insistence, Dr. Bass climbed the ladder and changed it himself. That was the last time anyone had to tell me that a bulb had burned out. I'd learned from the master.

Whenever Dr. Bass went out of town, I was the contact person for po-lice and medical examiners at the University of Tennessee if a floater turned up or if they needed assistance on a case. I'd been at the university for a couple of years when Dr. Bass and his wife asked me to house-sit for them while they went on a trip. Since my truck was in the shop, Dr. Bass left me the keys to his Chevy pickup, with permission to use it to go to the university and back, or to receive a body from the local police or medical examiner. One weekend I decided to go out to the facility to check on some bodies and clean up the area a bit. I spent the better part of a day collecting insects from one of the decomposing bodies. Then I raked leaves, picked up surgical gloves and body bags left lying in the cage, and threw away the trash. It was the middle of the summer, so the heat and humidity ensured that there would be plenty of maggots and flies to contend with, and my clothes had become saturated with the odor of decomposition. By the end of the day I'd stopped noticing the smell. Becoming desensitized to these odors can get you into trouble, especially if you stop at a gas station or convenience store on your way home. Sometimes we threw away clothes because we couldn't get the smell out, even after washing them. So many bodies had passed through the facility over the years that it always smelled like death, even when there weren't any bodies out there aboveground. Bodily fluids had soaked into the soil and the concrete and the wood of the cage; these materials held odors that you just couldn't eliminate with bleach and water.

When I finished working that day I climbed into the driver's seat of Dr. Bass's truck—he'd had it for only a couple of months—and drove back to his house to clean up both the truck and myself. I pulled out the floor mats, vacuumed the carpets and seats, aired it out a few hours, and thought I'd done a pretty good job of cleaning it. I rolled up the windows, locked the cab, and left it waiting for his return the following day. Not needing to be there when the Basses came home, I got a ride back to the funeral home where I lived and worked.

I checked in with Dr. Bass when I got to school the following Monday and was surprised when he asked, "Bob, what did you do to my truck?"

"Nothing," I replied with a lump in my throat the size of a baseball.

"Well, it sure smells," he said.

Clearly my attempt to clean it thoroughly had failed. Walking out to the truck, I told him about my trip to the facility. When he opened the door, we were hit by that horrendous smell. I sniffed around and discovered that it was coming from the plastic floor mat on the driver's side. In retrospect, I can see that walking around on the smelly, greasy concrete floor at the facility and on the ground where greasy bodily fluids had soaked into the soil had transferred the odor to my tennis shoes and from them to the floor mat. My sense of smell was so damaged by the end of that day that I wouldn't have known if I'd been sprayed by a skunk. With the truck locked up overnight, the odor had intensified. Unfortunately, I'd replaced his new car smell with dead body smell. Once again, the master taught me an important lesson—to take good care of other people's property. Dr. Bass is one of the most giving and forgiving people I've known in my entire life, but he raised three boys and believes that if you borrow something, you should return it in the same shape in which you received it.

Before the Body Farm, studies on postmortem decay used dogs and pigs, since human bodies were hard to come by and some people were appalled at the idea of allowing human beings to decompose in the open. I was skeptical that a thirty-five-pound dog would exhibit the same decomposition pattern and length of time to become skeletonized as a 150-pound human being, so I did my own study.

One summer, with Dr. Bass's permission, I obtained the remains of four euthanized dogs from the University of Tennessee veterinary school and placed them, two at a time, at the Body Farm, putting one dog on the ground and one on concrete. In this way, I replicated the surfaces on which most human remains are found, in wooded areas or on a paved surface. I visited the dog carcasses at the Body Farm every day and monitored their decay for more than a month. I photographed the dogs from various angles, recorded the number of days required for them to go from the "fresh" to the "dry" (skeletonized) stages, and collected insects in bottles for species identification.

Although I wasn't a forensic entomologist (my fellow student Bill Rodriguez had that field covered), I did want to learn more about flies and maggots and how they related to the length of time someone has been dead. My dog study demonstrated that, although the same species of insects visited dogs and human beings alike, coming in relays, one species after another, the rate of decomposition was not the same.

I think it's logical to expect such variation, given the difference in body size. The dogs weighed between forty and ninety-five pounds. One forty-pound dog, to my amazement, was completely skeletonized in three days. The maggots had picked the bones clean and the dog hair lay in a nearly perfect ring around the skeleton. Although they are nothing more than rice-shaped scavengers of the dead, the maggots' activity during feeding had pushed the dog's hair away from its body, resulting in the ring around the carcass. This ring of hair would be proof positive that the animal had decomposed in that very spot, not somewhere else.

Scientists would later apply this principle in human cases. I still use slides of this case when I speak to police and medical authorities on the postmortem interval. I ask if anyone can estimate how many days the dog has been dead. Invariably people guess one or two weeks. They find it hard to believe that the carcass of an animal can go from fresh to dry in only three days. While scientists have found that pigs decompose at about the same rate as human beings, the result of my dog study was to show that decay studies substituting dogs for human bodies must be viewed with caution, even with skepticism. That's the beauty of scientific experimentation: research and testing provide insights and knowledge that sometimes contradict common sense.

From this series of experiments I learned that the rate at which a body decays depends on a combination of factors, including ambient temperature, humidity, accessibility to insects, rainfall, the surface with which they are in contact, and whether penetrating wounds are present. Dr. Bill Rodriguez, a friend and colleague, once worked a case in which the body of a dead woman had been dumped in a wooded area. By the time authorities found her body, she had begun to decompose. Surprisingly, her hands had decomposed more rapidly than the rest of her body. Close inspection revealed the reason: her attempt to defend herself from the knife-wielding attacker resulted in cuts on her fingers. These open wounds had lured flies to lay their eggs on her hands, hence their rapid decomposition.

While it usually took weeks to months for a body to be stripped of flesh, some cases defied expectations. One of my early experiments at the Body Farm involved a twenty-one-year-old woman who had been raped and killed. She came to us after autopsy. I placed her in a black body bag on the ground in a shaded area at the Body Farm while police waited for someone to come forth and claim the remains. To allow insects access to the body, I unzipped the bag down to her knees and left it slightly open. The surroundings therefore were dark, warm, and moist—the ideal environment for decomposition. The medical examiner had removed her internal organs on autopsy. Digestive organs are full of bacteria, which are necessary to the process by which food breaks down and supplies nourishment. Ordinarily, the presence of bacteria in the abdomen after death results in the formation of gas and, consequently, bloating. This process hastens decomposition.

In this case, with the internal organs removed, the victim's body should have theoretically decomposed at a slower rate than one that had not been autopsied. But this woman was reduced to a skeleton in seven days. I could hardly believe my eyes. It was the quickest decomposition I'd ever witnessed. Being the good Dr. Bass student that I am, I have the photographs to prove it. The only way I can explain the speed with which the victim decomposed was the extreme heat and humidity of the immediate environment.

Climate and terrain have a great impact on the speed with which a body decomposes. If a body is deposited in a wooded area in upstate New York in the dead of winter, it's going to decompose much more slowly than one dumped in Florida woods in the summer. One reason is that flies and bacteria, the two main factors in turning a corpse into a skeleton, aren't active outdoors in cold weather. Research at the Body Farm showed that bodies placed outside in the winter don't bloat as much as those in the summer, and many of them turn what we refer to as "Halloween colors"—orange and black.

Although not every case holds true, bodies usually go through several predictable stages: fresh, bloated, and dry. At this last stage, the decomposition process has ceased, maggots have finished feeding, and, unless rodents and larger carnivores eat it, the corpse will change very little, even over a period of years. If there is any flesh left covering the skeleton, it will harden so that it will someday resemble leather or parchment paper. During the early stages of decomposition, internal gases bloat the abdomen, the skin stretches like plastic wrap, and the veins fill with bacteria, turning them green and black so they look like thin highways or the graining on marble—hence the term "marbling."

Sometimes, in as little time as two weeks, the face, chin, throat, groin, and abdomen become the first areas to skeletonize. The less meaty and, to maggots, less desirable areas, such as the arms and legs, often decompose last. When you lift a body to look under it, those areas of the body in contact with the ground often resemble Swiss cheese or wormwood; this is where maggots have left the body and burrowed into the ground. Contrary to common belief, hair and nails don't keep growing after death; it's the shrinkage of tissue that gives this illusion. Skin and hair are dead cells; they were dead before the individual died.

I learned several useful tips from studying bodies at the Body Farm. One is that the skin on the hands separates from the underlying surface and can be pulled off the corpse and slipped over one's own hand like a glove. That's one of the ways we roll fingerprints on badly decomposing bodies. There are a variety of ways to take someone's fingerprints after they're dead: by pulling off the "glove," slipping it onto someone else's hand, and rolling the prints; or cutting off the entire hand, putting it in alcohol, and sending it off to the police lab, where they roll the prints themselves. I've done both. Another thing I learned is that after a body decomposes for a few days, the head's hair falls off in a clump—or a hair mass, as we call it—under and around the skull. Finding the hair mass is important because, even if the skull rolls downhill, if you find the hair mass, you've found the spot where the body decomposed.

If the Body Farm sounds like a spooky place to visit during the day, imagine what it's like out there at night. One autumn night I decided to go there after dark to see whether insects behaved differently in the dark. It wasn't fear that had kept me away before this night—at least that's what I told myself. Instead, I liked to believe practicality had kept me away: Why should I go there in the dark when I wouldn't be able to see anything? But now I went because I wanted to know if flies laid eggs and maggots emerged from their daytime hiding places to feed on the outside of the body after dark. I'd examined many bodies during the day and knew that maggots don't like direct sunlight. Instead, they spent their time inside the body. I got to wondering whether insects worked in shifts—a day shift inside the body and a night shift outside. The only way I would know was to go out there and see for myself.

Curiosity is a powerful motivator. I drove out to the Body Farm alone around eight o'clock one night. As I made my way down the narrow dirt lane leading to the chain-link fence surrounding the facility, I kept looking to my left and right to see if anyone was hiding in the bushes. I pulled up to the gate, got out of my car, followed the headlight beam to the fence, and removed the lock. I quickly climbed back in my truck just as the hair on the back of my neck began standing on end. There was really nothing there to be afraid of; I was just spooking myself.

When I had calmed down, I drove through the gate, got out, and latched it behind me, then pulled up to the small clearing near the closet-size enclosure that was holding a couple of bodies. With light from a quarter moon and wind whisking past my face, things were beginning to look more like a horror movie than I'd anticipated. I was working and living at a funeral home, and I was very comfortable around dead bodies. But this place was giving me the creeps. To this day, one of the hazards of working on bloated bodies is that I occasionally wake up in the middle of the night thinking I'm lying on the ground with maggots crawling all over me.

I moved from my truck to where one of the bodies lay on top of the ground. It had been there a few weeks and was partially skeletonized. The skin of the face had been eaten away by maggots and some of the fingertips had been gnawed on by what I presumed were mice or rats. Armed with only a flashlight, I moved closer to the corpse, knelt beside it, and scanned the beam from her feet up toward her face, full of apprehension and expecting some creature to come rushing out from under or inside the body. To my relief, all I saw were flies and maggots doing the same thing that I'd seen them do during the day—flying, laying eggs, feeding. Nothing was different. I know this may sound like a revelation only to an idiot, but I've never felt comfortable talking about something that I haven't seen firsthand. Now, because I've seen it, I can say with certainty what happens to a corpse at night: exactly what happens during the day.

When I had first climbed out of the truck, I'd thought I'd heard something rustling in the leaves off to my left. I shined my light in that direction but saw nothing. Just before I finished examining the body, I again heard a rustling, this time in the bushes off to my right. Just as I was turning to flood the area with light, a rabbit scurried past me, kicking up leaves and twigs. It scared the wits out of me. I scurried back to the truck, jumped in, and locked the doors. It took me a couple of minutes to regain my composure and muster the courage to leave the relative safety of the truck to lock the gate so I could go home. Although I'd seen evidence of critters at the Body Farm before—a female opossum and her litter inside one of the chicken-wire cages that held a decaying body; a rat that ate a softball-size hole in the stomach of one of the cadavers—this was the first time I'd heard one. And that was the last time I ventured out to the Body Farm at night.

So well known and respected has the Body Farm become that people sometimes will their remains to it for study. One such person is the late Dr. Grover Krantz, the Washington State University anthropologist who made Big Foot a household name. His passion was searching for evidence of Big Foot; studying casts of impressions people claimed were made by the huge beast; and intriguing his students with tales of wonder, mystery, and exploration. Before he died of cancer a few years ago, Krantz willed his remains to the Body Farm for two years, specifying that his skeleton then be sent to the Smithsonian Institution. He also requested that the remains of his three beloved Irish wolfhounds be placed on the Smithsonian shelf beside him. Not many of us would choose to end up on a shelf in a museum. But considering the thought of being put inside a steel box and buried in perpetual darkness, I'm not sure it's all that bad of an idea after all. At least you wouldn't be alone.

4. THE CADES COVE MURDER

I'll be okay. I'm a big girl.

—ROSALYN GOODMAN

Dressed in a sweatshirt, jeans, and sneakers, Rosalyn "Rosie" Goodman, a thirty-five-year-old mother of two, left her Memphis, Tennessee, home on September 23, 1984. She told her mother she was going to Gatlinburg for a four-day hike in the Great Smoky Mountains National Park. Responding to her mother's concern, Rosie Goodman told her, "I'll be okay. I'm a big girl." She loaded her backpacking gear in her yellow 1970 Volkswagen and headed for Cades Cove, one of America's most popular scenic spots. On the way, she stopped in Jackson to see her brother and in Nashville to visit friends. Rosie spoke to her daughter when she called to say she'd be home the next night. After the call she was last seen in a Maryville restaurant, talking with an unidentified couple.

When Rosie didn't arrive home, local police were called in to investigate her apparent disappearance. A month later, when police leads had run out, Rosalyn's friends advertised in a Gatlinburg newspaper to ask for help finding her. Contacted by a reporter, park officials were unable to verify that Rosalyn had reached the park, but a painstaking search of three thousand park records would later reveal her handwritten registration card. As newspaper coverage continued, a Wisconsin couple called police to say they had seen Rosalyn with a man on September 28 or 29.

The *Knoxville Journal* said family members described Rosie as a free spirit, a warm and caring woman who trusted everyone and loved the great outdoors. She had just purchased a small house and a housecleaning business in Memphis and was loving life. But now, three months after having disappeared, Rosie was still missing. The case, like the Tennessee weather, was turning cold.

Then, on December 29, a family tracking a buck deer found a skeleton and women's clothing about a hundred yards from a cabin in Cades Cove. From the remains, authorities described the dead woman as about five feet four inches tall with shoulder-length brown hair. She had been wearing a red sweatshirt, green jacket, yellow vest, gray striped shirt, blue jeans, and tennis shoes. If she'd carried any personal items, they were missing. Someone seemed to have tried to conceal the body by placing it under a fallen tree. Although authorities found her clothing, whoever killed and robbed her had enough presence of mind to remove anything that could identify her.

I was still working at the Weaver Funeral Home and studying with Dr. Bill Bass at the University of Tennessee when Dr. Bass received a call from Jerry Hobbs, assistant chief park ranger at the Great Smoky Mountains National Park, asking for help in identifying a human skeleton found earlier in the day. Arrangements were made to have Ranger Robert Wightman deliver the remains to the University of Tennessee Department of Anthropology. With the remains came an evidence log and field map showing the location of every bone park rangers had found. Dr. Bass remarked that the way the park rangers handled the evidence demonstrated some of the best field techniques he'd seen in thirty years of forensic investigations. The rangers had been meticulous in their recovery and documentation.

A preliminary analysis done in the presence of Ranger Wightman revealed that the skeleton was a Caucasoid female who had probably been in her thirties when she died. The only white woman reported missing in

Cades Cove was Rosie Goodman. The remains were nearly without soft tissue; dried ligaments resembling leather held together some bones. A few maggots were still present inside the skull, and beetles were feeding on the maggots. Guided by research done on body decomposition at the Body Farm, we estimated she had been dead for three to five months. At that point, the combined evidence was already suggesting that we'd found Rosalyn. We laid out the remains in anatomical order on an examination table and began doing our analysis.

Canine puncture marks on many bones revealed that carnivores—dogs, raccoons, or bears—had chewed on them. Although none of the long bones of the arms or legs were complete, much of the skeleton was present. The next step was to conduct a systematic forensic anthropological examination in search of anything that might tell us who the person was or how she died. It was time to pull out the magnifying glasses.

Dr. Bass assigned the case to Steve Symes, Tony Falsetti, and me—all of us graduate students in forensic anthropology. Each of us was given responsibility for specific portions of the analysis. My assignment was to estimate her age and x-ray her hair mass. That's how I know she was wearing her hair in a ponytail when she died. I was looking for evidence of a shooting; what I found was a cloth-covered rubber band–type hair tie—or, more accurately, evidence of a hair tie. The metallic piece that connected the two ends of the rubber band showed up on the X-ray.

We did our own analysis, then checked one another's work for accuracy. We could tell the remains were female based on visual examination of the skull and pelvis, and a mathematical analysis of the skull measurements. The skull was small and lacked the heavy muscle markings typical of men. The frontal bone (forehead) was vertical, and the upper margins of the eye orbits were sharp; the mastoid processes (the "bump" behind each ear) were small. The chin was rounded (it is squarish in men) and the palate (the roof of the mouth) was short and narrow. The hips yielded additional female traits, including long pubic bones in the front; shallow, wide sciatic notches; and a buildup, or "platform," of bone where the sacrum attaches to the hips on either side. We had no doubt about the sex of the deceased person.

To eliminate the element of observer subjectivity, we used another technique that relies on eight cranial measurements taken with a simple measuring device known as calipers. The measurements are plugged into a mathematical formula that yields a number indicating whether the bones are probably those of a man or a woman. This method has an 86 percent accuracy rate and is widely used in anthropology. As we expected, the measurements told us the bones belonged to a woman. Both methods, statistical and visual, are based on the size and shape of the bones used. An experienced physical anthropologist can visually examine a skull and determine its age, race, and sex almost immediately. But statistical analysis confirms what the eye has seen.

We figured out the individual's race based on the features of the skull and hair. Examining the remains, we found the skull had features consistent with a Caucasoid person. It was short—front to back—and broad and rounded in the back. The jaws lacked alveolar prognathism, a forward jutting of the mouth commonly seen in blacks, and there was a slight dental overbite. The upper central incisors lacked shovel shaping; shovel-shaped incisors are a dental trait common to Asians, although they are sometimes found in whites and blacks.

Investigators often overlook hair at the scene, as it may blend in with soil and leaf litter. It can become almost invisible if it's the same color as the soil. Experienced observers, however, know exactly what to look for and search nearby trees as well as the ground, because birds sometimes use hair to build their nests. Occasionally, a careful observer will find a single hair inside the skull or wedged in an area of trauma such as a fracture or bullet hole. Microscopic examination of hair can provide information on race, hair length, hair color, whether the hair was bleached or commercially dyed, and approximately how long before death the individual had had a haircut. We were lucky this time; the rangers who dug up the remains found the hair.

Speaking of hair reminds me of something that has bothered me since the 2002 discovery of remains determined to be those of Chandra Levy—an intern at the Federal Bureau of Prisons in Washington, D.C., who was declared missing on May 1, 2001. Her remains were found more than a year later in Washington's Rock Creek Park, about six miles from her apartment. Police ruled her death a homicide, but no one has been charged. I wasn't involved in the case, but I find it perplexing that investigators never found her hair mass where they found her scattered remains. Although she had been lying dead in the woods for a year and three weeks, investigators ultimately recovered about 95 percent of her skeleton and some clothing, but no hair. Ms. Levy had long, dark hair. The lack of recovered hair suggests that the search party didn't know to look for a hair mass, or that the hair would still be there. Many people mistakenly think that hair disintegrates, or that maggots and other critters eat it, as they eat skin and other soft tissue. Perhaps the searchers did not recognize the hair, lying as it must have been among the deep leaf litter and other ground debris. The absence of hair mass might also mean that her body decomposed elsewhere, although this is less likely.

Since I wasn't involved in the search, I don't know how extensive or thorough it was. I'm simply trying to point out possible explanations for the absence of hair, not to second-guess the investigators in the Levy case. I've worked with many of the authorities in D.C., and they're very good. I have to keep reminding myself that they don't know what I know about what to look for. To me, the most compelling reason for finding Ms. Levy's hair is to find a clue as to what she was planning to do when she went to Rock Creek Park. Was her hair pulled back in a ponytail, suggesting that she had gone jogging? Or was it hanging loose, more likely indicating she had planned a social engagement?

Finding a victim's hair mass is what prompted a North Carolina man to investigate what he first thought was a wig that his two dogs had dragged into the yard. He discarded the brown hair mass, only to pull it out a few days later when he found his dog chewing on bone fragments. The bones and hair turned out to be those of nine-year-old Jennifer Short of Virginia. The girl's parents had been shot in their own home; Jennifer had been abducted and later shot in the head. If the man hadn't found the hair mass and questioned what it was, we might never have known what happened to that little girl.

Examining the remains from Cades Cove, we used the number of erupted teeth, growth changes in the pelvis associated with age, the closure of skull bones, and the level of arthritic changes in the spine and scapula (shoulder blade) to estimate the woman's age at the time of death. The third molars (wisdom teeth) were fully erupted and their roots fully formed, suggesting she was at least eighteen. Union of the bones of the hip, which are separate in children, and skull sutures suggested she was at least twenty-one when she died. The spine had mild arthritic changes that I would expect to see in someone more than thirty years old. Investigators would later learn that Rosie had sought relief from a chiropractor for her misaligned spine. The absence of arthritic changes in the shoulder and sacroiliac joints suggested an age of about thirty to thirty-four years, although this is only an estimate. Everything was pointing to the woman having been between thirty-two and thirty-six years old when she died. Rosie was thirty-five.

We next examined the bones and teeth for evidence of trauma. There were no signs that she was shot, stabbed, or bludgeoned. Bullet and stab wounds, if they strike bone, are easily recognizable. Although we found no evidence of perimortem trauma (injury around the time of death), the possibility remained that she had been strangled. The crescent-shaped hyoid bone, which sits high in the neck and is sometimes broken during strangulation, was not recovered with the remains. If it had been, we might have had a cause of death.

The woman's identity was established with the help of a dental chart and two bitewing X-rays obtained from her dentist by Shelby County detective J. E. Blackwell. Knoxville's forensic dentist Dr. William Powell examined the teeth and compared them with the chart and X-rays. Comparison of the before- and after-death X-rays revealed identical features in tooth shape, spacing, pulp cavity configuration, and fillings. Now we knew: the skeleton found in Cades Cove was Rosie Goodman.

Officials notified the family that Rosie had been found. What they did not know, however, was how and why she died. That her car had been found in an Alcoa, Tennessee, parking lot, far from Cades Cove, washed clean inside and out, seemed to suggest foul play. With all the publicity of Rosalyn's disappearance, why hadn't the man with whom she'd last been seen contacted the police? Though they had obtained the victim's identity, investigators now had more questions than answers.

We presented our findings to the police as they continued investigating the case. Park rangers were asking that anyone who took photographs or video recordings in the Cades Cove area around the time of Rosie's death come forward. The police hoped someone might have accidentally captured Rosie and her male companion on film. Based on newspaper photographs, most people were probably trying to remember a woman with her hair hanging freely across her shoulders. I hoped that the fact I'd discovered that Rosie wore her hair in a ponytail would help someone remember seeing her, but that didn't happen.

Four years passed and the Rosie Goodman case remained unsolved. Then, in June 1988, a Knoxville FBI agent named Grey Steed was watching *America's Most Wanted* when he recognized the face on the screen. The show was profiling William Hewlett, wanted for rape and assault in two states. But the agent knew the man not as William Hewlett, but as Harry Steven Mercer, whom the FBI wanted to interview in connection with the Cades Cove murder. The FBI had photos of both Hewlett and Mercer, but they didn't recognize that the two images were of the same man. Forty-four-year-old Hewlett and his thirty-four-year-old wife, Linda (her real name was Rebecca Jo Hewlett), often took restaurant jobs and moved every three months. They were a latter-day Bonnie and Clyde. (Harry Mercer used this description in a letter he sent from prison to his wife.) The FBI thought they were the couple seen with Rosie in Cades Cove prior to her disappearance.

In 1970, Mercer had walked into a West Virginia bank with a shotgun. Saying he was a Federal Deposit Insurance Corporation (FDIC) inspector, he closed the bank for what he called an audit. It was a bold move, but it fooled exactly nobody. He was convicted of bank robbery and hostage taking; he served five years and was paroled. After that, Mercer was on the U.S. Marshall Service's list of the fifteen most wanted criminals. An article published in the *Knoxville Journal* on Christmas Day, 1985, quoted an investigator as saying he considered Mercer and his wife key to the investigation, whether or not they had anything to do with her death. The Mercers could, the investigator said, cast light on her mood and what she was thinking while they were with her. In actuality, the investigator was being disingenuous. Mercer was a prime suspect in Rosie's death. After all, Mercer was also wanted in connection with a 1977 sexual assault in which the bones of a woman's face were fractured during repeated beatings. However, the Mercers' nomadic lifestyle kept them always one step ahead of their pursuers. The investigation into Rosie's death continued.

Four years and three episodes of *America's Most Wanted* later, authorities caught up with William Hewlett, aka Harry Steven Mercer, Billy Joe Edwards, Joseph Jackson Edwards, Louis Frederick, Richard Earl Crayton, William Joseph Thompson, and Joe Hudson. Despite changing his name so often, nothing could disguise his face or his heinous crimes. He was arrested in Gulfport, Mississippi, turned in to FBI authorities by friends in Biloxi, and brought back to Knoxville to stand trial for Rosie's murder. Hewlett later confessed to raping and, with a short piece of cord, strangling Rosie in Cades Cove. He was convicted of the murder and sentenced to life in prison without the possibility of parole. The Goodman family could finally rest assured that Rosie's killer was behind bars for the rest of his life, and that she received a proper burial. Hewlett spends his days in prison, with a tattoo of a Playboy bunny on one arm, a blue heart with an arrow in it on the other, and a large heart tattooed to the center of his chest—a killer with three hearts.

5. THE HALLOWEEN MUMMY

Science is the knowledge of Consequences,
and dependence of one fact upon another.
—THOMAS HOBBES, *Leviathan*

One of the most bizarre cases I worked as a student at the University of Tennessee stepped out of the darkness in 1986. A few days after Halloween, Knox County police called Dr. Bass, saying they'd found the upper half of a body wrapped in chains in the Hiwassee River. It was a Friday when the body was found, and the police planned to drag the river the following day for the lower half. Local television stations had already gotten word of the find and were pushing for answers. Authorities wanted Dr. Bass to get to the city morgue as fast as he could to help unravel the mystery of this body.

Since the body was already at the morgue, we didn't need to take the paraphernalia that made up our field kit—latex gloves, trowels, plastic bags for collecting evidence, permanent markers, and kite string and wooden stakes for laying out an archaeological grid. This time we would be working over a stainless steel autopsy table. We made the fifteen-minute drive to the University of Tennessee Hospital and its basement morgue, where the upper torso of a human mummy was waiting for us. Police had found this one wrapped in chains and weighed down with a cinder block. It seemed certain we had a murder on our hands.

When we got there, several forensic pathologists and police officers were already at the morgue, staring at the upper half of a dark-skinned mummy minus a right arm. Dr. Bass and I were equally captivated; the sight could have graced the cover of *National Geographic.* The mummy's skin was dry and hard, the eyes closed, the nose slightly flattened to one side, and there was hardly any head hair. The features of the skull usually critical in determining one's sex were so distorted by the effects of time that we couldn't immediately tell if it was a man or a woman, although at first glance we thought it belonged to a man. As you know by now, generally speaking, male skulls are larger and have more pronounced markings where the muscles attach to the bone; they also have larger mastoid processes (the bump behind the ear), blunt rims along the upper margins of the eye sockets, and square chins.

Most striking, however, was the absence of any odor of decay. When a body dries out over a long period of time, the skin shrinks tightly against the skeleton, making it look as if it's been shrink-wrapped over the bones. One of the effects of this drying is that the fat more or less melts away—breasts completely flatten and bulging bellies disappear. At this stage, other than the presence of genitalia, men and women are almost indistinguishable. In this case, the absence of the lower half of the body made whatever clues we could glean from the skull that much more significant.

Above all, the police wanted us to tell them how long this person had been dead. The time since death would be an important factor in weighing whether to declare the mummy a possible homicide victim and launch a search for the killer. If the person had been dead for decades, the police would still be interested in trying to figure out his or her identity, the cause of death, and how the body came to be found on the riverbank. A death that occurred many decades earlier wouldn't rule out foul play, but it would probably mean that all possible leads had gone cold and there would be little reason to pursue the case. The passing of time would have moved it from the front burner to the cold case file.

Dr. Bass and I moved closer to the torso, donned latex gloves so as not to contaminate it, and systematically began an examination. I slid one hand under its back and the other one under the head. Slowly I lifted the torso off the cold autopsy table to get a look at its back for possible evidence of trauma. It was amazingly light, weighing about as much as a pair of men's shoes. From the bottom of the torso, where the waist would have been on a full corpse, we could peer into the thorax as if we were looking into a cave. The organs were shriveled and paper thin. We were holding in our hands the shell of a person whose shriveled heart had once pumped blood through the body, whose desiccated lungs had expanded and contracted with each breath.

We moved our examination to the person's neck and were surprised to find along the right side a three-inch-long vertical cut, packed with cotton and stitched closed with thread. This suggested an embalmer's incision in the carotid artery—the main vessel supplying the brain—made to draw off the corpse's blood. The vertical orientation of the sutures and the incision's location along the neck were typical of embalming technique in the nineteenth and early twentieth centuries. I'd become familiar with embalming at the Weaver Funeral Home, where I had occasionally assisted the embalmers. I knew that contemporary embalmers made a horizontal incision above the right collarbone. Thus, we knew the person had been embalmed many years before the torso was found on the riverbank.

Next we made several X-rays of the chest, looking at the place where the ribs attach to the breastplate for evidence of age. In young people this attachment is smooth and even, but in old age the area's surface becomes irregular, and the cartilage connecting the ribs to the breastplate turns to bone. The pattern of ossification of this cartilage looks like lobster claws in men and like Swiss cheese in women. Within minutes we were ready to surmise that the mummy was that of a woman who had died in her seventies. Confident that we could find other indicators of this person's sex, we continued the examination.

Now we were more than intrigued, because the skull had made us think we were dealing with the corpse of a man. We turned our attention to the outside of the chest, where the evidence at first seemed utterly inconclusive. While there were no breasts, there was also no chest hair. Was this a flat-chested woman, or a hairless man? Once, at the Smithsonian Institution, I examined an Egyptian mummy of a pregnant teenage girl who had died more than three thousand years ago. Early researchers had cut into her stomach and removed the fetus but, fortunately, had kept it with her body. Though she was pregnant, she had absolutely flat breasts. The lesson is that we have to be very careful when judging the sex of a mummy based on the outward appearance of the chest.

Moving closer to the Halloween mummy we noticed that the areola and nipples were positioned very low on the chest, more like the sagging breasts of an old woman than a man. Not only were the silver-dollar-size areolas exceptionally low, but also the nipples themselves were too large for a man. When we put it all together, the evidence was most consistent with an elderly woman, but, scientifically speaking, it was too scant for us to be absolutely certain. Anthropologists typically work with bones; having to rely on the size and position of the nipples was a little out of our professional lane. While we included these soft-tissue clues in our assessment, this was unusual for a couple of bone detectives. Having hips to examine certainly would have clinched it. We told the police and pathologists our opinion on the mummy and went home.

A few days later police contacted Dr. Bass to say they'd identified the mummy as a Mrs. Eliza Leonard, a sixty-year-old white woman placed to rest in an aboveground crypt in 1901 with the family name etched above its entrance. We were astounded that they not only were able to identify her by name, but they also knew when and how she died, and when her body had been removed from the vault that was supposed to have been her final resting place. A police report explained that vandals had broken into Mrs. Leonard's crypt a few weeks before Halloween and stolen the upper half of her body. Summoned to the scene, investigators had photographed the damaged crypt, as well as the lower half of the body left behind.

The story of the mummified torso brought to the morgue jarred the memory of the detective investigating the vandalism, and everything started to fall into place. In his case file he had a Polaroid photo of the lower half of the mummified body, taken inside the crypt. There was no reason to doubt it belonged to the torso we'd examined. A search of the historical records revealed Mrs. Leonard's husband had been a physician in Monroe County, Tennessee, during the Civil War.

Mrs. Leonard's torso stayed in the care of Dr. Bass until 2001. He used her as a teaching specimen until her mausoleum was repaired. Dr. Bass said that he took Mrs. Leonard with him on many talks and that "Mrs. Leonard has taught a lot of policemen throughout Tennessee and North Carolina." He said that she probably traveled more after she died than she did when she was alive. He added that a funeral home donated a new casket when she was returned to her final resting place, with the hope that vandals would not repeat their ghoulish prank.

Our best guess as to how Mrs. Leonard ended up along the Hiwassee River was that the theft of the torso was a Halloween prank. To make it look like a murder, we think the mischief-makers used the chains and the cinder block, then placed her body on the bank where someone was likely to find her. Fortunately for us, however, there were two things the vandals didn't count on: the skills of forensic anthropologists and the memory of a police detective.

6. A MAN AND HIS CAR

Half the work that is done in the world is to make things appear what they are not.

—E. R. BEADLE

Johnson City, Tennessee, is a quiet town that contains large expanses of green lawns, thick woods, and an atmosphere of safety. It's a college town, home to East Tennessee State University (ETSU) and its medical school—the kind of place that seems ideal for raising children. However, on September 24, 1986, a man and his car would disrupt the serenity of this community in a most unpleasant way.

Walking along the winding road leading to the top of Cherokee Mountain, an area many called Lover's Leap, a young couple peered over the cliff and saw what looked like a black sports car some two hundred feet below in the ravine. They realized that the car had been burned. The young man made his way down to the car and found nothing more to identify it other than that it was a small sports car, probably an MGB. He climbed back up the mountainside and called the police, who sent a wrecker to pull the car up from its awkward resting place.

The wrecker attendant climbed down the mountain slope to attach a chain to the car's rear bumper. Back at the top of the cliff, he winched it up onto the narrow dirt road, aptly named Fire Tower Road, from where it had first been seen. As he walked by the rear end of the burned car, sheriff's sergeant Ed Graybeal noticed a repugnant odor. He opened the twisted steel trunk lid and discovered a human body, burned beyond recognition, rolled up in a carpet. Police secured the car and its contents, turning it into a crime scene so that nothing would be disturbed. Then they called the medical examiner's office. Within minutes the medical examiner called the Forensic Investigation Team from the University of Tennessee to help in the investigation. Dr. Bill Bass and three students—Henry Case, Mark Guilbeau, and I—grabbed the field kit and drove the four hours to the site.

Johnson City police officers met us at the base of Cherokee Mountain and escorted us up a long and winding road, at times breathtakingly close to sheer drop-offs. It was a remote area, thickly covered with vegetation— a perfect out-of-the-way spot for lovers, beer drinkers, and pot smokers. Used by young city dwellers and ETSU students, it offered privacy and a good view of anyone approaching on the dirt road. Local television and newspaper reporters were already at work, clicking cameras, rolling tape, and interviewing anyone willing to talk. Suddenly, the normally hidden Lover's Leap was the focal point of the small city.

The fire had burned everything but the car's rear bumper. All that remained of the tires were steel belts, which were now nothing more than multistrand cables encircling the rims. They reminded me of large silver rings on small fingers. So intense was the heat that most of the window glass had melted. Some of it settled in the bottom of the side doors, looking like frozen, cloudy water. The windshield had shattered from the drop over the cliff, and the rear plastic window, part of the convertible top, had melted away to nothing. Radio speakers mounted behind the seats had also melted, and only the two metal seat frames remained. The seat cushions, carpeting, and paint had completely burned away.

The car's bashed-in front end left no doubt it had gone over the cliff nose first, but the 1973 MGB had held together remarkably well, considering the impact of a two-hundred-foot fall. Only one thing was missing: the license plate that would have allowed the police to identify the car's owner—presumably the corpse in the trunk. The plate on the car was registered to another car and owner. Clearly, someone wanted to hand us a mystery. The only clue to the body's identity was the "ETSU Student" parking decal on the unburned rear bumper. No one looking at the body would be able to identify it. No one, that is, but a forensics expert.

Huddling around the car to block the view of the reporters, police removed the trunk lid while Mark and I began examining the body, which was on its back, its head on the driver's side. The hands, forearms, and lower legs were gone; such an intense fire often consumes areas where the skin is exposed. The facial features were unrecognizable: the mouth was drawn tightly closed in an eerie smile; and the ears, nose, and head hair were burned away. The corpse's large size suggested the victim was a man. Because the skin was burned black and the facial features were grossly distorted, at this stage of the examination we couldn't even guess at his race.

We lifted the body out of the trunk and placed it inside a body bag on the ground near the car. While police and arson investigators combed the debris in the trunk, I searched for skull fragments and tried to put the pieces back in place. I wanted to see if the bones gave any evidence of the cause of death; burning was only one possibility. Perhaps I would find evidence of blunt force injury such as a hammer blow or a gunshot wound. Dr. Bass and I had once worked another case where we sifted through the debris in a burned car, found in a rural part of Tennessee and believed to contain the body of a missing man. The police suspected someone might have killed the man as part of a Hatfields-and-McCoys–type feud. They handed us a piece of melted weather stripping used to hold the rear window in place, thinking it was a rib. Burned bone can be very difficult to identify visually, never mind identifying it as human.

That the skull in the MGB was in pieces was not unusual. Intense temperature causes the bones of the skull to split and break apart. But they do not explode, as some people say they do. The skull has plenty of openings that allow the release of pressure from escaping gases. When the skull burns, two processes take place simultaneously: the outer portions of the skull are exposed to higher temperatures than the inner portions, so they dry at a faster rate; and the brain and fluids inside the head boil and expand. However, even if a skull breaks apart and is nearly consumed by fire, finding evidence of injury is often possible. All we have to do is fit the pieces together and see what is missing. Burning doesn't necessarily destroy or even significantly alter evidence of a stabbing or gunshot wound. If the person was shot, we may see a bullet hole; if his head was crushed with a hammer, we may see hammer-shaped holes. I was looking for both.

I sat on the ground next to the body and began piecing the skull back together. The body had a strong odor, much like barbecued beef; it's an unsettling thought, but to human beings there are few visual or olfactory differences between burned flesh and cooked meat. I found the missing bones of the forearms and lower legs in many small pieces. Exposure to intense heat causes the muscles in the hands, forearms, feet, and lower legs to contract to the point at which the bones break. Often, if the bones don't shatter, the tightening of the muscles draws the forearms and hands—fists clenched—toward the head like a praying mantis. Forensic scientists often call this a "pugilistic pose," because it resembles a boxer's stance. I continued piecing together the skull while other members of the team searched for bone fragments and teeth among the burned debris in the trunk. We placed each piece in the body bag until we could get it all back to the morgue.

Within a few minutes, I saw what might be fractures and beveling consistent with a gunshot wound to the head, but without X-rays we couldn't be sure. It doesn't take a rocket scientist to know that the victim didn't climb in the trunk and lock it behind him, shoot himself in the head, set the car on fire, and then drive it over the cliff. He must have been shot first, placed in the car trunk, and then the car was set on fire. But how did it get to the bottom of the ravine?

While police were seeking to identify the MGB and anthropologists were gathering up the body parts, a Tennessee arson investigator was examining the car to figure out just what had happened. The melted tires and glass showed that the fire was intense and of long duration. Still, despite what Hollywood movies teach us, not all cars that go over a cliff necessarily catch on fire and explode. The investigator was looking for clues as to what had started the fire. The presence of blood pooled beneath the trunk liner said that the victim had bled profusely before the car was set on fire.

It didn't take long for the arson investigator to find what he was looking for: the pattern and distribution of burning were consistent with an accelerant. A flammable liquid, perhaps gasoline, had been used to burn the car. Someone had set the car on fire to destroy it and the body in the trunk. Few people realize how difficult it is to destroy a body completely. Something is always overlooked, no matter how determined or thorough the killer. That's the beauty of forensics. It allows us to find evidence even in the most hidden places. Forensic scientists hone their skills and learn from both the wisdom and mistakes of others as they work on hundreds of homicides.

When we had all finished our field analyses, authorities took the body to the morgue for autopsy. There X-rays of the head revealed a bullet lodged in the top of his spinal cord. The bullet had entered his neck from behind, fracturing the first and second cervical vertebrae and severing the spinal cord. Undoubtedly death had been immediate. Anthropological examination of the skeleton revealed the body was that of a young adult white man, twenty-five to thirty years old at death. The condition of the organs was consistent with a death that had occurred within the past few days.

Police checked their list of missing persons and got a listing of MGB owners in the area from the Tennessee Department of Safety. Within hours dental records allowed us to identify the body as a twenty-seven-year-old white male student at ETSU. The police investigation focused on the window between Wednesday night, when Janney was last seen at a cookout at his trailer park home, and Friday noon, when his body was found. Investigators soon found the killers, who told authorities that the victim had owed them money and that, after they shot him, they had rolled his body in a carpet and put it in the trunk of the car. They then removed the license plates so authorities would be unable to trace the vehicle. They doused the car with gasoline, put it in gear, and pushed it over the two-hundred-foot cliff. Just before it went over, they tossed in a match that caused it to burst into flames. The killers thought the fire would consume both the car and the body, to hide the man's identity and the cause of death. As it turned out, they were dead wrong.

7. A FLORIDA HANGING

The art of living is more like that of wrestling than of dancing. The main thing is to stand firm and be ready for an unforeseen attack.

—MARCUS AURELIUS

In October 1990, at the end of another hot summer, a man stumbled upon a skeleton in the Withlacoochee State Park in Pinellas, Florida. Police arriving at the scene found remains that seemed to be those of a man who either had been hanged or had hanged himself. A rope and simple noose were still looped over the branch of a Florida live oak, some thirty or forty feet off the ground. A plant had taken root on the branch where the rope touched it. Bones and a man's clothing were scattered on the ground. Nothing capable of identifying the victim could be found.

Although I had seen a few cases of suicide and of male autoerotic asphyxia (accidental death by hanging during masturbation, intended to heighten orgasm), this was the first I'd seen in which the remains were skeletonized. The other hangings I'd worked were recent deaths for which the medical examiner could determine the manner—was it self-inflicted or caused by an outside agent? In one case a man had hanged himself in an orange orchard in Florida and was still hanging from the tree when he was found. His neck was grotesquely elongated and his mummified body remained mostly intact. Because a medical examiner works by examining soft tissue and none was present in the case I'm about to describe, it was outside his expertise. But it was right up the alley of a forensic anthropologist. So, too, was the Pinellas skeleton.

Using kite string and stakes, the police laid out a series of squares that covered the crime scene. They intended to use this archaeological grid as a point of reference, much like graph paper, for recording the exact location of every piece of potential evidence that had been found on top of or dug up from the ground. This technique, combined with photographs and a site sketch, would provide the documentation necessary to reconstruct, even months or years later, the events surrounding the death. Investigators found most of the skeleton, clothing, and tennis shoes scattered over a small area on the ground. The height of the noose, twelve feet up, meant that the dead man's toes had been more than six feet above the ground— not an easy position to get into. There were only three possibilities: he had climbed the tree with a rope around his neck and jumped; he had stood on the roof of a truck or the top of a car, although none was found at the scene; or someone had helped him, willingly or unwillingly. The first two possibilities were suicide; the third, even if the person helped with the hanging at the deceased's request, was homicide. At the Smithsonian, Doug Owsley and I were asked to help figure out which it was.

What was most unusual about the case was that one of the seven bones of the neck, a cervical vertebra broken on one side, was still in the noose when the police arrived at the scene. All of the other bones had fallen to the ground like so many leaves. We hoped this crushed bone held enough information to tell us whether the person's death was self-inflicted. But there was more. Near the remains police found three pieces of electrician's tape still stuck together, a piece of fabric, four cans of motor oil, a deodorant container, a pair of swimmer's goggles with black electrician's tape covering its lenses, a thin leather thong stuck to one of his wrist bones, two knives, and a box cutter. These items weren't what you'd expect to find in the woods at the base of a tall tree. It was possible that some items were associated with the hanging and some weren't. It would be up to the police to sort the trash from the evidence.

One piece of information critical to solving the case was how long the man had been dead. Police could tell by the condition of the clothing and the skeletonized state of the body that the man had been dead a few months at least. But if there was to be a court case, prosecutors would need a more detailed estimate of the time since death. They also needed to know whether the man had died where his skeleton was found. He could have been brought there sometime after his death. For help, we turned to the surroundings. When a body is found in the woods, plants often supply the answer.

A botanist is a scientist who specializes in studying plants and trees. Botanists can look at a leaf, a vine, a piece of bark, an acorn, or a root and name the species of plant or tree from which it came. Often, a botanist can tell you how long it takes for a plant's root, trunk, or branch to grow an inch. If a root grows one inch a month, then each inch of root that has grown into a bone at a crime scene signifies a month in which the bone has lain undisturbed. Determining how long a plant has been alive allows a scientist to learn how long a body lying on the plant has been dead. Here the botanist estimated that the plant growing around the rope was between one and two years old. Our guy had been hanging there for one to two years, if not longer.

Since there was no soft tissue and, thus, no sign of bullet holes, stab wounds, bruises, or rope burns, the typical signs of murderous intention could not be found. Maggots had eaten the most crucial evidence. There were no marks or grooves around the bones of the neck. If tissue had remained on the skull we might have found petechia, small red dots caused by increased blood pressure to the head, but there were none. Only the skeleton would tell us what happened to this man.

Death by hanging can result from asphyxia as the throat is squeezed. It can also occur if the spinal cord breaks, shutting down the brain and bringing to a halt all of life's functions. Failing those two possibilities, the body's drop may crush one or more cervical (neck) vertebrae, with consequent fatal damage to the spinal cord. When a person is sentenced to death by hanging—which at the time of this writing is still on the books in Delaware, New Hampshire, and Washington—authorities take the person's weight and height into consideration to ensure that the fall literally breaks the neck. The goal of a legal hanging is to cause death without decapitation or unnecessary suffering from strangulation. In fact, drop distance tables compiled by the U.S. Army specify exactly how far the condemned should fall to ensure a humane death.

The "drop," based on the person's height and weight, is computed so as to deliver 1,260 pounds of force to the neck. For example, a person weighing 150 pounds should drop six feet, seven inches. Not that you'd necessarily want to know, but to compute your "drop height" in feet and inches, divide 1,260 by your weight. A greater height might cause decapitation and a lower one might induce slow strangulation. Done properly, hanging should cause separation between the third and fourth cervical vertebrae (in medical terms, between C-3 and C-4). Gradual pressure to the neck, on the other hand—such as what happens in autoerotic asphyxia or manual strangulation—won't damage the vertebrae. In the case at hand, the single vertebra stuck to the noose would prove crucial to our interpretation of the manner of death.

When we received the remains and material evidence, Doug Owsley and I laid the bones out on the laboratory tables and began our examination. Doug estimated the person's age, race, sex, and stature while I looked for evidence of skeletal and dental trauma and studied the material evidence found at the scene. The problem with this type of puzzle is that it doesn't come with directions, so it involves some guesswork—the "art" of Forensic Anthropology—on our part. Still, it wasn't long before we knew the bones were those of a thirty- to thirty-five-year-old white man who stood about five feet nine inches tall.

We next needed to decide whether the found objects were somehow related to the dead man. First I examined the black electrical tape. Three pieces, each about six inches long, were overlapped along their lengthwise edges, making a single strip about as wide as the three fingers extended in a Boy Scout's salute. In the middle of the tape was a raised area, a sort of bump. I soon realized that the bump had a very specific and recognizable shape. It was formed like a nose, suggesting that the tape had been used to cover the decedent's face. Because it didn't make sense that he would have taped his own nose and mouth, the possibility was emerging that the man had been tortured before being killed.

I next examined the thin leather thong stuck to one of his left wrist bones, the lunate, a crescent-shaped bone resembling the moon. Its irregular shape often causes it to be mistaken for a small rock or a piece of wood. The thong was old and rubbed smooth in places, suggesting that it had been on his wrist for many months prior to his death. The police had first wondered if it had been used to tie his wrists to prevent him from struggling. Its polished appearance, however, suggested that the dead man wore it as bracelet. My attention then went to the swimmer's goggles. They were typical plastic goggles that any swimmer might wear to protect his eyes against chlorine. Since the decedent had been found in a wooded area, far from the ocean or even any swimming pool, we deduced that the killer had the goggles on hand when he hanged the victim, but that they didn't belong to the victim. The electrician's tape on the lenses seemed intended to cover the man's eyes before he died. Here was a second piece of evidence suggesting the man had been tortured or, at the very least, blindfolded. The bottles of motor oil, deodorant, and fabric, possibly from a curtain, yielded no explanation for their own presence. Our only guess was that the fabric might have been used either as a gag or to bind the man's hands or feet.

The knives added another sinister dimension. They might have been used to torture the man, or to stab him after he was hanged. If the man had been stabbed we might expect to find cuts in his bones, something for which we would look closely. But knives don't always strike bone. I thought it unlikely that the knives had been used only to scare the man. Whoever had killed him wasn't fooling around with pranks or idle threats—the result proved that they meant business. His clothing showed no evidence of stab or gunshot wounds. The size of the victim's pants waist and length confirmed Doug's judgment that he was of medium height, five feet nine being average for adult men in the United States, and I found no marks or unusual characteristics in the clothing that might help us narrow our search.

The skeleton was nearly complete but gave no evidence of carnivore activity, a fact that I found surprising. My own experience with bodies in wooded and marshy areas of Tennessee, the Carolinas, Louisiana, and Texas had taught me that large and small carnivores alike feed on human bodies, especially their bones. Meat-eating animals chew on the soft parts of these bones, leaving visible scratches, grooves, and puncture marks with their teeth. The absence of such activity in this case made me think he'd been dead less than two years.

Some of the man's ribs had been broken at or near the time of death. The broken ribs were still relatively intact but there were long fractures, showing that these bones had been subjected to force sufficient to make them bend to the point of splitting. If the ribs had been broken months after death the breaks would have looked different; the bones would have snapped in two and not merely split and stayed together. It was clear he had been beaten either just before or soon after he was hanged. In other words, everything we found was weighing in favor of the conclusion that he was a victim of homicidal—not suicidal—hanging.

The presence of one or more broken ribs in a case like this is certainly an attention grabber for anyone looking for evidence of trauma to help determine the cause or manner of death. Bones broken more than about ten days before death usually show evidence of healing; breakage occurring just a few days prior to death does not. That's why a broken bone without evidence of healing catches our eye and heightens our suspicion that the injury was related to the person's death. However, something I heard at a forensic anthropology seminar in New Orleans in February 2005 has forever changed the way I look at broken bones.

I remember my jaw dropping as I listened to a young graduate student describe her research at the Body Farm. During her research on the nocturnal activities of raccoons, she captured behavior on film that, to my knowledge, had never been seen before. A cuddly raccoon waddled up to a decomposing human corpse covered with what appeared to be chicken wire (presumably to keep out large carnivores and prevent them from dragging away body parts), reached its hand into the abdominal cavity, wrenched out one of the person's ribs, and began chewing on the end of it. The student had also captured raccoons on film as they grabbed handfuls of maggots out of body cavities and ate them. I really wouldn't have believed it if I hadn't seen the video myself, and I won't be surprised if someday a clever defense attorney uses this information to suggest to a jury that a rib might have been broken postmortem by raccoons feeding on the body, rather than by an assailant at the time the victim died. In the present case, if raccoons were involved, they would have had to wait until the body decomposed and fell to the ground. Of course, this doesn't guarantee that animals are responsible for all bone breakage, only that we have one more possibility to consider. In this case, I still think the damage to this man's ribs was due to someone beating him.

The bone in the noose was next on my to-do list. It was one of the seven cervical vertebrae in the neck and had stayed within the noose through a combination of luck and bodily decomposition—luck because the wind and rain didn't knock it out of the noose, and bodily decomposition because the tissues of the neck and throat created a sticky substance that held it in place. The fact that the bone was found this way made it particularly interesting to me. I knew it might tell us whether the victim had been dropped from a height or slowly lowered to his death. I found that one of the two holes—foramina or canals, in medical terms—carrying the vertebral artery down his neck had been crushed. Although the left foramen was circular and normal, the right one, about as wide as a drinking straw, had been squeezed so tightly and with such force that it had collapsed. That alone would have resulted in death.

Stacking the seven cervical bones like poker chips, I found that the bone stuck in the noose was C-4. The force of the drop had caused the man's neck bones to separate between C-3 and C-4, just as they're supposed to do in a legal hanging. But of course the law doesn't allow a man to be hanged in a Florida state park.

Looking at a photograph of the neck bone in the noose we could figure out the man's body position at the moment he was hanged. The pressure and force of the knot had crushed the right side of this man's fourth cervical vertebra. When a killer puts the noose around a victim's neck, the knot is usually placed to the side of the victim's neck. Think of the Westerns you've seen; the cowboy, hands tied behind his back, is seated on his horse. The noose is always to his side, not the back of his neck. In legal hangings the knot is usually placed behind the left ear. The position of the noose in most suicidal hangings, in comparison, is such that the knot is placed at the back of the neck. So although no soft tissue remained, we could reconstruct this murder. The bare bone evidence, so to speak, from the scene provided unequivocal proof that someone had placed the noose around the man's neck; his death was not self-inflicted. That the right vertebral canal had been crushed left no doubt he had been dropped from a height and not slowly lowered when he was hanged. All of the evidence suggested murder.

We even got a good idea of what the man looked like. Doug and I took the skull, with its unusually long and narrow features, across Constitution Avenue to a computer specialist at FBI Headquarters, where he superimposed on the skull a photograph of the man believed by the Pinellas County Police to be the victim. Everything fit. The size and position of the eyes fit the sockets of the skull; the mouth and teeth fit; the skull was the proper size and proportion with respect to the photo. The ghostly image of the skull visible behind the photographic image on the computer, like the face of a drowned man at the bottom of a swimming pool, was that of a thirty-two-year-old drifter named Randall Andrews. An FBI forensic odontologist compared the teeth recovered from the scene with dental records and X-rays and confirmed the identification.

Our examination complete, we wrote up our findings and presented them to the Pinellas police. We said the evidence suggested the victim had been beaten before being hanged, given that his ribs had been broken and he hadn't survived long enough for them to heal. Additionally, we said that he had been dropped from a height sufficient to cause crushing of his neck vertebrae. However, we could not say how far he fell.

Our report confirmed the suspicions of the police. By this time they had several murder suspects in custody. A man arrested on unrelated charges had telephoned his girlfriend and told her that he and three other men had hanged a man. She, in turn, told someone who told someone else, and, eventually, this information got to the police. The prisoner said that the victim had accidentally stumbled onto a marijuana farm. The assailants beat the victim before killing him, according to this informant. That explained the victim's broken ribs and the taped goggles, electrician's tape, fabric, and knives. Most likely one man climbed the tree and looped the noose-ended rope over the tree limb, while the others lifted the victim off the ground as high as they could and dropped him, or lifted him to the fork in the tree and pushed him off from there. Both of those are just theories, but they potentially explain how his fourth cervical vertebra was crushed and separated from the rest of his spine.

The men were charged with Andrews's murder, but prosecutors were unable to get a grand jury to hand up an indictment. Without enough evidence of guilt to satisfy a jury, the suspects were not tried. In 2002, twelve years after working the case, I phoned Florida detectives Tim Whitfield and Gary Kimble for an update. So far, it seems, some men—it had to have been more than one, and probably more than two—have beaten the system. At this point, they've gotten away with murder.

8. A QUESTION OF MURDER

When you have eliminated the impossible, whatever remains,
however improbable, must be the truth.
—SIR ARTHUR CONAN DOYLE

A couple of months after he'd brought Steven Hicks's remains to the Smithsonian Institution for analysis, Ohio medical examiner Dr. William Cox brought us another set of bones. A farmer plowing his field had found the skeletonized remains and, near them, a twelve-gauge shotgun with an empty casing in the chamber. Also present were some tattered clothing, a belt, shoes, a wallet, a ring of rusty and bent keys, a Saint Christopher's medallion, and a plastic nasal spray bottle. I think Dr. Cox had been pleased with the way we'd handled the case of Jeffrey Dahmer's first victim and knew that we would again be thorough in our analysis. He wanted to know whether the man had committed suicide or had been murdered. This highly unusual case reveals why things aren't always the way they seem.

Unpacking the remains, we found that the skull was in pieces. When we reconstructed it, we found that some pieces were bleached white from exposure to the sun while others were dark brown from being buried just below the surface of the soil. Bones, like photographs and wallpaper, fade when exposed to direct sunlight. Neither I nor Doug Owsley, my boss in the lab, had any doubt that the skull had been broken several years ago—long enough, at least, for it to become bleached. Another indication that the remains had been on the ground not for weeks or months but for years was that the cotton portion of what was obviously a pair of men's underwear had completely disintegrated, leaving only the waistband with a Jockey logo.

Doug and I put together the biological profile of a white man who had been dead for three to five years. The skull was broken in a way suggesting that he had suffered a gunshot wound to the face. To test our suicide hypothesis, we used a low-power microscope to look up into his frontal sinuses—the cavernous area above the eye orbits—where we found a small piece of nitrate cellulose, commonly known as gunpowder. The way we saw it, the gunpowder could have gotten so far up in his frontal sinuses only if the shotgun barrel was in his mouth or under his chin when it discharged, so that the bullet(s) and gunpowder traveled *upward* more than *backward*, lodging in the frontal bone and not the occipital bone. Later, we learned that when he was last seen, the man, despondent over a failed marriage, had gone hunting. Four and a half years passed before he reappeared.

Finished with the skull, we moved our examination down to the spine and arms, and then to the hips and legs. What we found was baffling. Several of the arm and leg bones had recent cuts spaced exactly eighteen inches apart. The hip bones, which were bleached white from the sun, had lead pellets in them—bird shot. The problem was that the shotgun found beside the body had fired not bird shot but a "pumpkin ball," a rifled slug about the size of a large marble. More important, the degree of damage to the skull indicated that there was no way that this man could have shot himself twice in the head, although multiple head shots are sometimes found in a suicide, where the bullets don't have enough power to break through the skull and enter the brain, but merely slide under the scalp. I took X-rays of the hips and spine and found they were riddled with bird shot, an image reminiscent of billiard balls scattered across a pool table. I taped the two hip bones to the sacrum so that they were anatomically correct and inserted thin wooden dowels into the pellet holes to see if I could figure out the angle at which the pellets had entered the bones.

By the time I was done, the pelvis looked like a white porcupine with red quills sticking out of it. Using our three-dimensional courtroom model to describe the pellets' movement, we could show they had traveled from the victim's head toward his toes, from behind to front, and from right to left. What was most telling, however, was that some pellets had penetrated the head of the femur, but not the hip socket. The only way this could have happened was if the man's hip was already separated when the bird shot hit. Otherwise, the pellets had to pass through the hip socket to burrow their way into the femur head.

When we had finished our investigation, we could tell the Ohio medical examiner and the local county coroner more than they'd expected. This was no run-of-the-mill forensic case, for several reasons. The remains were indeed those of the man whom Dr. Cox suspected. They had lain on the ground for three to five years. Doug and I thought it was a likely suicide, although, in the absence of a witness or scientific proof, we could not rule out the possibility that the gun had accidentally discharged as the man dropped it or tripped. In any case, we were sure it was not homicide, so the authorities could call off the investigators searching for a motive and a killer. What was surprising was that the man's remains had been shot several years *after* his death; this probable suicide was followed by a postmortem shooting. Although we'll never know for sure, we guessed that a hunter had shot the skeleton not knowing it was human, perhaps during target practice or while shooting at birds or rabbits. The disclike tractor blades had made the shallow parallel cuts in the bones when the farmer cultivated his field. A photo of the tractor in the field, towing a plow with disc-shaped tines, alerted us to the cause of the cuts. We asked one of the detectives to measure the distance between the tines and found they exactly matched the spaces between the cuts in the bones.

In the absence of scientific proof or the testimony of a witness, the county coroner was reluctant to declare the death a suicide, nor would he certify that the shooting was accidental. Instead, he ruled the cause of death as undetermined. Using only bones, we had reconstructed the sequence of events and could tell that a couple of years after this poor man died he was shot with bird shot, then later run over by a tractor. No one who set out to complicate an investigation could have done a better job than the farmer and the hunter did with this one—the stuff of novels, no doubt.

9. SEARCHING FOR A FRIEND'S GRAVE

Be not unkind or proud,
But think about old friends the most.

—WILLIAM BUTLER YEATS, *The Wind Among the Reeds*

For people who have never fought in a war, it is difficult, maybe impossible, to fathom the strength of the bonds military comrades form and the passion with which they seek closure when one of them is killed or goes missing in action. This is the story of such a bond, and of the determination of one fighting man to find and bring home the remains of another. It is also the story of one of my many treks through the jungles of Vietnam, and the surprising way in which the lost Marine was found.

Dennis Wayne Hammond was born April 26, 1946, in Madisonville, Texas, to Opal and Ernest Hammond. He was the baby of the family. His brother, Willie, was seven and his sister, Carlene, was thirteen when Denny was born. Fourteen months later, the Hammonds moved to Detroit, where Ernest went to work in an automobile plant. Denny grew up in Detroit, went through the public school system, and became a star at hockey and football. A tall, lean, good-looking man, he hunted and fished, and he dreamed of owning a Corvette, buying land in Canada, and working as a hunting guide or forest ranger. But first he would enlist in the Marines and fight in the war in Vietnam. Debate over the rightness of the war that would lead to demonstrations and riots in the coming years was just beginning to make newspaper headlines. Hammond believed the cause was just, and he wanted to be part of it.

Denny Hammond went to Vietnam in 1966, two years out of high school and twenty years of age. Before long he earned what many thought was a cushy assignment as a member of the Marines' new Combined Action Program (CAP). CAP squads, composed of a small group of Marines and a navy medic, lived in rural villages in South Vietnam, getting to know the local people, fighting alongside the South Vietnamese Popular Forces (SVPF). Their purpose was to earn the confidence and respect of the Vietnamese for the government in Saigon while they boosted the spirits and fighting ability of the PF troops. The Vietnamese soldiers were skittish at first, reluctant to fight beside the Marines. However, as the months went by they grew in confidence and bravery, inspired by the friendly but disciplined Americans. At the height of the program, 114 CAP teams were in place in South Vietnam.

It took an exemplary record to be accepted into the CAP program: four months' experience in combat; a high recommendation from a commanding officer; no record of disciplinary action; and, above all, no evidence of prejudice against the Vietnamese people. Hammond volunteered for CAP duty, met the criteria, and was assigned to CAP Echo 2, situated a few miles from the Danang Airbase and eight thousand miles from his boyhood Detroit home.

CAP team members learned to bow in greeting; to shake hands in the Vietnamese way, using both hands; and to refrain from crossing their legs when they sat, a gesture considered rude in much of Southeast Asia, although not in Vietnam. The young Americans earned the affection and respect of the villagers by sharing with them the deprivations and risks of the war raging around them. Later, one CAP veteran would say that CAP team members knew that if their village came under attack, help was unlikely to arrive in time to save them.

If Denny Hammond, by this time a Marine corporal, believed this, he kept it to himself. In early February 1968, Echo 4, another of the CAP teams, came under attack by the North Vietnamese Army and Vietcong. The Tet Offensive was in full swing, and the North Vietnamese were intent on capturing the airfield at Danang. Echo 4 stood in the way. By February 8, Echo 4 was running out of ammunition. The situation looked grim. Captain Howard L. Joselane, the Echo teams' commanding officer, sent out a call to Echos 1, 2, and 3 for volunteers to come to the aid of Echo 4. The result was a seventeen-man reaction force, which Joselane himself would lead. The men assembled at Echo headquarters in Hoa Vang.

Hammond, twenty-one, with only days left on his tour of duty, was one of the volunteers. Mike Readinger, a radio operator at Echo headquarters, noticed Hammond when his truck pulled up. Readinger and Hammond had become friends, and the radioman, using Hammond's nickname, Ham-bone, asked him why he was volunteering for the detail. Hammond replied, according to Readinger, that he'd been in Vietnam for two years and hadn't accomplished anything. "This will be my last chance," Readinger quotes his friend as having said.

The reaction force worked its way across rice paddies and open terrain to an irrigation ditch a few yards from the jungle where Echo 4 was trapped. Suddenly they were in the midst of an ambush by an estimated two hundred to three hundred North Vietnamese soldiers. Twelve of the men who had set out to rescue Echo 4 were killed. Three—Dennis Hammond, Joseph Zawtocki, and Don Talbot—were captured. Only two Marines escaped the ambush. Talbot escaped from captivity later that day. The date was February 8, 1968. Hammond would have gone home eight days later.

Life as a prisoner of war is no stroll in the park, even under the most humane conditions. For Americans captured in South Vietnam, brutality, physical and psychological torture, and diseases born of an inadequate and unfamiliar diet were the main components of daily life. The men were reduced to little more than skeletons within a few months' time. Vietnamese POW camps were makeshift affairs; prisoners were moved often to avoid detection by U.S. troops that might have rescued them. Occasionally the camps themselves were caught up in U.S. bombing raids. Simply talking with another prisoner could lead to being beaten, caged, or deprived of food and water. Survival often became the prisoner's only goal, docility the only way to achieve it, calm but unwavering resistance the only means of staying strong.

Against this background, Hammond and fellow Marine Private First Class Earl Clyde Weatherman attempted an escape on April 1. Within an hour, their captors rounded them up. One account says Weatherman was executed on the spot; another says he was seen in the early 1970s, living with a woman in Vietnam. Hammond, shot in the back of his lower leg while trying to escape, was tied to a branch and carried like a pig back to the camp. There he was beaten in front of the rest of the prisoners, placed in stocks, and fed a coffee cup of rotten rice daily. Captain Hal Kushner, another prisoner, later wrote that Hammond was forced to defecate into his hands and throw the waste away as far as he could. Hammond spent two weeks in this situation. Somehow, he survived for nearly two more years. In early 1970, an emaciated Denny Hammond fell ill with dysentery. The disease overwhelmed him; he died on March 7 or 8. Fellow prisoners buried him in the Quang Nam jungle near the camp. Joseph Zawtocki, the Marine captured at the same time as Hammond, followed him in December and was also buried in the jungle, a few feet from Hammond. Zawtocki's remains were later recovered and repatriated to his family in 1985. Although one of the prisoners who helped bury Hammond thought he knew where his remains would be found, several attempts— starting in 1975 and repeated over the next twenty years—failed to recover them.

Army sergeant Thomas J. Davis was one of the prisoners who witnessed Hammond's death. The circumstances under which the two men were captured were strikingly similar. Like Hammond, Davis was part of a platoon sent to rescue a group that was under fire. Like Hammond's platoon, the men in Davis's group walked into an ambush and were captured in Happy Valley. Davis's capture came in March 1968, a month after Hammond's. Hammond was in the Quang Nam camp when Davis got there. The two men became friends. After Hammond died, Davis spent another three years as a POW in various Vietnamese prison camps.

Looking out of a hotel room that faced the polluted Han River in downtown Danang, I saw nearly deserted streets and very little activity. It was five-thirty A.M. on June 24, 1995. Two teenage girls squatted on their haunches beneath a tree, watching the sunrise. A large fishing boat lay motionless on the water as a wide swath of sunlight reflected brightly off the river. A light cloud of mist hung low on the mountains surrounding the harbor.

With me were U.S. Army captain James McGinnis, team leader for this Central Identification Laboratory (CIL) expedition, and Sergeant Randy Brown, also in the army and attached to the CIL. We were in Vietnam awaiting authorization to excavate another aircraft crash site in Quang Binh Province, a six-hour drive to the north. Such waits are common in our work. We can't simply go into an area and start digging; we have to get permission from representatives of the host country for everything we plan to do. In addition to the months of planning, coordination, and discussions before we arrive to dig a site, when we get there we have to meet with officials from the province, district, city, town, village, and hamlet. There we discuss topics such as how many local laborers we'll need to assist us, how long it will take, how much wood or bamboo we'll need, and where we'll be staying. It's a Communist country and we're their guests. Very little gets done without their permission and support.

Also in Danang was a team from JTF-FA (Joint Task Force—Full Accounting), our sister military organization at Camp Smith on Oahu. JTF-FA was responsible for investigating cases and providing investigative teams to locate unmarked graves of U.S. soldiers and aircraft crash sites in Southeast Asia. They also manned oral history teams to search historical documents and war records in museums in Vietnam, Laos, and Cambodia. Led by Chief Warrant Officer 2 Tony Banks, the JTF-FA's Research and Investigation Team (RIT) was there to investigate a jungle site and look for a grave that the CIL would later excavate if the RIT search succeeded. Banks asked the CIL team to go along to provide technical advice. The expedition was meant to help Command Sergeant Major Thomas J. Davis find the grave of his former POW buddy, Marine corporal Dennis Hammond.

Davis, who was liberated from captivity during Operation Homecoming in 1973, was in 1995 the only U.S. army sergeant major and former Vietnam war POW still on active duty. He had recently helped a U.S. team find the grave of another of his friends. That success led him to hope he could do what several other teams had failed to do: find Denny Hammond's remains and bring them home to his family. Twenty-five years had passed since the sergeant major had been at the POW camp.

Although every site I've worked on in Southeast Asia has its own particular significance, the grave of a former POW seems to evoke a special combination of emotion and mystique. Not only did POWs fight in the war, but they also endured the pain and degradation of physical deprivation and both physical and emotional torture. The previous night I had sat at my desk trying to imagine the unimaginable, what it must have been like to be a POW. Now my focus was on the hope that we'd find Denny Hammond's grave. We'd know in a few hours whether that hope had any chance of becoming a reality.

We left the hotel in two vans, bound for the Danang airport, where we boarded a Russian-built Mi-17 (pronounced "M-eye-seventeen") helicopter for the thirty-minute ride to Quang Nam Province to the south. (Quang Binh, where my team was to go, was in Communist-controlled North Vietnam. During the war it was the most heavily bombed province in all of Vietnam. Quang Nam and Quang Ngai, the two provinces where the events in this chapter took place, border each other in what was then South Vietnam. Quang Ngai is the province where the My Lai massacre occurred—an entire village of men, women, and children that was wiped out by U.S. soldiers.) The helicopter shook and rattled so much that it seemed as if we were flying in an antiquated washing machine. We followed the coastline and then turned inland, flying low over a few scattered hamlets and streams and then over the thick mountainous jungle of Vietnam. The view was incredible; it looked like a picture postcard of the Amazon. Our landing zone was in a sawgrass clearing that villagers had prepared in anticipation of our arrival.

When we touched down, the Mi-17 was surrounded by curious men, children, and women carrying infants on their backs or in slings at their chests. They were among the poorest people I'd seen in Vietnam. Their dark skins made them look more like the Lao I had often worked with than Vietnamese. Their clothing was dirty and tattered; many of the teenage girls were braless, which is unusual in Vietnam. Some boys and men carried small, crudely carved crossbows of the sort used for hunting birds and small game. They spoke a hill tribe dialect that left our American linguists unable to converse with them. We could all have been mute or deaf and it wouldn't have mattered at all. Luckily, we had some Vietnamese interpreters with us.

We gathered our supplies, and a local man led us to the site of the POW camp where Davis, Hammond, and Zawtocki were held and where the latter two had died and were buried. The thirty-minute walk took us through sawgrass taller than any of us. Sawgrass is well named; it cuts through the skin when it makes contact. The cuts don't close easily, and when sweat gets into them they sting miserably. We navigated along narrow rocky paths slippery with the morning dew, across two streams, and up a mountainside to a clearing where the POW camp used to be. At any one time, the camp housed from three to fifteen POWs, including Americans, Germans, and ARVN (Army of the Republic of Vietnam) soldiers who fought on the American side. Five German missionaries—three women and two men—sent to Vietnam under West Germany's aid program, had also been held in the camp. They were supposed to be considered neutral because they treated all who were wounded, regardless of which government they served. Three of the missionaries were later released; two women died in captivity and were buried in this POW camp. Both of their bodies were found and repatriated to Germany; the remains of at least one of the female nurses came through the CIL before going home to Germany.

Tom Davis, a man in his late forties, had a knife on his belt, a Washington Redskins baseball cap on his head, and a Sony camcorder slung from his left shoulder. He had spent nearly a year of his youth on this lonely mountain. Davis had described the way he and his fellow POWs had looked like emaciated hobos, the result of subsisting primarily on rice and manioc, with an occasional bite or two of chicken. Although I wanted to know more about life in the POW camp, I couldn't bring myself to intrude on Davis in that way.

Nothing was left of the POW camp—no house frames, fence debris, or familiar landmarks. If the Vietnamese hadn't taken us to the clearing where the camp once stood, we would never have known it existed. The vegetation had changed, the area had been cleared for growing rice, the villagers had felled a large tree that lay across the open area, and there was now a small bamboo house fifty meters uphill from where the ramshackle POW shelters once stood. The only evidence we had that soldiers had ever been there was a rusty bolt from a Chinese rifle. It felt, quite literally, like standing in the middle of a ghost town.

For fifteen minutes, Davis walked around the cleared area, sparsely cultivated with rice plants struggling to survive in the dry soil. Then he told us nothing looked the same to him. When he was held prisoner there in the late 1960s, he said, there was nothing but triple canopy jungle, a few bamboo shacks for the POWs and guards, and a fence around it all. The clearing altered the landscape dramatically. The Vietnamese had used the thick jungle as concealment.

"You'd never build a POW camp in a clearing like this," Davis told us.

We took a few photographs of the area and the villagers who had accompanied us, and the sergeant major recorded it all on videotape. After about a half hour at the site and a discussion with Chief Warrant Officer Banks, we decided to move on and search elsewhere for Corporal Hammond's grave. We retraced our steps along the slippery path, which was infested with leeches, biting ants, and mosquitoes. I felt as though I were a scientific specimen in a bell jar filled with hungry insects. Turning left onto another small path, one of the villagers led us to a small stream. I moved quickly along the moist path like a barefoot man walking on hot coals.

. . .

If I had to choose between sawgrass and leeches, I think I'd take the saw-grass. Lucky me, though—in the jungles of Vietnam I got both.

I was wearing the same style of green combat jungle boots that U.S. troops wore during the war. One of the bad things about these boots is that they have a perforated vent along the instep to allow the foot to breathe and water to drain after the soldiers have crossed streams. Unfortunately, these metallic vents often fall out, leaving a perfect opening the diameter of a cigarette. Leeches can work their way through almost any barrier, as long as there is room for them to squeeze their nasty, wriggly little bodies. They're everywhere along stream banks and jungles, wherever the ground is shady and moist.

Years ago during a trip to Southeast Asia I noticed an unusual odor while we walked in some parts of the jungle; I soon learned that was my signal to start looking for leeches. Later I deduced that the pungent aroma came from decaying foliage. Jungle leeches cling to low-lying branches, vines, and leaves fallen to the ground. They stand up on their hind ends and wriggle, waiting for just the right moment to climb aboard a passerby. If your boot or clothing brushes against them, they'll grab on and immediately try to push their way through any opening to get to your skin. They can flatten out and climb their way through boot eyelets, up the tongue of your tennis shoe or boot and up your pants legs, even if they're tucked into your socks. If we suspect there are leeches in an area that we'll be going into, we tuck the cuffs of our pants into our socks and use duct tape to close off the opening between the two fabrics. Ground troops refer to duct tape as "hundred-mile-an-hour tape" because it's said to hold down anything in winds up to one hundred miles per hour. I don't know if all that's true, but hundred-mile-an-hour tape was our best chance against leeches.

Jungle leeches (as opposed to the leeches we sometimes find in rice paddies, which are about the size of earthworms) are about the size of a toothpick before they latch onto you, suck your blood, and swell to the thickness of a pencil before dropping off on the ground. Some parts of the jungle, and even some well-worn paths between villages, are infested with these wriggling critters. I'm a leech magnet and tend to be the first in my team to get sucked on. When walking in the jungle, you can see dozens of them standing up on rotten vegetation and soil, swaying to and fro like miniature cobras seeking their prey. If you stand still for a moment, you'll see five or ten of them inching their way toward your boots.

Leeches seem to prefer the warm, lower parts of your body, such as the ankles and calves, but they are just as happy to dig into your groin and stomach if they get the chance. The truth is, they'll gladly attach themselves to any part of your anatomy. They stay attached for a few minutes as they become engorged with blood and then drop off fat, full, and happy. They're stealthy, and you never even know they're crawling on you—you can't feel them at all. They inject a chemical into your bloodstream that both numbs the area so you don't feel the bite and keeps the blood from clotting. Your blood runs free until they're done sucking and drop off. You stop bleeding a few minutes later. That's usually when you notice you've been bitten— either when you feel the blood running down your skin like a bead of sweat, or when you or someone else sees a red spot on your pants or shirt. One bite can leave a bloody patch the size of an orange on your clothes.

The Vietnamese usually roll their pant legs up and take off their socks so they can see the leeches as soon as they climb on their skin, and then knock them off with their fingers, a twig, or a knife. Americans, on the other hand, try to prevent them from climbing on board in the first place. We also use spray bug repellent, which doesn't seem to work, to try to keep them from climbing aboard. The best way to make them drop off once they've become attached and are in the act of sucking your blood is to burn them off with a lit cigarette. You simply touch them with the hot tip, and they fall off immediately. You're then wise to chop them in half with your machete; if not, they'll be back on you within seconds.

Our villager guide was telling our linguists that he'd seen a grave marked with American writing near the stream, but Davis knew this wasn't Corporal Hammond's grave.

"There would have been no reason for us to come down to this stream.

There's no bamboo for us to collect around here and no plants for food; and it's too far from the POW camp. The guards would never take us this far from the camp, and we sure weren't allowed to simply walk around on our own," he explained. "We marked the grave with a simple bamboo cross and nothing else."

With that, we headed back to the Mi-17 to eat lunch and gather our thoughts. We'd failed to find the grave, but no one was about to give up.

Back at the helicopter, all the expedition members settled down to the few cans of food some had brought with them or to a lunch of small squares of cooked egg and glutinous rice wrapped inside green banana leaves. The only beverage was warm bottled water, and our dining hall was the inside of a sweltering helicopter. The only option was an outdoor seat in the sawgrass. Although the rice cakes weren't the tastiest that I'd had, they did fill my hungry stomach.

A few minutes later Banks's research and investigation team decided to examine another possible temporary POW camp an hour and a half from the Mi-17. Unfortunately, Captain McGinnis, Sergeant Brown, and I had not come prepared for two long walks, and we were running low on drinking water. The sun was intense, and we were all in danger of dehydration. If one of us ran out of water during the trek, we would compound the problem by having to drink somebody else's, so the three of us decided to wait at the helicopter until the others completed their search. They returned in ninety minutes, saying the Vietnamese guide had again taken them to the wrong POW camp. The camp that had held the sergeant major was to the north, and they'd been taken south. Although the area had once been a temporary camp where Americans passed through, it was the wrong camp.

At that point we'd done all we could do. We'd run down all available leads to where the POW camps and alleged graves were, and could go no further without more information. We'd suspected all along that the guide was taking us the wrong way, but we needed to go along with him to prove the point and rule out any possibility of error in memory or direction.

In the helicopter I stared blindly out the window as our airborne washing machine labored on. I mulled over what I'd seen at the POW camp and again wondered what Tom Davis was thinking after revisiting the POW camp. I wondered if it had been difficult for him to maintain his composure when he first stepped into the jungle clearing where he had spent nearly a year as a prisoner. Did his visit to the camp bring up vivid memories that had rested in his mind for twenty-five years? Was it as traumatic as he might have anticipated? What kind of frustration did he feel at not being able to find the grave of his friend? My questions were answered when I glanced over at this gentle man with graying temples and gold-rimmed glasses. His head was slumped forward, and he was asleep. A chill ran up my spine as I thought about how lucky we were: Davis for having survived, and in such good spirits; myself for never having been in his situation.

Once on the ground in Danang, we headed back to the hotel, where the RIT would write their report on what they had and had not found that day. Although we had hit a dry hole, the search was far from over. Another investigation for another jungle POW camp in the province would begin in two days. On that trip, Banks's team found a jackfruit tree with the name of Dennis Hammond and an arrow carved into its trunk. Davis didn't remember who had done the carving. A search-and-recovery team dug around the tree, but found no evidence of Hammond's remains. The search continued. The sergeant major was determined not to give up until he found Corporal Hammond's grave.

In October 2003 we got a blind hit on some bones we cut and sampled for mitochondrial deoxyribonucleic acid (mtDNA). A blind hit is a match made by submitting a DNA sequence from a bone or tooth sample and comparing it against the entire DNA database without knowing to whom it belongs. It's like asking a large crowd if there's anyone out there named John Smith and having someone stand up and say yes. Once we get a mitochondrial sequence, it can be compared with all the database's DNA sequences from Southeast Asia housed at the Armed Forces DNA Identification Laboratory (AFDIL) to see if it matches any of them. In this case, Dennis Hammond's sequence popped up. It was unique in the database.

This finding prompted us to reexamine the skeleton from which the mtDNA came, compile a biological profile, and see if it matched that of Hammond. It did. Then CIL forensic anthropologist Dr. Brad Adams superimposed the skull on top of a photograph of Hammond. In the photo, Hammond's head was shaved, making it easy to see its exact shape. The two images fit perfectly; in fact, it was the best match I'd ever seen with a skull and photograph. We now knew that while Tom Davis and I were searching for Hammond's grave in the jungles of Vietnam in 1995, his remains were sitting on a shelf at the CIL. The Vietnamese had turned them over to U.S. authorities back in 1989, but we hadn't been able to identify Hammond at the time. No teeth had come with the remains, and mtDNA technology had been in its infancy at the time. We were missing too many pieces of the puzzle. But with a little patience, a bit of luck, and developments in DNA analysis, we could identify this soldier, who had been much closer to home than anyone knew. Although a decade had passed since we'd searched for him, I'd often wondered if we would ever find him. Now we had. After being gone for thirty-six years, Dennis Wayne Hammond of Detroit, Michigan, had come home.

10. THE LAST UNKNOWN

Things are not what they seem; or, to be more accurate, they are not only what they seem, but very much else besides.

—ALDOUS HUXLEY, *Vedanta for the Western World*

One month and a week after his twenty-fourth birthday, Mike Blassie, a lieutenant in the U.S. Air Force, spent the last night of his life in the alert barracks at the Bien Hoa Air Base in Vietnam. The base, just north of Saigon, had a long history in the Vietnam War, beginning when the United States started building its air power after the Tonkin Gulf incident of 1964. From there, Blassie would take off at dawn the next morning, May 11, 1972, in his A-37 aircraft, a converted trainer renamed the "Dragonfly" and equipped to drop bombs. His mission was to fly about sixty miles north to An Loc, a provincial capital that was home to some seven thousand people. The city had been under siege by North Vietnamese forces for more than a month. Blassie's mission was to drop a load of napalm and return to the base.

His partner on the trip, flying another plane, remembers seeing Blassie's jet fly low to bomb his target. Suddenly, a plume of white vapor spurted from the olive-drab aircraft. It rolled to the right, dove into the trees, and exploded in a ball of flame. His plane crashed into enemy-controlled territory, making a recovery effort impossible. Because someone witnessed the crash, Blassie was classified Killed in Action, Body Not Recovered (KIA/BNR).

. . .

The oldest of five children, Michael Joseph Blassie was born in St. Louis, Missouri, on April 4, 1948, the son of Jean and George C. Blassie. His father was a staff sergeant in the army air corps during World War II and was working as a meat cutter when Michael died. Friends remember Michael's love of laughter, of tennis and soccer, and of tuna fish and macaroni casseroles. He played the bassoon and saxophone in high school. People knew him as a boy who always did his best. Years later, a friend would tell of how Michael got him so involved in soccer that he was now running a program for two thousand young players.

Michael went from high school to the Air Force Academy, where in 1968 his superiors assigned him to be Lucille Ball's official escort while she was there on location for the movie *Yours, Mine and Ours*. After graduation from the academy Blassie went to pilot training, survival school, and Vietnam. In his four and a half months in the combat zone he flew 132 missions, mostly to support troops fighting on the ground. "Why am I trying to live if I'm just living to die?" Michael Blassie wrote in one of his last letters to Lou Adams Pennebaker, the woman he was planning to marry. "I'll keep on living to fight as long as there's a fighting reason to live or for others to live." The letter was quoted in the June 1, 2003, issue of *Citizen Airman*, a magazine for nonmilitary pilots.

To honor his lost son, George Blassie set up a memorial display in the basement of the family home displaying Michael's awards, photographs, and medals. The military had awarded Michael the Distinguished Flying Cross, a Purple Heart for wounds received in action, the Silver Star for gallantry in action, and an Air Medal with four Oak Leaf Clusters for meritorious achievement during flight. George Blassie took to raising the American flag, illuminated by a floodlight, in the front yard every morning. Every night he took it down.

South Vietnamese and American forces eventually won back control of An Loc Province, and authorities mounted a search to recover the remains of those killed in action. On October 31, 1972, five months after Michael Blassie's plane was shot down, a Vietnamese Army search party found a handful of bones—four ribs, two from the right side and two from the left; a pelvic bone; and the right humerus, the bone in the upper arm—and a few objects that seemed to belong to an airplane or its pilot. Listed as found were an airplane ejection seat, pieces of fabric from a flight suit and some from a parachute, a pistol holder, a one-man inflatable raft, two compasses, a flag, and a wallet with an identification card bearing Blassie's name. The remains were labeled "BTB [believed to be] Blassie, Michael Joseph," and shipped to the U.S. Army mortuary at Tan Son Nhut Air Base in Saigon, for examination. Somehow, the wallet and ID card disappeared, either stolen or lost. In 1976, the remains, still believed to be those of Michael Blassie, were sent to the Central Identification Laboratory in Thailand.

It was the laboratory's job to confirm or refute the identity of the bones. If the bones were Blassie's, how could the authorities prove it? Did the Vietnamese patrol really find the bones and identification card together, or did they find them in different places and put them all in a single bag? Standard practice now is for a team from the CIL to go to the site when remains are found, supervise the recovery, and take custody of the remains so there is no question of the integrity of the results in the laboratory. Here, that didn't happen. If someone responsible for graves registration had been there when the remains were collected, perhaps the wallet and identity card would not have disappeared. Having these two items would have been useful in identifying the remains, even though they would not have been sufficient to prove the dead man's identity. What the forensic anthropologist seeks in the identification process is enough evidence to back up testimony under oath as to the identity of the remains. A single piece of evidence, no matter how convincing, is not sufficient.

Forensic anthropologists routinely develop a biological profile—an estimate of the person's age, race, sex, height, and blood type—from skeletal remains. Although Blassie's ID card was missing, his medical records, containing that information, were on file with the air force. The procedure called for analysis of the remains believed to be Blassie's without reference to the air force files. Only after they analyzed the bones would the scientists consult the records. The lab results suggested the bones were those of someone between five feet six inches and five feet eleven inches, who was thirty to forty years old at death. Analysis of a leg hair found inside the flight suit showed the man's blood to be type O. Blassie, whose medical record set his height at between five feet eleven inches and six feet tall, was twenty-four when he died, and his medical records said he had type A blood. The only evidence matching the remains to Blassie in a scientifically convincing way was that the bones almost certainly were those of a man.

The discrepancies raised serious questions in the minds of the CIL's identification specialists. Establishing the sex of the deceased person is not difficult. Men have larger joints than women, and so the ends of their bones are larger. There are also several features in the hip bones that distinguish between the two sexes. Apart from the individual's sex, the biological profiles were entirely different, but even that didn't prove the bones weren't Blassie's. The differences between actual and estimated age and height are easy to explain as normal human skeletal variation.

For example, the average femur (thighbone) measuring 19.1 inches (486 millimeters) comes from a person five feet nine and a half inches tall (1.76 meters). On average, a person of that height will have a humerus (upper arm bone) measuring 14.3 inches (363 millimeters), but some people will be shorter and some taller. Leg length is only one factor in determining a person's height. The size of the pelvic bone, the size and shape of the head, and the size of each of the twenty-four vertebrae in the spine are also part of the story. Using just a single arm bone to arrive at a person's height, as was done in the believed-to-be Blassie case, may result in an estimate that is off by as much as a few inches.

When it comes to estimating a person's age, lifestyle can profoundly affect the bones. For example, a lifetime of vigorous physical activity, or chronic drug or alcohol abuse, can make a person's bones seem older than they really are. For reasons such as this, some people's bones don't fit the expected pattern.

Finally, analysts can obtain blood type from bone marrow, but usually not from bone itself unless the bone is unusually well preserved and in good condition. Finding a leg hair was a real coup, but typing blood from any tissue can yield inaccurate results as much as a third of the time. Here, exposure aboveground in the harsh Vietnamese weather could have caused the loss or alteration of the antigens that serve as evidence of blood type, making any blood look like type O.

Although forensic anthropology is founded in science, there is still some art and subjective professional judgment to it. One always has to be aware of the limited degree of precision inherent in drawing conclusions about a dead person's biological profile based on skeletal features. From the information available, scientists could neither prove nor disprove that the remains were Blassie's. If the remains were not Blassie's, whose could they be? Eight other fliers had crashed in the area during battle, but only one had characteristics that might match those of the remains: Captain Rodney Strobridge, thirty, of Torrance, California, whose Cobra went down on the same day, two miles from the site of Blassie's wreck. However, nothing else found with the bones made sense if the remains were those of Strobridge. Most problematical was the remnant of a one-man life raft. Strobridge's helicopter would not have carried one.

In 1979, seven years after the remains believed to be Blassie's were found, the Pentagon declared they could not identify the remains and labeled the contents of the box X-26. The box was placed on a shelf at the CIL, stored for the time when advances in technology might make a more certain identification possible. Never during the period between Michael Blassie's death and the reclassification of remains originally thought to be his was his family informed that some of what might be his body and a few belongings had been found.

In 1973, Congress had enacted a law ordering the interment at Arlington Cemetery of an unknown soldier from the Vietnam War to rest with the unknowns from America's two world wars and the Korean conflict. To qualify for the honor, the remains had to be those of an American known to have died in action, for whom all efforts at identification had failed. By convention, although not by law, at least 80 percent of the skeletal remains had to be present. The order did not set a date for the interment, however. It wasn't until 1980 that Vietnam veterans, some major veterans' organizations, and a few members of Congress began to press for the selection and burial of a Vietnam unknown.

At first glance the idea of a Vietnam unknown seems noncontroversial. The United States has a tradition of honoring its military dead dating from the establishment of Memorial Day in 1868, three years after the Civil War ended. The argument surrounding U.S. involvement in Southeast Asia, in contrast to Americans' near-unanimous approval of fighting the two world wars and even the more controversial Korean War, only heightened the desire of many to honor Vietnam veterans by singling out one who was unidentified and could stand for all who fought there. These veterans saw the government's delay naming a Vietnam unknown as a sign of disrespect for the sacrifices they had made for their country. Yet those most deeply affected by the Vietnam War didn't speak with one voice. Many families who had lost loved ones in the war, to whom remains had never been returned, argued against naming a Vietnam unknown. Burying a set of unidentified remains would mean denying some bereaved family the chance to bury those remains close to home and experience the closure that a funeral brings. Also, some family members feared selecting a Vietnam unknown would lead to a slackening of government efforts to search for military personnel remaining unaccounted for.

In 1982 the veterans' voices prevailed, and President Ronald Reagan saw the burial of an unknown soldier from the Vietnam War as a way to heal the still-festering scars the war had left on the collective American psyche. The plan was to select the unknown from among all unidentified remains, and bury at sea those not chosen. This raised an alarm within the National League of POW/MIA Families, whose representatives contacted the National Security Council and, through that agency, the Reagan White House, protesting that the government was overlooking the needs of bereaved families. The administration responded by ordering that the selected remains must be not only unidentified but also unidentifiable. Had the original plan been carried out, more than one family would never get to collect the remnants of a loved one's life, the league said later.

The idea of honoring the unknown dead of World War I originated in Europe. France buried an unknown soldier at the Arc de Triomphe and England buried one at Westminster Abbey on November 11, 1920, two years after the signing of the armistice—an agreement to stop fighting, not the actual peace treaty, which the United States signed in 1921—between the Allies and Germany. Italy and other European nations honored their unknown soldiers soon after that. When the idea was presented to the army's chief of staff, he rejected it, citing the lack of a suitable burial place. He suggested that eventually the U.S. Army's Graves Registration Service was likely to be able to identify all of the American soldiers who had died in battle.

Some six weeks after the French and English ceremonies, Representative Hamilton Fish Jr., of New York, introduced a resolution in Congress. It called for the selection of an unknown American soldier killed in France to be buried with appropriate ceremony in a tomb that would be constructed at the Memorial Amphitheater at Arlington National Cemetery, on a hill overlooking the District of Columbia. Congress approved the measure on March 4, 1921, and, in 1926, authorized spending fifty thousand dollars to place a suitable monument over the tomb.

A design contest was held. The winning design was the work of Thomas Hudson Jones, a sculptor, and Lorimer Rich, an architect. Made of four pieces of Colorado marble, the same kind used in the Lincoln Memorial, it stands eleven feet high, eight feet wide, and fourteen feet long at the base. Panels on both sides are divided into three sections, each carved with a wreath. On the back is the inscription HERE RESTS IN HONORED GLORY AN AMERICAN SOLDIER KNOWN BUT TO GOD. On the front, facing the Potomac and the city of Washington, are three figures signifying Victory, Valor, and Peace. Specially trained members of the Third United States Infantry, nicknamed "The Old Guard," stand watch over the tomb every minute of the year.

The process by which the first American unknown soldier would be chosen began September 9, 1921, when the U.S. War Department ordered the quartermaster general to carry out the task. After a search of records of the unknown dead to be sure there was no evidence of identity, four bodies were exhumed on October 22, one from each of the American cemeteries in France. Another four were selected as alternates, against the possibility that identifying information on the first four should come to light when their bodies were exhumed. After a final examination to be sure the men had belonged to the American Expeditionary Forces, that they had died of wounds received in combat, and that there was no possibility they could be identified, the corpses were placed in identical coffins and shipping cases and carried by truck to the city hall in Châlons-sur-Marne for the selection ceremony.

Outside, the city hall was hung with French and American flags; inside, potted palms and flags decorated the halls and aisles. After entering the building, officials rearranged the caskets and shipping cases to make it unlikely that anyone could tell which body came from which cemetery. Following the tradition established by the French, an enlisted man— Sergeant Edward F. Younger of Headquarters Company, 2nd Battalion, 50th Infantry, American Forces in Germany—was chosen to select the coffin to be buried as the American unknown. While a French military band in the city hall courtyard played a hymn, Younger walked around the caskets several times. Then he placed a spray of white roses on one of them to show his choice and saluted the chosen unknown American. The roses were later buried with the unknown soldier in Arlington. The caskets of the three remaining soldiers were loaded onto trucks and taken to Romagne Cemetery, 152 miles east of Paris, for burial.

There followed a series of ceremonies leading to the departure of the chosen unknown soldier from the town hall and its arrival at the navy yard in Washington, D.C., aboard the USS *Olympia*, Admiral George Dewey's old flagship, on a rainy November 9, 1921. The next day, the flag-draped coffin, placed on the same catafalque that once held the coffin of Abraham Lincoln, stood in the rotunda of the Capitol so that members of the public, walking four abreast, could file past and pay their respects. Capitol guards at the time estimated that some ninety thousand persons passed the bier in the sixteen-hour period.

The next morning's three-hour funeral procession moved, largely on foot, from the Capitol past the White House and across the Potomac River to the Arlington Cemetery's newly dedicated Memorial Amphitheater. President Warren G. Harding presided over the funeral, which featured a military band playing funeral marches and hymns, multiple artillery salutes, a quartet of singers from the Metropolitan Opera Company, eulogies, prayers, and the singing of "Nearer My God to Thee" by the audience. The band played "Lead Kindly Light" as the audience moved from the amphitheater to the area around the tomb for the burial service. A bugler played taps, and the ceremony ended with a twenty-one-gun salute.

In 1956, President Dwight D. Eisenhower signed a congressional resolution to select and honor unknown soldiers from World War II and the Korean conflict. With precautions similar to those used in selecting the World War I unknown, two more sets of unidentifiable remains were chosen, and laid to rest in the amphitheater plaza on Memorial Day, 1958.

Since 1926 a military honor guard has minded the tomb twenty-four hours a day. The changing of the guard at the Tomb of the Unknowns is a popular tourist attraction. It is conducted every hour on the hour from October 1 to March 31, and every half hour from April 1 to September 30. While guarding the tomb, the sentinel on duty takes twenty-one steps across a sixty-three-foot rubber-surfaced walkway in each direction. At each end of the walkway, the guard faces the tomb for twenty-one seconds, turns, pauses another twenty-one seconds, and then resumes his pacing. The use of the number twenty-one is symbolic, representing America's highest military honor, the twenty-one-gun salute.

The CIL, known as CIL-THAI when it was located in Thailand before its move to Hawaii in 1976, had on hand only four boxes of unidentified remains when the order came down from the White House to choose the Vietnam unknown soldier. In the lab's view, some of these remains had characteristics that might someday make it possible to identify them. The government's first choice were the remains in a box labeled X-15. They came from the mortuary in Saigon and could have been from an American soldier, but they didn't match the records of anyone listed as missing and unaccounted for. That suggested the dead soldier might have been a deserter, since the CIL received all records of those killed or missing in action. But the bones were plentiful, and there were even teeth, which would have made identification much easier. Major Johnie Webb Jr., the laboratory's commanding officer, could not in good conscience certify that the deceased was unidentifiable.

Webb was right. Not only were the remains identifiable, but identifying them cleared the name of Private First Class Alan Keith Barton, of St. Charles Township, Michigan, whom the army had indeed listed as a deserter from the time he was reported missing, on July 28, 1970, from Camp Radcliff, his military installation near the village of An Khe, in the central coastal region of South Vietnam. A month later, Barton's mother received a letter from Captain Marty C. Keef, the young man's commanding officer, telling her Barton had been absent without leave for thirty days and was therefore classified as a deserter. "I believe that you should advise him to return," Keef said in the letter. "The longer he stays away, the more severe will be his punishment if and when he is apprehended." Barton was eighteen years old when he disappeared. His father had served a twenty-year stint in the army, and Barton himself volunteered to fight in Vietnam after serving for a time in Germany. His aunt, Shirley Burgoyne, an attorney, tried to get the army to clear his name.

On March 28, 1972, skeletal remains with three steel pellets embedded in the right arm were found at the edge of Camp Radcliff's grounds. The corner of an envelope postmarked Saginaw, Michigan, was also found. The next day, more bones and personal belongings were discovered, but these items were lost in an army mail room. The remains were sent to the CIL to be identified. In 1983, when dental records and bone analysis showed the remains to be Barton's, his body was returned to his family. He was buried with full military honors, and his name can be found engraved on the wall of the Vietnam Memorial in Washington, D.C. According to Major George Stinnett, an army spokesman, he hadn't been identified earlier because the army tries to identify only remains of soldiers reported missing in action. Stinnett said Barton probably met his death by tripping a land mine.

The next box chosen contained bones that came with a dog tag bearing the name William McRae. However, as far as anyone knew, McRae's remains had long since been identified and were buried in a Boston cemetery, so the bones in the CIL's possession were considered unidentified. McRae had served time in the Long Binh "jail," a military stockade on the road between Bien Hoa and Saigon, most likely for being absent without leave (AWOL) more than once. The army offered him early release from the prison if he rejoined his unit and went back on duty. The practice of offering AWOL soldiers the opportunity to redeem themselves was common at the time. The war was heating up, and the military needed as many soldiers in action as possible.

McRae was released from Long Binh on August 9, 1967. He boarded a Huey helicopter to be flown back to his unit. The helicopter's passenger manifest listed four crew members and McRae. Almost as soon as it was airborne, the Huey collided with an F-101, a single-seat aircraft. The pilot of the F-101 ejected and survived. The helicopter crashed and burned with all five men on board. The four crewmen were easily identified; the fifth body was badly burned, but forensic analysis fit McRae's age, race, hair color, and height. The body was wearing army fatigues and boots, but the uniform bore no insignia. This was not unusual for someone just out of the stockade. Based on this evidence, the corpse was identified as McRae, and the remains were sent to his family for burial in a Boston cemetery.

Four months later, a patrol in the area where the Huey had crashed discovered a sixth body, now badly decomposed. At the Tan Son Nhut mortuary, investigators discovered the body wore McRae's dog tags. Since McRae had already been identified and buried, this corpse was designated as unidentified, given the designation X-32, and shipped to the CIL in Thailand to await identification. The box of bones named X-32 rested on a shelf at the CIL in Hawaii until 1982, when the first candidate for Vietnam unknown was rejected. It was X-32's turn to be considered. Scientists either had to identify the remains or certify them as unidentifiable. When they opened the box and found McRae's dog tags, the staff launched a search for his dental records and, through them, positively identified the remains as those of William McRae. His family was notified. The body in the Boston grave was exhumed and McRae's bones took its place. X-32 was replaced with a corpse the CIL staff affectionately named Boston Billy.

When X-32 was found to be McRae, a search of all missing persons thought to be lost near the Huey helicopter crash revealed only one possible alternative, a civilian named Jerry Degnan, who came from Ohio. Degnan was an independent contractor who worked for a company called Decca Navigation Systems. Degnan's job was to train aviators to use Decca's sophisticated aircraft piloting system. Every week he sent his family an audiotape about his experiences in Vietnam. The tapes stopped coming in July, but the family didn't think much of the lapse at first, assuming Degnan was simply too busy with his work. By late August, though, his family got in touch with Decca's office in Saigon. Someone there said they'd have Degnan call home when he got back to the office. A week later the family called again, and Decca realized nobody had seen Degnan for too long a time. In the subsequent investigation, launched September 20 after Decca filed a missing persons report with the U.S. Embassy in Saigon, an office manager gave a sworn statement that made clear he'd seen Degnan and another Decca employee outside a hotel in Saigon on August 14, which was five days after the Huey crashed. The manager was sure of the date, he said, because the next day he left for Hong Kong on leave.

Authorities listed Degnan as missing and unaccounted for and the matter remained such until 1974. Then Degnan's family went to court to have him legally declared dead. They had been paying Degnan's life insurance premiums for the past seven years and apparently thought it was time to collect. Had Degnan been in the military, officials would have looked into his disappearance long since and a board of inquiry would have declared him dead. However, Degnan's disappearance was a civil matter. The court record includes testimony from the man thought to be with Degnan in Saigon in August 1967. This man, a pilot, had checked his flight log and could say with certainty that he was nowhere near Saigon on that day. The office manager who had identified him was mistaken. Based on this testimony, the court declared Degnan legally dead. However, because Degnan was a civilian, the CIL never received this information.

It wasn't until 2002 that Boston Billy's identity became known, largely the result of some supersleuthing done by CIL analyst Bob "Bulldog" Maves. Periodically, lab staff members take old boxes off the shelves to see if any new technology might help identify their contents. One of those was Boston Billy. All that Maves knew was that the remains had been found at the site of the August 9 helicopter crash, and that the five men on the passenger manifest had been identified. Maves began to doubt the accuracy of the helicopter's passenger manifest. A search was undertaken to eliminate from consideration everyone lost in Vietnam in August and September 1967. The only person who could not be accounted for was twenty-eight-year-old Jerry Degnan. This was not sufficient evidence for a scientific identification, however, so the lab began to correspond with Degnan's family. Forensic analysis of the remains provided a match with Degnan's age, race, and height. The family provided a chest X-ray, and Degnan's brother sent a blood sample, which proved to be the conclusive evidence: a DNA match between Degnan and his brother. Since Jerry Degnan trained helicopter pilots, they all knew him. Hopping a ride with one of them wasn't unusual for him.

Because identifying the body in the second box as that of an American soldier killed in action was impossible, the CIL moved on to the third box of bones. This set was part of a unilateral turnover of remains by the government of Laos—unilateral meaning that no Americans were involved in the recovery of the remains and thus there was no chain of custody to rely on. The CIL's commander pointed out that these remains did not satisfy the law's requirements, since there was no way to be sure they were indeed those of an American fighting man.

At this point the Pentagon once again proposed X-15 from An Khe for the honor, because it represented the largest complement of bones. But the fact that there were teeth—a promising source of DNA, although the technique to extract it was not yet known—led Webb once again to refuse to sign off on the remains, repeating that it was likely they could eventually be identified. This time his refusal led to a visit from a Pentagon general, who said, in effect, if you're so sure you can identify the body, you have six months to do it. It was within that time period the CIL was able to identify the remains as those of eighteen-year-old Private First Class Alan Keith Barton, the soldier who had incorrectly been listed as an army deserter.

That left only the fourth box, the one marked X-26, which had once been thought to contain the remains of Michael Blassie. Believing the bones could not be identified with the technology available at the time, Webb reluctantly signed the required document declaring them to be unidentifiable, but not before making one last attempt to keep them from being selected as the Vietnam unknown. He sent a memo to the highest level of army leadership, urging that the remains be rejected because they had at one time been associated with the names of Blassie and Strobridge.

Despite Webb's objections, the remains were formally selected by a Medal of Honor recipient, as had been done with the unknowns from World War II and Korea, in a dockside ceremony at the Pearl Harbor Naval Base. On May 17, 1984, Marine Corps sergeant major Allan J. Kellogg, who had earned the honor in Vietnam in 1970 by throwing himself on a Vietnamese hand grenade, put a wreath at the foot of the casket. Then the casket was placed on board the USS *Brewton,* which carried it to Alameda Naval Base in California. From there, the remains went to Travis Air Force Base, and were flown to Andrews Air Force Base in Maryland the next day. On May 25, a motorcade escorted the casket to the Capitol, where it lay in state in the Rotunda while thousands of veterans and tourists filed by to pay their respects.

At noon on Memorial Day, May 28, 1984, a military procession carried the casket to Arlington National Cemetery. Uncounted thousands watched the funeral service, attended by hundreds of guests, including more than a hundred Medal of Honor recipients from all U.S. wars, as President Ronald Reagan presented the Unknown Soldier with the Medal of Honor. Then came the traditional heartbreaking ceremony in which a member of the honor guard, in full formal military dress, knelt before Reagan, who was representing the bereaved next of kin, and reverently offered up the trifolded flag that had covered the casket. Although no one could have guessed at the time, some of Reagan's words predicted the future of the Vietnam unknown. "We write no last chapters," he said. "We close no books. We put away no final memories."

Michael Blassie had been dead for twenty-two years when the July 1994 issue of the newsletter *U.S. Veteran Dispatch* carried an article saying that the bones buried in the Tomb of the Unknown Vietnam Soldier might be his. Ted Sampley, a former Vietnam-era Green Beret who publishes *Dispatch,* wrote the story. Sampley is also the founder and head of Last Firebase Veterans Archives Project, an advocacy group speaking for Vietnam prisoners of war and those carried on Pentagon records as missing in action. The group maintains a large collection of POW/MIA files.

Before he published the article, Sampley phoned Jean Blassie, Michael's mother, in St. Louis and told her what he was about to reveal. When the piece was in print, Sampley hand delivered a copy to officials at the Pentagon. Michael's sister Pat, an air force captain at the time, called the Air Force Casualty Office hoping to confirm Sampley's report. Instead she was told there was no information to back up Sampley's claims. The Blassie family let the matter drop. Three years later, Sampley reprinted the story and posted it on the *Dispatch's* web site. Vince Gonzales, a reporter for *CBS News,* read the story there and got in touch with the Blassie family. The Blassies agreed to help Gonzales investigate further and develop a story for broadcast.

The news report, broadcast on CBS stations on January 19, 1998, began this way: "A seven-month *CBS News* investigation has revealed that the identity of [the Vietnam] unknown soldier is almost certainly known and that some military officials, for whatever reason, knew it all along and tried to hide it." Jean and Pat Blassie, Michael's mother and sister, appeared in the segment, urging the government to disinter the unknown soldier and try again to identify him, using DNA testing techniques not available at the time he was buried. "Everything leads to the tomb," Pat Blassie told the CBS interviewer. "If it's Michael, he is not unknown."

Predictably, the broadcast caused a stir, especially among veterans' groups and families of still-unaccounted-for Vietnam soldiers. Quoted in the *Washington Times* a few days later, navy captain Michael Doubleday, speaking for the Pentagon, summed up the government's dilemma. "We have an obligation to family members who have unresolved questions," he said. "We also have an obligation to all of those who have served in wars in the past and who view this site as very hallowed ground."

Secretary of Defense William Cohen appointed a working group to review available evidence and assess the possibility that the remains of the Vietnam unknown could be identified using new DNA testing techniques. Headed by Rudy de Leon, the undersecretary of defense for personnel and readiness, and Jan Lodal, the principal deputy undersecretary of defense for policy, the group met with members of Congress, scientists responsible for choosing the remains, and representatives of various veterans' organizations.

At an April 27 briefing, a member of the working group described in detail the recovery of the remains once believed to be Blassie's. Speaking on background, which meant the reporters present could not identify him by name, the Pentagon official revealed that a U.S. Army lieutenant named Chris Calhoun had received the remains and personal effects from the Vietnamese patrol that discovered them in 1972. The bones and some of the personal items were placed in one bag and other effects were placed in a separate bag. The official said Calhoun described to him a chaotic scene in which a helicopter landed in the jungle and, while Vietnamese refugees and deserters rushed the craft, hoping to fly away from the war scene, Calhoun tossed a bag of remains to the helicopter crew chief. "And that was essentially the process of delivery of these remains," the official said. On

May 7, the Pentagon announced Cohen's decision to open the tomb a week later, leaving time for the Pentagon to design an appropriate ceremony for the disinterment.

Dave Rankin, another CIL anthropologist, was in Washington, D.C., for two days before I got there, although we'd left the CIL at the same time. On the way, I stopped in Oregon to meet with the family of a missing Vietnam pilot. Dave went straight to D.C. and took part in the May 7 Pentagon press briefing announcing Secretary Cohen's decision to open the tomb. By the time I got there, the plans to open the Tomb of the Unknown Soldier of Vietnam were well under way. The event was attracting attention worldwide. The international media would cover it; the White House would watch closely. None of us could afford to do or say anything wrong.

The day after I arrived both of us attended another Pentagon press briefing, held in the studio instantly recognizable to everyone who watches the nightly news on television, the oval Pentagon seal prominent behind the dais. The setting made me feel like a dignitary. The briefing—with its herd of camera crews, the cameras, the boom mikes hanging over our heads like jungle snakes—was something I'll never forget. Here we were, the people on whom everything hinged, in a case involving perhaps the most famous grave in the United States.

The planners had every detail under control. A contractor would build an eight-foot white plywood fence around the tomb to preserve its dignity and sanctity while it was opened. One of the fence's functions was to stymie the efforts of news photographers, who wanted to take pictures of the actual removal of the casket from the crypt, something the Pentagon brass judged inappropriate. Workers even strung up a piece of camouflage netting so that no one could photograph the work from an airplane or helicopter. Another contractor, experienced at handling marble, concrete, and granite structures, would open the crypt and extract the casket that held the remains. The honor guard and its changing-of-the-guard ceremonies would be moved to the east end of the tomb for the duration.

Opening the tomb was painstaking work. The concrete pavement sur-

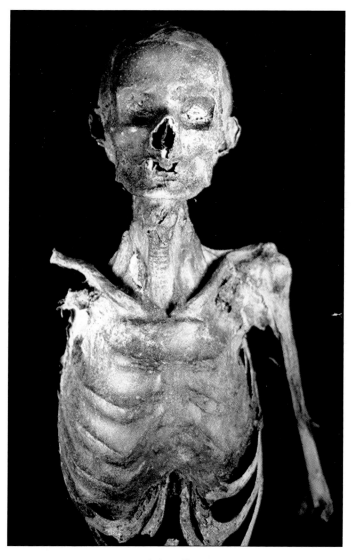

Mrs. Leonard, the Halloween mummy.

Some of the items excavated from Jeffrey Dahmer's Ohio backyard in 1991.

Lt. Michael J. Blassie, disinterred from the Tomb of the Unknown
Soldier of Vietnam in 1998. Anthropological and mtDNA
analysis led to his identification.

Kendall Francois's backyard and home—the House of Horrors—at 99 Fulton Avenue.

Parachute recovered beside U.S. Marine radar operator S.Sgt. James Harrell in Pangpo Beach, South Korea. He was missing since 1953, and his remains were found eroding on the beach in 2001.

A cloth map of Korea found with Staff Sergeant Harrell's remains.

Apprentice Seaman Thomas Hembree in uniform, soon after entering the navy at age seventeen.

Thomas Hembree (*second from right*) with family, visiting from Grand Coulee Dam, in 1940, the year before he died. Thomas's mother is holding Marion Price.

The Hembree family at Thomas's burial, which finally occurred in 2002.

Headstone of Pearl Harbor
sailor Thomas Hembree in the
National Cemetery of the
Pacific, Hawaii.

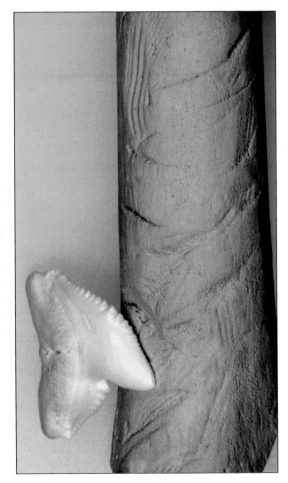

Tiger shark tooth marks along the back of the femur from the Toilet Bowl. Note how the serrated edge of the shark tooth, which is about the size of a half dollar, matches the gouges in the bone.

COURTESY BOB MANN

rounding it had to be cut carefully so that the blocks could be reused. A crane would remove the crypt cover and place it off to the side. The casket would be lifted to ground level and placed on a portable cart. Then the crypt would be closed and the paving replaced so that it would look as though no one had ever disturbed it. That process was to take between twenty-four and thirty-six hours. It continued through the night of May 13 and the early hours of May 14 so that everything would be ready for the ceremony over which Secretary Cohen was to preside later on May 14. The casket came out of the ground near midnight.

Dave's job was to ensure that the casket was properly sealed with evidence tape the moment it came out of the ground. Establishing a chain of custody from the moment of recovery or receipt of any remains or material evidence is the first step in our procedure. The 1995 verdict in the O. J. Simpson murder trial had given everyone involved in forensics a refresher course in the crucial importance of proper evidence handling. The jury's verdict then was heavily influenced by the laxity with which the Los Angeles police took care of important pieces of evidence. Jurors were justified in questioning the authenticity and accuracy of the laboratory test results because of shoddy evidence management. We at the CIL were going to make sure we didn't follow in the footsteps of the L.A. police. Joining Dave and me in assuring the chain of evidence were two independent observers who were with us every step of the way.

My primary job was to act as the senior anthropologist, overseeing the anthropological work that would provide specimens for examination once the remains arrived at the Armed Forces Institute of Pathology (AFIP) in Washington. The AFIP had gone to great lengths in instituting security safeguards to protect the integrity of the evidentiary process. They gave Dave and me security badges, allowing us unrestricted access to the facilities. They changed the lock on the door to the laboratory in which we would work on the remains, and gave us the only key for use while we were working. Everyone involved in even the smallest way wanted to be sure there were no mistakes. Can you imagine trying to explain a mistake handling remains from the Tomb of the Unknown Soldier in this most public of processes?

Using a diamond-tipped cutting tool, private contractors took more than four hours to slice through ten inches of granite slab around the crypt's marble cover. By dawn on May 14, the casket, wrapped in an American flag, was resting on a platform in front of the tomb. At ten A.M., as the sun broke through an early morning fog, an army chaplain prayed, "If it be your holy will, make known the identity of this unknown Vietnam serviceman and bring peace of mind to an American family. But if the answer we seek is not ours to know, let us hold fast to our belief that this serviceman's name is known to you, O God."

Defense Secretary William Cohen said the tomb was opened with "profound reluctance," but in keeping with the military's promise to identify every one of its fallen soldiers. "If advance in technology can ease the lingering anguish of even one family, then our path is clear. We yield to the promise of science, with the hope that the heavy burden of doubt may be lifted from a family's heart." A military band played "Amazing Grace," and the coffin was loaded into a hearse for a stately motorcade past Rock Creek Park to the Armed Forces Institute of Pathology at Walter Reed Hospital. The line of cars and police escorts stretched on for blocks.

At the hospital we were swarmed by photographers and television news crews. They scurried about for the best camera angles as the flag-draped casket was removed from the black army hearse and carried into the auditorium, where the seal would be broken. This was the point at which Dave Rankin and I would take over.

The silver-blue steel casket was rusty but in good condition. Opened, however, the casket told a different story. Moisture had caused the liner of the inner enclosure to fall away from the lid. We found a U.S. Army–issue olive-drab wool blanket pinned shut along all sides. Carefully we removed the rusty safety pins and, upon opening the blanket, saw the six bones and several fragments of military equipment. We supposed these items had been found with the remains in 1972. I was surprised not to find the Medal of Honor awarded the deceased soldier, but later learned the Pentagon had ruled that the medal was to stay with the tomb, not the service member, a matter that caused some controversy at the time.

Dave and I finished our preliminary examination of the remains in the auditorium, observed by eight or nine military brass and a few enlisted soldiers. Then we hand carried the remains up to the laboratory, where we began the anthropological analysis and cut the bones for DNA testing. Dave and I examined the six bones independently and came up with our own biological profiles of the person's age, stature, and sex. We finished our examinations before discussing our findings. During our analysis we also looked for evidence of trauma that the pilot may have sustained at or near the time of his death.

Our findings were identical. We both believed that the individual was between thirty and forty years old when he died, stood approximately five feet eight inches, and showed no skeletal evidence of trauma sustained at the time of death. Our analysis also revealed that a small wedge had been cut from each of the six bones in the manner used in the 1970s to analyze the person's blood type. Choosing where to cut bone samples for identification purposes focused on preserving available information about the person's age, height, and sex.

Dave cut a fragment weighing approximately two to two and a half ounces (between five and seven grams) from each bone, using a small Dremel tool. We placed the bone samples, which were about the size of postage stamps, in individual plastic bags sealed with evidence tape, signed and dated across the seal and labeled with a preselected number that would, in effect, make it impossible for the DNA laboratory to know the origin of the specimen. This was another way of preventing any bias or suspicion from getting into the equation. We also inventoried and photographed the remains, as was done in the 1970s when they were found in the jungle.

Dave and I completed our analysis later that day and locked the bone samples in an empty vault on another floor in the building. Dave was the only person with the combination to the vault, until he turned it over to the AFIP's registrar of records so that Dr. Mitchell Holland, chief of the Armed Forces DNA Identification Laboratory (AFDIL) could perform the actual DNA analysis. After that, we returned to our hotel to prepare for our trip home.

.   .   .

The human body consists of approximately 100 trillion cells. The nucleus of each cell contains a double spiral composed of molecules of deoxyribonucleic acid, which holds the genetic code that makes each of us unique. Approximately 99.9 percent of the DNA in the human body is identical from person to person. It's the remaining one tenth of 1 percent that makes us who we are.

Scientists first identified DNA in 1944. Much more recently, early in the twenty-first century, scientists successfully mapped the entire human genome, the sequence of genes on each DNA strand. DNA is found in skin cells, hair, blood, semen, saliva, even teeth and bone, and analysis of it is carried out by using a computer to compare and attempt to match two samples. We shed old skin cells and hair constantly, which is why DNA is so often found at the scene of a crime, and DNA samples can be obtained by swabbing inside the cheek or from an unwitting suspect's cigarette butt, coffee cup, or toothbrush.

Only identical twins and clones have identical DNA. For anyone not a twin, finding a match between one's DNA and a specimen found at a crime site is as close as one can get to proof that the person was involved in the crime. It's still circumstantial evidence, but juries tend to find it sufficient to convict a defendant. In the last few years, hundreds of convicted felons have been pardoned and released from prison because analysis failed to find a match with their DNA and that left at a crime scene.

But DNA is easily destroyed, and the DNA found in bones at the site where an airplane crashed and burned can safely be presumed to be contaminated. That's why the remnants of X-26 remained unidentified for twenty-six years, and why the director of the Central Identification Laboratory could certify in 1984 that the remains were unidentifiable. However, by the time X-26 was exhumed in 1998, an advance in technology made it reasonable to think that the bones could indeed be identified. It is also the reason there will probably never again be a designated unknown soldier. Another kind of DNA—mitochondrial DNA, as opposed to nuclear DNA—was identified in the early 1990s.

Each of the body's cells contains one nucleus and thus one set of DNA containing roughly a hundred thousand genes. Other genes can be found in the fluid called cytoplasm that surrounds the cell nucleus. These genes exist in the mitochondria, tiny organs that serve as the cells' power plants. Mitochondria convert the energy from the food we eat into a fuel called adenosine triphosphate (ATP), which provides our bodies with energy. ATP and the function of the mitochondria are crucial to life. The poison cyanide kills by preventing the mitochondria from doing their job. Without ATP, you can't scratch your head or swing a baseball bat; you can't even move a muscle or breathe. Mitochondrial DNA contains only thirty-seven genes, far less than 1 percent of all genes in the body. These genes are not responsible for traits we normally associate with genes, such as eye color, height, or the tendency to be overweight. The mitochondrial genes encode only the instructions that the mitochondria need to do their job. That, however, is far from trivial, given the importance of ATP for sustaining life.

Mitochondrial DNA has two important characteristics that make it particularly useful in identifying older skeletal remains. Firstly, it is more plentiful than nuclear DNA; there are hundreds of copies of mtDNA to each copy of nuclear DNA. Secondly, while nuclear DNA is a combination of genes from an individual's biological mother and father, mtDNA comes from the mother alone. The DNA of brothers and sisters, even of fraternal (not identical) twins, is different from one to another, but every child's mtDNA is identical to his or her mother's and his or her siblings, and the mtDNA of a woman's offspring is identical to hers and to her mother's. Thus, while the only match for nuclear DNA comes from the same individual or an identical twin, mtDNA matches can come from the mother of the person whose remains are under analysis, or from any of her first-degree relatives—her mother, her brothers and sisters, and her other children.

The process of testing mtDNA consists of four steps. About one square inch or two grams of bone is collected from the remains. To ensure accuracy, it is customary at the CIL to collect at least twice that amount, so that more than one test can be conducted. Then specific regions of the mtDNA are chosen for copying, using a process known as the polymerase chain reaction (PCR). This is a commonly used genetic testing tool that makes it possible to analyze even minute amounts of genetic material, even if it has been damaged, by replicating the material in the study sample as much as a billion times. It does this by exploiting the natural function of enzymes known as polymerases, which are present in all living things. Their job is to copy genetic material, and to proofread and correct the copies to ensure they match the original.

To perform PCR, the scientist needs the material that is to be duplicated, known as the template, and two short chains of the four chemical components that make up any strand of genetic material, called primers. These are arranged to match the sequence in which the components appear on either side of the sample of interest. The template is heated and its two spiral-shaped strands are unwound. Then each strand of DNA is joined with one of the primers. Now the polymerase is introduced; it reads the template and creates an identical strand, replacing the original double spiral with two identical strands of DNA. The process of doubling a bit of DNA takes between one and three minutes; in an hour you can have millions of copies of a DNA strand, all identical to the tiny fragment with which the process began. Once there is enough mtDNA to read the genetic code and be certain the reading is accurate, the sequence can be compared with the mtDNA of people thought to be related to the person whose remains are being identified.

AFDIL began doing mtDNA testing in 1991; the process gained formal approval from the Defense Science Board in 1995. Since then, more than two hundred identifications at the CIL have involved mtDNA analysis. While a mitochondrial DNA match is not absolute proof of identity, it is a strong piece of evidence when combined with other scientific and circumstantial evidence. Nuclear DNA is the unique combination of the DNA of two individuals, a mother and a father, and the likelihood that more than one individual will have a specific genetic sequence is roughly one in a trillion. The fact that mtDNA contains a comparatively tiny number of genes makes a match between two unrelated individuals quite a bit more likely. Just as some names are more common than others, some DNA sequences are more common than others. For example, some mtDNA sequences occur in 20 percent of all Caucasians. There is a worldwide database of DNA sequences that scientists can use to figure out how common a particular sequence is, and this analysis provides an idea of how reliable a particular match is.

Dave Rankin and I flew back to Hawaii the day after sampling the bones and settled back into our normal routine. Everyone in the lab was eager to know if the remains buried in the Tomb of the Unknown Soldier could be identified, but we simply had to wait. AFDIL was to compare the mtDNA in the bone samples with that in a blood specimen Blassie's sister Pat had donated. Additionally, they would compare the mtDNA from the tomb with mtDNA from samples given by maternal relatives of the eight other fliers lost in the same general area at the time Blassie's plane went down.

As part of the search for unidentifiable remains, the government in the early 1980s had searched in a twenty-five-mile radius from the place where Blassie's plane crashed, trying to identify other soldiers who might have crashed between the day Blassie was lost and when the remains believed to be his were found. Records turned up the names of eight other servicemen reported missing in the area. Only one, Captain Rodney Strobridge, fit the description of age, height, and blood type developed by the forensic anthropologists examining the X-26 remains. Still, the scientists at AFDIL were determined to ensure that they had overlooked no possibility.

I didn't expect that they would identify the bones in the tomb as Blassie's because of the discrepancies in earlier examinations between estimates of the age, height, and blood type drawn from the remains and those in Blassie's medical records, but I also knew that just about anything was possible—anything from a positive identification to the inability to draw any conclusions. I knew that the scientists at AFDIL were working as fast as they could without making any mistakes. Getting a mitochondrial DNA sequence from a bone sample is a very complicated process. If you move too fast or cut a corner, the sample may be contaminated. Simply touching a bone with bare hands will transfer more of your own DNA onto the bone than what the sample itself contains. Having learned from our own mistakes, we now wear surgical gloves, gowns, goggles, and masks.

In June 1998, the results came to CIL scientific director Dr. Tom Holland. Sitting at his desk behind a mound of paperwork and a desk lamp that I like to call his "hanging Rolodex"—its shade is covered by a patchwork of yellow and pink Post-it notes—he scrutinized the document from top to bottom. The X-26 samples and a second set of bone samples had been examined by scientists who had no information on the possible identity of either set, in what scientists call a double blind study. They also compared the mtDNA sequences derived from these samples with mtDNA samples from maternal relatives of Strobridge and six other servicemen. All had gone missing around the same time, within the same twenty-five mile radius.

The mtDNA from the second set of samples didn't match any of the reference samples; those from X-26 exactly matched the samples submitted by Blassie's sister. Dr. Holland studied the report for minutes before peering over his seldom-worn spectacles. Then he said, "It's him. It's Blassie." Although he had rested on U.S. soil for nearly three decades, Michael Blassie had yet to make it all the way home. Perseverance by his family and developments in DNA technology finally made identification possible. Both ingredients, one from the heart and one from the head, had come together to answer what had once seemed an impossible question.

The Pentagon notified Michael Blassie's family of the finding on June 30, 1998. On July 11, a cloudy day in St. Louis, his remains were finally buried in Jackson Barracks National Cemetery, the nation's second-largest cemetery. It is home to more than 125,000 veterans of various U.S. wars, including some three thousand still unidentified. Observers estimated that between two thousand and four thousand people attended. There were government officials, including Secretary of Defense William Cohen and Representative Dick Gephardt, the congressman from St. Louis and the minority leader of the House. There were a flock of aging Vietnam veterans on motorcycles, wearing army fatigues and T-shirts with battle zone maps drawn on them. There were entire families—fathers and mothers clutching the hands of small children.

At ten A.M. the funeral procession began to arrive. Old soldiers saluted smartly as the gold hearse moved slowly to the grave site. Michael's mother accepted the embrace of Defense Secretary Cohen, then took her seat beneath a flower-decked canopy, joining other members of the family. The honor guard began a stately march to the hearse, eased out the coffin, and carried it to the grave's edge. A military band played "Amazing Grace," then four F-15 Eagle fighter planes flew low over the cemetery. One Eagle broke formation and shot straight up through the low ceiling of gray clouds, in the traditional salute to a lost pilot. St. Louis archbishop Justin Rigali prayed over the casket. This time Jean Blassie received the folded flag that had covered the casket. Twenty-six years had passed since a handful of bones believed to be those of Michael James Blassie had been found in the jungle near the town of An Loc. At last the Blassie family had the closure every grieving family craves and deserves.

That closure has never come for Rodney Strobridge's widow. The former Pat Mulligan, at the time an elementary school teacher in Monterrey, California, married Strobridge in the summer of 1970. Strobridge had already served a tour in Vietnam as an army pilot flying fixed-wing aircraft. In 1971, the army sent him to helicopter school. Shortly after Christmas of 1971 he left for a second tour in Vietnam. Pat Strobridge never saw her husband again. He was declared missing and presumed dead on Mother's Day, May 14, 1972. By the time the quest to identify the Vietnam unknown soldier got under way, Pat Strobridge had remarried and was no longer considered next of kin. Notice that the remains were Blassie's was delivered to Strobridge's mother, Althea, in Perry, Iowa.

"He's still MIA," she said. "I don't know whether to cry or be happy."

Since the late 1990s, all service members have donated blood samples to a DNA registry. The technology of forensic identification leads authorities to believe that eventually they will identify the remains of most soldiers missing in action in Vietnam. In February 1998, two months before Blassie's remains were identified, the Department of Defense announced it would not place another body in the crypt. Instead, on September 17, 1999, POW/MIA Day, the Department of Defense held yet another ceremony, this time to dedicate a new inscription on the empty crypt of the Vietnam unknown: HONORING AND KEEPING FAITH WITH AMERICA'S MISSING SERVICEMEN.

Speaking at the ceremony, along with Georgia senator Max Cleland, who suffered multiple wounds during his service in Vietnam, Defense Secretary Cohen said, "The words that now grace the Vietnam Tomb . . . are carved in stone. Their permanence, like our remembrance of America's fallen soldiers, sailors, airmen, and Marines, will be a measure of this nation's profound reverence and respect. . . . Science helped ease the sorrow and suffering of a family and return their son to his rightful place, and science may one day help ease the weight of grief of those who wait and wonder."

11. HOUSE OF HORRORS
THE POUGHKEEPSIE SERIAL KILLER

It's a perfect night for mystery and horror.
The air itself is filled with monsters.
—ELSA LANCHESTER (as Mary Shelley), *The Bride of Frankenstein*

The first to disappear was Wendy Meyers, white, slim, thirty years old, with short brown hair. She was reported missing in Ulster County, New York, in October 1996. Two months later, twenty-nine-year-old Gina Barone's mother asked police in nearby Poughkeepsie, New York, to find her daughter. Like Wendy Meyers, Gina Barone was a slightly built Caucasian brunette. Police learned she was last seen on a Poughkeepsie street corner, apparently arguing with a man, on November 29. Another two months passed, and Kathleen Hurley, forty-seven, white, short, and slim, with brown hair, went missing. She had last been seen walking along Main Street in downtown Poughkeepsie. With two Poughkeepsie women missing and the third, Wendy Meyers, known to hang out in the same part of the city, an area frequented by prostitutes and the men who bought their services, detectives in the Poughkeepsie police department thought the three disappearances were more than a coincidence. Still, no bodies had been found, and there was no evidence of a crime. Police could do nothing but wait.

Two months later, on March 7, 1997, another missing persons report came in, this one from the mother of Catherine Marsh. She was another regular visitor to the same downtown area, last seen in November of the previous year. Like Wendy, Gina, and Kathleen, Catherine was white, small in stature, with short brown hair. Two more disappearances followed in the autumn of 1997.

Police detectives identified several possible suspects, men who frequented the area: a man from the South who had been convicted of rape and had come to Poughkeepsie in the summer of 1997; the boyfriend of one of the missing women; another man arrested for rape and assault; yet another who had a long rap sheet that included assault on women; and a local man who lived a few minutes from the area in which two of the women had last been seen. One by one each of these men was dropped from the list—except a local man named Kendall Francois, against whom a prostitute had recently filed an assault complaint. The woman said Francois had picked her up in January 1998 and taken her to his home. There they argued; the man punched her in the face and began choking her. She agreed to have sex with him. When he was done, he took her back to the street where he had found her. On May 5 he pleaded guilty to third-degree assault, a misdemeanor, and spent fifteen days in jail.

Three weeks later, Sandra Jean French, fifty-one, was reported missing from her home in a small town just east of Poughkeepsie. She, too, was small and white. Her car was found abandoned a few blocks from the Francois home. Her disappearance was followed two months later by that of Catina Newmaster, twenty-five, like most of the others slightly built with short brown hair. Fear gripped Poughkeepsie, especially among the women who did business on the streets downtown.

Earlier in January, before his assault arrest, police had staked out the Francois home, to no effect. Then they asked Francois if he was willing to undergo an interview. He came to the police station willingly, his demeanor calm and respectful. He answered everything asked of him, let them come to his house, even to his bedroom, and said nothing that aroused suspicion. The most outstanding aspect of the interview, according to a police report, was that the house was littered with garbage and smelled terrible. Still, the troubling facts persisted: all of the missing women were short and slim, all were white, all had brown hair, all were last seen where sex workers were known to hang out, some had been arrested for prostitution, and most were not in regular contact with their families. Poughkeepsie, a usually quiet college town, seemed to have become home to a serial killer.

The two-story house at 99 Fulton Avenue, where Kendall Francois lived with his parents and teenage sister, was the kind of place with which children like to scare themselves, calling it a haunted house. Unlike most of the homes in the middle-class neighborhood, a few blocks from the Vassar College campus, it looked as though it was about to fall down. Paint was peeling off the faded green clapboard siding, the yard was overgrown with weeds, and trash littered the ground. It looked like something out of a horror movie. It smelled even worse.

Now twenty-seven, the six-foot four-inch, three-hundred-pound Francois had worked until January 1997 as a hall monitor at Arlington Middle School. A dark-skinned Haitian native, he must have looked like a giant to the children he watched over, but they didn't seem to fear him. Their nickname for him was "Stinky." Neither the children nor their teachers had any idea that Francois had started picking up female sex workers in downtown Poughkeepsie in 1996. From time to time, over a period of more than twenty-two months, he would take the prostitutes home for sex, then kill them.

His ninth encounter turned violent when he began strangling his intended victim in his second-story bedroom. Using a combination of pleading and wily manipulation, she broke free and persuaded Francois to drive her back to Main Street, where he had picked her up. As they pulled into a nearby Sunoco gas station, the woman jumped out of the car and ran off.

Coincidentally, two detectives were nearby, preparing to hand out flyers asking for help in finding Catina Newmaster. They saw Francois driving by and waved to him. Francois waved back, recognizing one of the detectives from his interview. The detectives pulled into the same gas station from which the woman had just run away, and a man there told the police that a woman had just said she had been assaulted. The two detectives found the woman walking down a nearby street. She confirmed the attack and accompanied the men to the police station to file a complaint against Francois. Police arrested him and searched his home, where they discovered eight bodies in various states of decomposition.

Serial killers tend to establish a pattern. Were this not so, the fact that the murders were done by a single person might well escape police notice. Francois's pattern was to have sex with the prostitutes in the small, detached garage adjacent to his family's home, in the house's basement, or in one of the house's bedrooms, then strangle and dismember them. He hid one body under a mattress on the garage floor until a storm partially destroyed the structure. He then moved the body into the house. After killing five of the victims, he cut them up and put their body parts into one of three plastic containers—a small trash can, a child's swimming pool with white ghostly figures on it, and a black trash bag—where they decomposed. The stench in and around the house was almost unbearable. Neighbors thought the odor resulted from filthy living conditions inside the house. They had no idea what lay beneath it. No one associated the odor with decomposing flesh.

Tom Holland and I became involved in the case through a request from the New York State Police. Dr. Lowell Levine, a CIL consultant, called to ask if we could reassociate the body parts and assist in identifying the victims. Although Dr. Barbara Wolf, the state police medical examiner in Poughkeepsie, was thoroughly experienced, she wanted help with what would prove to be one of the most unusual cases in her professional career. The stimulus for bringing us into the case came when Dr. Wolf removed several right legs from a single trash bag in the morgue and realized that she was dealing with a jumble of body parts. Eight Poughkeepsie women were missing. The common thread binding these unfortunate women, Dr. Levine told me, was their occupation. Furthermore, except for one, they were in their mid-twenties, white, and crack cocaine users. And they all had the ill fortune to go home with a man who had more than sex on his mind.

Anthropology would play a major role in the case because most of the victims were skeletonized and, other than a few decaying tattoos, no identifying media were found with the bodies. Although the skilled Dr. Levine could positively identify the women's skulls from their dental records, there was no way for either him or the medical examiner to reassociate the five skulls with the dismembered skeletons that were found in various containers in the attic. Three corpses buried in a crawl space under the house, on the other hand, were sufficiently intact, their bones not mixed.

My job was to reattach the 206 bones constituting each woman's skeleton, starting with the skull and ending with the toes. The plan was for me to go to Poughkeepsie and do the initial assessment of the body parts. Tom would come up later and give the remains a second look and, as it turned out, reassociate the bones that stumped me or that needed a second opinion.

By the time I arrived, the bodies and body parts had been removed from the house on Fulton Avenue and taken to St. Francis Hospital morgue for autopsy. The bodies were waiting for me in several refrigerators. After I put on scrubs and gloves, Dr. Wolf gave me an overview of what we were dealing with, and I jumped right in. I first needed to identify which body parts were present and which were missing. The possibility existed that some parts might have been discarded elsewhere, perhaps at the local dump, as in the Jeffrey Dahmer case. My second step was to reassociate each bone with the appropriate skull, then completely reassemble each skeleton. Third, I would document which of the three plastic containers each part had come from. Knowing that a person's arm and leg came from two different containers would help police reconstruct the gruesome details.

Although I had plenty of experience identifying bones and reassembling skeletons, this case was more difficult and complicated than most because some of the arms and legs were still covered with decaying soft tissue. Lying on the five gurneys were the lifeless bodies of at least five victims. Trying to match up the body parts of the five victims that Francois had dismembered was going to be like trying to distinguish the pieces from five jigsaw puzzles when all the pieces had been mixed together in one box. Looking around the morgue, I saw one gurney loaded down with more than a hundred bones. There were hands, feet, legs, arms, and everything in between. A quick glance revealed that each gurney held the remains of more than one person. One table had three skulls, on another were the legs of at least three people, and yet another held a jumble of arms, legs, spines, ribs, hands, and feet, some still wearing socks. Complicating the process of sorting the remains was that the victims were all female and all about the same body size and race, so I couldn't use those two criteria for sorting the bones.

As we sort remains, we rely as much on bone size as anything else. Often we can differentiate between the bones of a six-foot man and those of a six-foot woman because a man's joints are usually larger than a woman's. This is especially true of the head of the femur, which fits into the hip socket. The most difficult cases are when two people of the same sex are also the same size and age. Confronted with this situation, anthropologists must draw upon their experience and look for subtle differences. Increasingly, mitochondrial DNA can answer many questions, but the technique is costly and slows the identification process. MtDNA is, however, a great way to reassociate and sort remains. In fact, we can even use mtDNA to determine if an arm bone goes with a leg bone, a hip, a skull, or even a toe, even if all 206 bones are present. For example, imagine that a serial killer has mixed the bones of two or more of his victims. If we suspect that what appears to be a single skeleton consists of the bones of more than one person, we can test some of the bones to see if there is only one DNA sequence. If not, the bones have either been contaminated by someone handling them or have come from more than one person.

Lifting the stiff arms and legs covered with dark brown, leathery skin, I saw maggots dropping everywhere. The maggots gave proof that the bodies had been exposed to the elements long enough for flies to lay eggs on

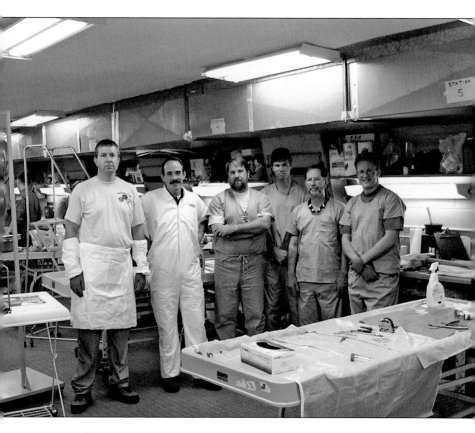

Some of the anthropologists who assisted with the identification of victims killed at the Pentagon and in Pennsylvania on 9/11. *Left to right:* Max Houck, Bill Rodriguez, Tom Holland, John Byrd, Bob Mann, and Andy Tyrrell.

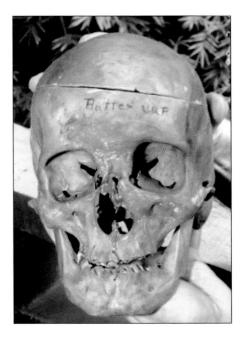

Butter Cup, showing badly broken nasal bones and a skull cut from the autopsy.

Four shrapnel holes, indicated by red probes, in the WWII helmet of Private Horner.

Lieutenant Clement's ejection seat found more than fifty years after his aircraft went missing over northern Japan. The crewman's remains were found sitting in the seat.

COURTESY JPAC

Search-and-recovery team members going over the side of a steep mountain in Laos in search of remains in 1994. The drop-off is more than 5,000 feet.

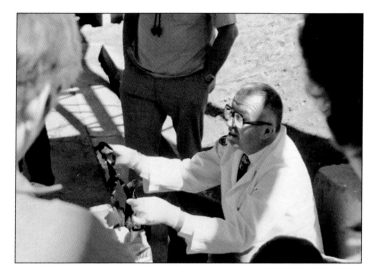

Dr. Bill Bass discussing a new forensic case with graduate students and members of the Tennessee Bureau of Investigation, Knoxville.

COURTESY BILL BASS

The Joint POW/MIA Accounting Command's Central Identification Laboratory in Hawaii.

COURTESY BOB MANN

The author (*left*) and Doug Owsley examining skeletal remains in the late 1980s.

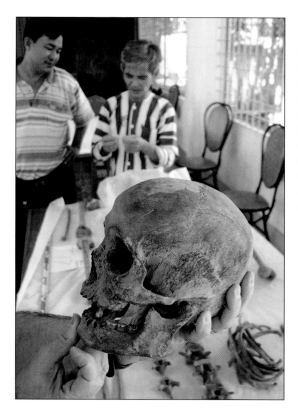

A Vietnamese policeman and a prisoner, who was incarcerated for being part of a group involved in the illegal practice of selling human remains, stand by as the author examines a skull alleged to be that of an American listed as missing in action. PHOTO BY KEN DUNN

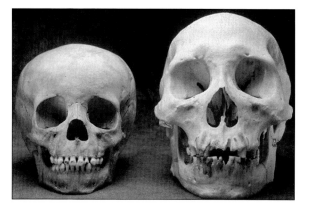

Child's skull (*left*) compared to that of an adult (*right*).
COURTESY BOB MANN

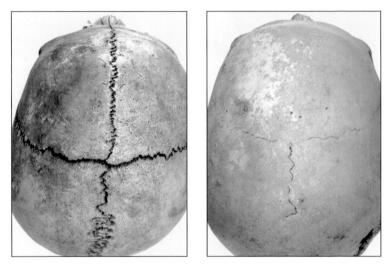

Although it is a generally unreliable method, the openness of
cranial sutures continues to be used as a relative gauge of whether someone
is a young adult (*left*) or an elderly person. The sutures consist of interlocking joints
that usually begin to disappear, as in the photo at right, in the thirties.

Differences in the size and shape of the nasal bones
of Asian, white, and black individuals.

them. These body parts had not been put into the containers in which they were found until some time after the victims died. We knew this because the maggots were visible in the first-floor ceiling. We could have had a forensic entomologist examine these wriggling creatures to tell us their age based on their stage of development, but police already had a confession from the murderer and the victims' time since death was not in question. Whether we could put them back together was.

Looking around, I saw a few body parts in the late stages of decay, and greasy bones that were nearly without tissue. The evidence was consistent with the victims having died at different times over a period of at least a year, and having been left to the natural process of decay. There was also evidence that Francois had used a saw to dismember his victims. Police recovered several saws from the filthy house, which was cluttered with partially eaten food, rat droppings, victims' underwear, and driver's licenses. I visited the Fulton Avenue house to see where the bodies had been kept. We who entered the house were required to put on a white Tyvek jumpsuit and latex gloves and to cover our hair. Because people shed hair and skin cells continually, care was required to avoid contaminating the scene with evidence of our presence.

Everywhere were old newspapers, unwashed silverware, pots and pans, cobwebs, bare electrical wires hanging from the ceiling, cabinets without doors, and used condoms. Clearly, Francois came from a family of pack rats. One of the most interesting items in the house was a brochure that appeared to be a self-help guide, entitled "Who Am I and Why Am I in Treatment?" perched precariously atop a stack of books in one of the bedrooms. The inside of the house looked like a trash Dumpster that doubled as a home for vagrants. How anyone could live in such filth was beyond comprehension.

Using colored markers, I shaded in the skeletal diagrams showing which bones were present and in which container each was found: red for the garbage can, green for the trash bag, and yellow for the child's swimming pool. I used five skeletal charts, one for each victim. The trash bag had parts of all five victims. The swimming pool held pieces of four. The bright colors made it easy to see where each bone had been found, and which bones remained missing.

Eventually, five forearm bones and eleven pieces of femoral shafts were sent to anthropologist Dr. Steve Symes at the University of Tennessee, Memphis, for cut-mark analysis. Steve, a gregarious scientist with a passion for volleyball whom I knew from my days in Tennessee, did his dissertation on sawed bones and has become the world's expert on the subject, even serving as a consultant to author Patricia Cornwell. He examined the pattern of parallel cuts in the ends of the bones and provided two critical pieces of evidence. First, the women's bodies were dismembered by someone using a new hacksaw blade. Second, the same person sawed all the bones.

Steve compared the pattern of striations, starts, and stops in the cut ends under a microscope and could see that whoever wielded the saw consistently changed direction about one third of the way through the bone. Also, he didn't saw all the way through the bone. Instead, he stopped when he was nearly finished and snapped the bone in two. Steve told me this was the first time he was able to determine personal behavior based on sawed bones, because this was the first case for which he had so many sawed bones to compare. We all know the significance of bloody footprints, spent bullet casings, and tire tracks in solving crimes, but who would have thought that saw marks could yield so much information about a person's behavior?

To my way of thinking, the most bizarre part of this case is the fact that Francois may have dismembered some of his victims while members of his family were in the house. It's clear he left his victims in the attic to rot and grow rank. Photographs of the scene showed that the swimming pool, trash bag, and garbage can were left in plain sight. In fact, one would have had to climb over these stinking bags of body parts to get into the attic. A detective on the case told me that Francois's family pointed out that "the ceiling was moving with maggots." Francois's calm response was that some raccoons had gotten into the attic and died. At his family's request he sprayed the rooms with bleach, but the maggots and mystery stench simply wouldn't go away.

The remains of the five victims were reassociated, identified, and returned to their families for proper burial. Francois was arraigned, tried, and found guilty of the first-degree murder of all eight women. He was sentenced to life without parole and incarcerated in Attica, New York's toughest prison, where he remains, known now as prisoner A4160.

12. THE FATE OF A SKYKNIGHT

Night, when words fade and things come alive, when the destructive
analysis of day is done, and all that is truly important becomes
whole and sound again. When a man reassembles his
fragmentary self and grows with the calm of a tree.

—ANTOINE DE SAINT-EXUPÉRY

As the scientific spokesman at a family update meeting, anthropologist
Tom Holland gave the best description I've ever heard of what it's like trying to reconstruct the broken skeleton of a plane crash victim. The CIL
participates in such meetings, hosted periodically by several government
organizations for the families of service members killed or missing in action. Holland asked the audience to imagine a thousand-piece jigsaw puzzle still in the box. Let someone remove seven hundred of the pieces at
random, and throw them away. Take what is left and scatter the pieces over
an area the size of a football field and then set the ground on fire five or ten
times. Go back twenty-seven years later and see how many pieces of the
puzzle you can find, and then put them back together. I can tell you from
experience: that pretty much sums it up.

On the morning of July 27, 2001, Albert McFarland, the mortuary officer in Seoul, South Korea, called me on the phone. A few days earlier, a vacationing South Korean man had found what appeared to be the remains
of an American soldier, along with his parachute, boots, dog tags, a cloth
flight map, and tattered pieces of a flight suit. The man called the local po-

lice, who notified the Republic of Korea (ROK) Army, which brought the U.S. Army Mortuary into the picture. Al was excited and almost breathless as he described what the villager had discovered: erosion on the side of a small, sandy hill at Pangpo Beach, some 150 miles south of Seoul, had partially uncovered the remains. Al knew from the dog tags that the body was that of an airman who had gone missing at the end of a combat mission on May 30, 1953. Forty-eight years later, we were about to learn what had become of S.Sgt. James Vaughn Harrell, a twenty-one-year-old Marine radar operator at the time of his death. Harrell, whom his buddies called "Red," was one of seven Americans from Shreveport, Louisiana, who died in the Korean War.

Along with his pilot, Captain James B. Brown, and another plane from the Marine All Weather Fighter Squadron 513, nicknamed the "Flying Nightmares," Harrell's mission that night was to escort a flight of B-29 bombers to their targets over North Korea. Harrell and Brown's aircraft was a twin-engine Douglas F3D-2 Skyknight, described as a sort of "primitive" jet plane. On the return run, heading toward Kunsan Air Base, designated K-8, Harrell's plane fell in behind another Skyknight, which carried radar operator Ron Stout. The crews identified themselves to each other. The last radio transmission came just before midnight, when Harrell reported the Skyknight had twenty minutes' worth of fuel remaining and had been cleared to land at the K-8 airfield. Stout was the last person to hear Harrell's voice. The plane that carried him and Brown never reached K-8. They simply vanished. The only clue to their fate came five days later when a flight crew saw an oil slick on water over which the plane had been flying.

The remains and artifacts found at Pangpo Beach arrived at the CIL in a silver Batesville casket provided by the Seoul mortuary. We removed the green body bag from the casket and laid everything out on an examination table. Enclosed were several plastic bags containing bones as well as artifacts that the long-missing airman had carried with him that day in 1953. Equipment intended for life support had been at his side all those years and had suffered the same conditions that had reduced the body to bones. His skeleton, stained brown by the moist soil and split by small roots that had pierced it over the past half century, was fragile and incomplete.

Looking at them, I saw that the size and development of the bones was consistent with those of a male. A racial determination was more tenuous because we had neither skull nor teeth. The mild degree of front-to-back curving of the femurs, however, was most consistent with those of a Caucasian man. The youthful condition of the collarbones and spine suggested that he had been in his early twenties when he died. A measurement of one of the leg bones suggested a stature of five feet seven inches, about average height for a man of his generation. Many bones showed fractures and injuries typical of an aircraft crash. I made a note that my preliminary examination of the bones suggested that they were those of a young white male adult who sustained injuries consistent with a high-speed impact incident. The pattern, distribution, and severity of his injuries, however, suggested that he was not in the airplane when he died.

I moved on to the other artifacts. The first thing to catch my attention was the U.S. Air Force cloth map. Although torn, tattered, and missing small sections, it was in very good condition considering that it had been exposed to fluctuating temperatures, freezing rain, and roots growing in acidic soil for more than four decades. It was unburned. I carefully picked up this silk treasure and spread it out on the table to see if it was a map of North or South Korea. Seeing Pyongyang, I immediately knew it was of the North. The 38th parallel running near the bottom of the map's tattered edge revealed the crew's destination and intention. Being familiar with maps, I scanned its margins and along the bottom saw "SEPT 1951." Sitting back in my chair, I realized that I had been only two years old when this map was printed and only four years old when it went out of service. None of this information, however, solved the mystery surrounding the plane's disappearance.

Examining the remains, I mulled over several questions, some of which the evidence within my reach would not likely answer. I wondered why the crewman had bailed out and how he had ended up in the side of a hill. The place where his remains were found and their condition suggested that one of two things had happened: either someone buried him soon after he died, or he became buried as years of soil erosion gradually covered his body while it lay on the hill. Although either scenario was possible, I favored the former. The ROK soldiers had done the actual recovery of the remains. What they had uncovered was not a crash site but a grave, whether natural or man-made. The absence of aircraft wreckage left no doubt that the airplane had expelled its crew and traveled on to another resting place. To my knowledge, the aircraft has never been found. It could be at the bottom of the sea or buried beneath years of leaves somewhere in the mountains of Korea.

I guessed that the crew had bailed out just before the plane ditched in the Yellow Sea. The escape system in this type of aircraft was unusual because the crew got out through a bailout chute, an opening in the bottom of the fuselage. In most planes, crewmen bailed out through one of the side doors in the aircraft, the same way they got into the plane. In others, escape was made with an ejection seat that propelled the pilot or copilot out of the top of the aircraft. In the F3D "bubble chaser," as one pilot put it to me, the plane had an escape chute in the center rear of the cockpit. To get out of the aircraft, the pilot pulled a D-ring handle on the center console that caused a door to drop off the bottom of the aircraft, and a door opened in the cockpit through which he would drop. The question of why the crew bailed out nagged at me. They apparently thought something terrible was about to happen, and they did their best to get out of the aircraft. But what, exactly, did they know?

In the laboratory I moved from one artifact to the other, looking for useful clues. The artifacts consisted of two dog tags bearing the name of James Vaughan Harrell, USMC; a fragment of a leather name patch worn on the flight suit with the letters "J.V.HA . . . , AIO" (Airborne Intercept Operator) in gold lettering; and a piece of flight suit material and corroded zipper that appeared to be from the chest region. Also present were two size-nine boots, a green plastic U.S. Navy whistle, a nearly intact yellow life vest, a back-style parachute, pieces of a life raft, a signal strobe light, and a few snaps and buttons. But his pistol, watch, wallet, and other personal items that he might have been carrying were missing. We'll never know, but my guess is that the person who first found his body had removed them as souvenirs. The Korean authorities several times put out flyers and sent local news outlets requests for information on the case, but got no replies. It wasn't likely that anyone would remember the incident or, for that matter, even be alive, fifty years after the crash. We would have to rely on the evidence at hand to tell us what happened.

Although the Korean soldiers had unpacked it in South Korea, we took the parachute out back of the CIL and stretched it across the ground to make sure no bones remained inside. I also wanted to see if it held the name of the manufacturer or a serial number, two clues to its date and place of manufacture. We were also looking for a parachute packing log that might have been in a small pocket in the outer parachute bag. This log was normally filled out by whoever packed the chute and served as a record. We didn't find one. Although the harness straps were in relatively good condition, the buckles were no more than rusted lumps of metal. Close examination of the cream-colored canopy that, once laid out on the concrete, resembled a cloth Portuguese man-of-war, revealed a pattern of rust stains indicating that it had spent many years compressed inside the back-style parachute. When we held up the parachute to the light, several thin rip-stop panels revealed the markings "U.S. NAVY PARACHUTE NO." and "PIONEER PARACHUTE CO. INC." but no serial number. Several of us wrestled with the tangled parachute in gusting winds as we examined every nook and cranny of the harness and canopy for even a shred of evidence about what had happened to the crewman. The bent steel D-shaped rip-cord handle bore witness that the parachute had not been deployed.

I returned the artifacts to their respective bags and began the painstaking process of inventorying the bones. I laid out each bone in anatomical position and, upon completing my inventory, saw that most of the skull and some of the spine, lower right leg, hands, and teeth were missing. At that point there was no way of knowing whether the two Korean soldiers who collected the remains missed some of the bones when they removed the body from the ground, or if the natural process of decay and decomposition had claimed them. Again I suspected the former.

We had bones, but no usable DNA. We had a parachute, but no serial number, which would have yielded evidence of the flyer to whom it was issued. We had dog tags, but no wallet or identity card. I thought that the totality of the evidence, including the dog tags, date of the map, type of parachute, and area of recovery would be strong enough to support an identification and ran this possibility by our scientific director, Tom Holland. He thought we should see what other evidence might appear. The only way to tell would be for a CIL team to travel to South Korea to do a systematic recovery. I'd already begun the analysis and was the logical person to do the recovery, so I planned a trip for the following week, and finding a tooth or two was high on my investigatory wish list.

After pulling together the equipment necessary to excavate a burial, three of us boarded Northwest Airlines for the eight-and-a-half-hour flight to Kansai, Japan, followed by a short commuter hop into Seoul. We checked into our hotel Friday night and were on our way to Anmyon Island the next morning. The drive, which took us 150 miles south through some of the most picturesque parts of Korea, should have taken only five hours, not eight, as it turned out to do. The drive to Taean Town along the western coast answered my previous night's question of why the streets of Seoul lacked their usual traffic jams and congestion. Everyone was heading out of the city. As we would soon learn, it was peak vacation time, and everyone who could possibly do so had made a hasty retreat to the countryside. It seemed that Anmyon Do, an island resort in the South, was a popular destination at that time of the year. We were sharing the road with a horde of relaxed vacationers who, it was clear, were in no hurry whatsoever.

We finally made it to our destination and received a police escort to the site. As we turned off the highway and made our way down a narrow dirt road lined on both sides with pine trees, we were met with a pleasant surprise. At first we seemed to be headed for a dig site in the middle of the woods, but soon we came to the end of the road and saw that it opened onto a beautiful rocky beach. We'd left Hawaii and flown nearly five thousand miles to a site that could rival in beauty any postcard from our own home state. We parked our cars and vans in a small family campground. Tents were scattered about the area, and families huddled inside around their cookstoves. It was cool, breezy, and damp, but not cold. It seems that the objective of a family outing in Korea is the same as in the States— eating food cooked over a campfire, less conveniently than at home.

We tried to be unobtrusive as we walked past the tents and made our way to the ocean's edge, where we were met by Korean police who had secured the area, a few local officials, and one of the Republic of Korea soldiers who had excavated the burial less than two weeks before. After the usual introductions we walked over to the burial site, which had become as well known as the resort when the remains were discovered. Once alerted that an American team would be returning to the area to dig, the police marked off the area with rope and prevented anyone from tampering with the site. Walking over to the place where the remains had been found, which was at the base of a small hill facing the Yellow Sea, I immediately recognized a small piece of innominate (hip) bone lying on the ground. Within inches of it were a few pieces of ribs and to the right was a small piece of a vertebra.

We were right thinking that the ROK soldiers, who at first suspected that the remains were those of a North Korean infiltrator who had died trying to make it to the coast, had overlooked at least some of the remains. In fact, they only realized that it was an American when they uncovered his dog tags and read the "USMC" initials on them. Although the ROK soldiers had done a superb job of recovering the remains, they had overlooked a few of the smaller pieces of bone and teeth. It's easy to understand why they missed the teeth. I think many people imagine a search for teeth on the ground ends with the discovery of a full and shining smile lying there, waiting to be picked up. The problem is that a person's smile is actually made up of two rows of teeth held tightly in their bony sockets. Once the flesh of the gums is gone, many of the teeth can fall out of their sockets as easily as pencils from a cup.

After I noted the location of the teeth on my site sketch, we gathered up the few pieces of bone and another fragment of a cloth map and went to the hotel to prepare for the next day's work. The hotel was less than a two-minute drive from the site. We checked in, got a good night's rest, and returned to the site ready to work the next morning.

Working in a light drizzling rain, we unloaded the excavation equipment—including our shovels, trowels, and buckets—and set up an archaeological grid with the burial spot at its center. Even as we laid out the grid, with wooden stakes and string to outline where we would be digging, we encountered small pieces of bone. We marked their location within the grid, and the excavation was in full swing, despite a light drizzle that moved in and then away. By lunchtime we'd recovered several pieces of bone from the spine, ribs, legs, feet, and hips. We also began finding pieces of boot leather with corroded eyelets still attached; part of a flight suit zipper stained green from oxidation caused by contact with the salt water of the Yellow Sea; a piece of a black plastic comb; a rusty buckle that looked as if it had come from either the parachute harness or belt; and a piece of what seemed to be stainless steel, shaped roughly like an L. My first thought was that this piece was from a flight helmet, or that it had been used to attach something to the life raft that the flyer would have been sitting on when he dropped through the ejection chute. The bone and other material evidence weren't concentrated in any one area; rather, they were spread throughout the grid. These pieces appeared to have been scattered twice—first when the two ROK soldiers excavated the burial; and again when they refilled the hole with soil, thinking that they would never dig it again.

The highlight of the first day came in the early afternoon when one of our team members found a tooth in the lower right quadrant of our grid. She was moving along, thinking that she had dug deep enough that she wouldn't find anything more, when it "just jumped out at me," she told us as a small crowd huddled over her shoulder. It was the first tooth that she'd ever found, and her enthusiasm showed. It was a molar without any fillings in it. Although I, too, was delighted with the finding, I would have preferred one that had a filling in it so we might have used it to positively identify the crewman from his dental records. But the tooth renewed my team's optimism. We were all hoping to be the one to find the next tooth. We soon realized, however, that the second tooth would have to wait until tomorrow. Or longer.

We were back at it again at eight o'clock the next morning. The previous day's rain having done nothing to dampen our spirits, we clambered down the dirt road to the site and picked up where we'd left off. Every now and again I'd look around at the beautiful scenery and try to figure out why this young crewman had bailed out. There was no way for me to know for sure what happened on that fateful night in 1953, but I had to wonder what went wrong for this Skyknight.

The aircraft was far from the fighting in the North, so my best guess was that it developed mechanical problems or ran out of fuel and the crew of two was forced to bail out, too late and too low. I was aware that this was only a guess, and would forever remain so. If our sergeant bailed out over the Yellow Sea, he may not have had enough time to pull the rip cord and deploy his parachute before striking the water. I figured he parachuted out over the water and his body washed up on the beach. Someone strolling along the beach or looking out over the sea from the surrounding hills probably found his body and buried him near its base. Whoever had buried him was kind enough not to remove his identification—his dog tags and the leather name patch on his flight suit. It was these two small pieces of metal that, nearly fifty years later, would provide the link to his remains and his identity—and, we hoped, bring him back to his family. If someone hadn't buried his body, we probably would have never found him or been able to deduce what had happened to end his life.

Continuing the dig, we made slow progress due to the many rocks and pebbles scattered throughout the soil. By the end of the first day we'd dug more than half the project area and planned to complete work the second day—that is, of course, if nothing went wrong. Near the end of the first day, the slow drizzling rain finally stopped and we could remove the plastic canopy that we'd stretched overhead to keep the site dry. When the soil got wet, it turned to soft, oozing mud that we couldn't push through the sifting screens. We did our best to keep the ground dry and work around the discomfort of sitting on rocks all day with muddy butts and numb legs.

As the excavation pace slowed at the end of the day, my mind again turned to the bailout. But try as I might, I just couldn't find that one magical piece that would bring the puzzle together. Behind me was the calm Yellow Sea, the northernmost part of the vast China Sea, with its jagged limestone towers stretching skyward like a giant's chess pieces on a massive and watery chessboard. Although it was cloudy, I still managed to catch a few glimpses of a vibrant sky trying to break through. The hill where the crewman was buried was covered with trees and grass, and the long beach in front of it was littered with rocks ranging in size from eggs to footballs. Beneath all this ruggedness was a soft bed of fine sand. But my mind soon returned to the task at hand. Our airman was still waiting on us to take him home, so we continued digging.

The third morning found us focusing on the burial pit. We'd closed the other four grid squares and had this last one to do. The ROK soldier told us that he'd found the remains a bit more than three feet (about one meter) from the rocky beach. This part of the hill had a gentle slope and was sparsely covered with grasses. At that height, the tide would have only occasionally been able to reach the burial place, so erosion would have been slow. This explains why nearly fifty years had passed before any evidence of the burial became exposed. Although the morning of that third day started cool, breezy, and dry, within an hour the light, misty drizzle had returned. The usual throng of vacationers walking along the shore, skipping stones on the glassy sea, or sitting in brightly colored tents along the shore was replaced with swarms of dragonflies.

Over the years I'd come to associate the first appearance of these insectivorous helicopters with serious rain. I first noticed this connection while working in Vietnam. As usual, the dragonflies' appearance correctly foretold the weather. The rain made its way to our part of Pangpo Beach within the hour. Although the precipitation kept it cool and made it pleasant to work, it once again turned the brown soil into soft mud. Pushing mud through a sifting screen is no easy task; at times it was like screening modeling clay.

I climbed into the mouth of the small burial pit and, lying on my side, began slowly digging myself deeper into the side of the hill. One unpleasant part of the dig was the large centipedes that slithered out of the hill through cracks in the ground and from between the rocks. I used my trowel either to toss them out of my way or cut them in half, not wanting to become a victim of their painful bite. Meanwhile, the rest of my team was doing their best to sift the muddy soil and maintain a positive attitude while standing in the rain. We still hoped to find more teeth, but prospects were growing dim. Before lunch we'd dug into the burial pit to a depth where the skull and teeth, if still present, should have been found. Since the burial had already been dug and most of the skeleton removed, we had little more to go on than what the ROK soldier had told us. I hated to admit it, but this was one of those cases where the anthropologist couldn't "read the soil."

Reading the soil is a phrase anthropologists use to describe how they interpret what they see in the ground. Depending on the area, the ground may be composed of distinct layers of soil like a layered cake—the top layer, richest in organics, is usually darker than the layers below it. The second layer might consist of light sand and the third, a layer of grayish, moist clay. Imagine digging through the three layers and mixing them as you bury a body—you dig a hole and remove the soil, put a body in it, and fill the hole with the same soil. In essence, you've mixed the three layers of soil, destroying nature's careful sequence. In the surrounding soil, the stratification remains unaltered. A trained eye can recognize this disturbance in the form of marbled, mottled, or swirled soil. It's the same concept as those glasses containing different-colored sand that were popular in the Southwest in the seventies. If you go back to find the grave ten years later and skim off the top three to four inches of soil in an area of sufficient size, you're likely to see a place where the body decomposed and darkened the soil. Reading the soil is no more than exposing it and looking for evidence of disturbance. It's rather easy to do if you've got the proper training, know what to look for, and prepare the soil properly.

In the present case, the soil on the side of the hill was all the same color, so I couldn't see any differences in disturbance based on soil type, consistency, or color. At one point, however, our hopes were revived as we found a bone from the left hand, a few ribs, and the sternum (breastplate), in that order. Many of the bones showed small green stains, which signified where the copper leached out of the metal zippers or copper bullet casings— we had recovered a leather bandolier about as wide as a belt that contained what I believe were twelve corroded .38-caliber bullets in it; it had been in contact with bone since being buried—and turned them green. We often see the stains of copper salts on bones buried in moist soil for many years; the copper salts inhibit bacterial growth, preserve bone very well, and sometimes mummify a dime- or quarter-size piece of skin or head hair that the bullet has been resting up against.

Although it seemed that we were moving up the skeleton from the hands to the chest to the head and were just about to hit the teeth, instead we hit sand. The sand made digging and sifting easier, but it also meant that we'd dug out the entire burial site and were into what archaeologists call sterile soil—sterile in the sense that the soil was undisturbed. We'd come to the end of the burial pit and we had nowhere else to dig. Fortunately, the rain had let up, and the sun broke through to warm things a bit. It was a welcome change from the previous two wet days.

A bit disappointed, we broke for lunch while part of our crew got on the road back to Seoul. We ate and then returned to work, preparing the site for final photographs and measurements of the grids and the burial pit. This is all part of an archaeological dig: we prepare site sketches to document not only how much and where we've dug, but as a plot of where each item was found in relation to all others—what we call their provenience (an alternative form of the more commonly used "provenance"). Midafternoon found us troweling and brushing the soil off the rocks to expose everything for photographs. I pulled out my trusty 35 millimeter camera, took the closing photos of the site, and we were done. We would include these photographs in the search-and-recovery report, and they would become part of the identification packet given to the family, if there was a positive identification. I admit to being both surprised and disappointed at not finding more teeth and hand bones. I thought for sure that after sifting every inch of the soil we'd find the other 20 to 30 percent of the skeleton. But it wasn't to be.

Back at the mortuary laboratory, still in Korea, I washed the soil from the remains and laid them out to air dry. Drying bones too quickly, such as in an oven or in direct sunlight, may cause them to split. Drying too slowly causes them to get moldy. The best way is to lay them out on a towel or newspaper and let them dry overnight. I did another inventory to see what portions of the skeleton we'd recovered on our trip while anthropologist Jim Pokines did the material evidence. There were pieces of ribs, vertebrae, feet, at least one hand, one tooth, the breastplate, and, surprisingly, small pieces of the left and right temporal bones. The temporal bones were proof that we'd recovered at least part of the airman's skull. But the location of the rest of the skull remained anybody's guess. Still, the evidence suggested that Staff Sergeant Harrell had suffered a head injury, perhaps when he ejected the Skyknight. The remains that we'd recovered didn't provide much more information, but at least we'd gotten everything there was of Staff Sergeant Harrell. I was confident that we'd excavated the entire burial and hadn't missed any bones or teeth in the soil or surrounding area. I would be hand carrying everything—the remains and material evidence that we'd found at the site—on the flight back to Hawaii to see if we had enough evidence for a presumptive or, as some call it, a circumstantial identification. I hoped that Staff Sergeant Harrell was indeed waiting for me in Hawaii, one island closer to home.

Once I arrived back at the CIL, I laid the bones we'd recovered on the table along with the remains that the ROK soldiers had recovered a few weeks before. Sitting at the table, I compared the bone fragments to see if I could put any more back together. I was especially eager to see if we'd recovered any of the skull or other portions, such as the easily damaged pubic bones of the hips, which might help me narrow the age of the individual. Starting with the bones of the head, I slowly held each piece next to what we'd already recovered and immediately found some matches. I didn't glue anything together yet because I wanted to take photographs of what the Korean soldiers had recovered to compare to photographs of what my team had recovered, to determine what the Koreans had missed. My goal was to document the kinds of bones that inexperienced people overlook, which might be useful in future recoveries.

After a few hours of comparing bone fragments, I had a good picture of what we had—about 90 percent of the skeleton, including the sternum and more of the spine, hands, and feet. The really telling pieces of the puzzle were two irregularly shaped pieces of bone, which composed the auditory canal. Here was proof positive that at least part of the individual's head was present when he was buried. The perplexing part of the story, however, was that we found only one of his teeth and very little else of his head. The recovery of these small pieces of bone and one tooth suggested that he had in fact sustained head trauma at or near the time he escaped from the aircraft. I couldn't, however, tell exactly what had happened.

After reconstructing the approximately one hundred pieces of bone from Korea, which I noted on a skeletal drawing, the biological profile was completed. My initial analysis hadn't changed. This was a white male who was eighteen to twenty-five years old when he went missing and who stood about five feet seven inches. Everything about the bones matched what was recorded in Staff Sergeant Harrell's medical and personnel files except what appeared to be an old, healed fracture of his upper left fibula. It's not unusual, however, for old fractures to be omitted from both civilian and military records. People forget to mention them at an induction physical, and if there has been no reason to X-ray the area, the fracture will go unnoticed.

Researching the parachute, I found that it had been manufactured before 1953 and was indeed a back-style parachute that would have required the crewman to open it manually. The question of why he hadn't pulled the rip cord would go unanswered because there was simply no way to be certain what happened that Monday in 1953. Perhaps he was knocked unconscious as he bailed out of the aircraft, or he bailed out too low. Even after examining all the pieces of the puzzle, some answers were beyond the grasp of science.

Once we'd finished our analysis and were confident that the remains were those of Staff Sergeant Harrell, we contacted the U.S. Marine Corps service representative to move the case on to the next step, notifying the family that their loved one had been found and identified. The service representative's job would be to find Staff Sergeant Harrell's next of kin, whether it was his brother or sister, or perhaps an aunt or uncle. Because he had died forty-seven years earlier, it was unlikely that his mother and father were still living. We contacted the service representative and held our breath, hoping for good news. Luckily, they were able to find his sister, still living in Louisiana. Staff Sergeant Harrell's remains left the CIL by special escort on January 28, 2002, bound for Arlington National Cemetery. He was laid to rest with a new U.S. Marine Corps uniform and with full honors on Friday, February 1, 2002. More than thirty people, including former members of his unit and two retired generals, came to pay their respects.

Ron Stout, the radar operator whose plane preceded Harrell's, later wrote, "If you have never seen the Washington, D.C. Marines render honors then you have missed one of life's most stirring sights. In a pouring rain not one of them so much as blinked. After the rifle volleys they presented the empty casings to the family."

Harrell's great-niece Jimmie McClung, named for him, received the traditionally folded flag draped over Red Harrell's casket. She had been two years old when he disappeared.

This American airman from Shreveport, Louisiana, had been missing long enough for Neil Armstrong to walk on the moon, for Ford Mustangs to achieve their own prominence in history, and for the Beatles to come and go. Pangpo Beach is a lovely place, but I'm sure that after his forty-seven-year stay, S.Sgt. James V. Harrell was glad to be home.

13. A LEG IN THE TOILET BOWL

Now comes the mystery.
—HENRY WARD BEECHER

Watching the nightly news on the evening of March 3, 2001, I was surprised to see that a human leg had been found off the eastern coast of Oahu in a place known as the Toilet Bowl. Situated along the rim of the gorgeous Hanauma Bay, the Toilet Bowl is a natural pool; water enters and leaves it in rhythm with the waves, ebbing and flowing with the tides. The effect is much like the flush of a toilet. When the tide is low and surf is not too rough, you can sit in the pool and float up and down.

Hanauma Bay is full of small inlets and cratered pockets of seawater. It is a popular place for swimming, snorkeling, and scuba diving. Until the early 1990s, you could buy fish food and swim among fish with names such as humuhumu-nukunuku-a-pua'a (you really can pronounce it; just take it a syllable at a time), parrot fish, and triggerfish. I imagine it feels like swimming with a school of piranhas—the difference, of course, is that these fish don't bite, and, other than a little nibble on the finger here and there, they're not dangerous. As for the human leg, five divers had found it about a hundred feet offshore at a depth of about thirty feet. The news said that the medical examiner would be asking the Central Identification Laboratory for help identifying whose leg it was.

The first thing I did when I got to work the next morning was phone Susan Siu, the senior crime scene investigator at the Honolulu Medical Examiner's Office, to ask what we could do to help. I'd worked several cases with Susan and was well aware of her enthusiasm and tenacity in solving such mysteries. She's certainly not a quitter. A few minutes later John Byrd, another of the CIL's forensic anthropologists, and I were on our way to the medical examiner's office.

We met Dr. Kanthi von Guenthner, a native of Sri Lanka and the chief medical examiner for the City and County of Honolulu, as she was coming down the stairs. We entered the morgue off to our right; one of the dieners (morgue assistants) went into the back room and came out pushing a stainless steel tray. On it was a large plastic bag that contained the leg.

When we opened the bag, the odor of decomposition filled the room. Lying in front of us was a left leg consisting of the femur, tibia, fibula, patella (knee cap), and foot. The leg had been separated from the person's body at the hip socket. The only soft tissue remaining on the bones was on the foot and a small mound encompassing the patella. A few tendons and ligaments remained, holding the bones together at the ankle and knee. The leg looked as though someone had stripped off the flesh with a serrated knife. The strong odor and decomposed nature of the soft tissue suggested that the person had been dead for weeks or months, not days. The medical examiner's office wanted me to give them a biological profile of the person, based on what I could determine from the leg—the person's sex, stature, ethnicity, age at the time of death—as well as an estimate of how long ago death had occurred, and anything else that might lead to an identification. We hoped we could figure out how he or she ended up at the bottom of the ocean. The police had a short list of people missing from the islands, and a few suspects who might have been involved in a murder.

It was possible that the leg was from someone who had not been reported missing, or even someone who might have fallen off a passing ship. Our thoughts turned to the Japanese training vessel *Ehime Maru*, which had been sunk less than a month before, on the afternoon of February 9, when the USS *Greeneville*, a nuclear-powered fast attack submarine, surfaced from below the 174-foot ship and sank it. Among the thirty-five people on board were thirteen students from the Uwajima Fishery High School, in the southwestern prefecture of Ehime. The training ship sank within ten minutes of the accident. Twenty-six people were rescued. Four seventeen-year-old students, two teachers, and three crew members perished. The United States had raised the ship the following year, recovering and identifying all but one of the bodies.

A quick inspection of the leg bones showed that the fibula, the outer of the two bones that runs from knee to ankle, was broken at midshaft. X-rays would later reveal that the bone, roughly the size and shape of an arrow, was completely healed and must have been broken at least several years before its owner died. I found it interesting that only the fibula was broken. If the bone had been broken as a result of most types of motor vehicle accidents, I would have expected either the femur or tibia to have been broken as well. This fracture suggested either a severe twisting of the ankle, or a direct injury to the outer leg such as the kind that could happen if someone had been hit with a baseball bat.

On closer examination we noticed many cuts, striations, and gouges in the femur (the upper leg bone). Its shaft was scarred, as if a boat propeller had run it over, or, perhaps, someone had defleshed it before throwing it into the ocean. A closer look, however, persuaded me that the teeth of a shark had made the gouges. The entire surface of the femur was covered with shallow cuts, deep gouges, and fine regular grooves, suggesting that teeth ridged like a serrated knife had made them. The cuts reminded me of another case involving the severed leg of a young surfer from the Big Island. The pattern of cuts in the case from the Toilet Bowl left little doubt that a shark had been feeding on the leg. I couldn't be sure, however, whether the shark had killed the victim or simply fed on the body after the person was dead. That answer would probably have to come from a shark expert.

Using a scalpel, the diener removed a small piece of red muscle from the foot for DNA testing. Once that was done, we signed a chain-of-custody form and returned to the CIL with the leg. Within minutes I'd removed the foot, put it in the refrigerator, and begun cutting away as much of the remaining soft tissue from the knee as I could. When there was nothing left that I could cut, I used a Crock-Pot to simmer away the soft tissue. We try to avoid boiling since that tends to push the fats deeper into the bone and softens the bone's spongy ends. I placed the pot under one of our fume hoods to reduce the odor and keep the lab from smelling like a decaying corpse, which would have made me unpopular with the rest of the staff. This process took two days. The last step was to immerse the ends of the bones in a pot of household bleach to remove the last of the soft tissue and cartilage—cartilage being the hardest thing to remove from a body. By day three the leg was free of all soft tissue. I laid the three bones—the tibia, fibula, and femur—on paper to absorb the last of the water and speed the drying process. At last I could handle the bones without gloves and get a clear picture of the cuts. Now my task was to estimate the person's height by measuring the femur; draw in each of the tooth marks on a skeletal diagram; figure out the time since death; and decipher the person's age at death, sex, and ethnicity. Using an osteometric board (a wooden measuring device marked off in centimeters), I found that the femur was just over eighteen inches (forty-six centimeters) long. The mathematical formula that forensic anthropologists use to estimate a person's height from the length of the femur yielded a stature of five feet eight inches, with a probable range of five feet six to five feet ten.

I next turned my attention to the person's age at death, sex, and ethnicity. Other than in broad estimates, leg bones don't provide much information about a person's age after about twenty-one. As with height, instead we look for indications of a minimum and maximum age. Here, the growth caps were completely fused, and there wasn't any evidence of arthritis on the joints. That told us the person was probably twenty-five to forty-five years old. I suspected the younger end of the range, but since the ends of the bones were fused, indicating that growth had ceased, I was certain the leg belonged to none of the lost fishery students.

The diameter of the femoral head was less than two inches (forty-seven millimeters), suggesting the person was male; the head of a woman's femur would be smaller. The front-to-back curvature of the femoral shaft was most consistent with someone who was Caucasian, Asian, or Hispanic. The femurs of people of African origin (the technical term is still Negroid) tend be very straight. So, although we couldn't provide anything definitive on this person's racial origin, we could rule out the possibility that he was African or African American. This piece of information eliminated many possibilities among the police department's file of missing persons. Although we could see white skin on the foot, we always have to consider the possibility that the outer layer of skin has fallen off, which would make even a pure-blooded African look white. A person's pigmentation is carried solely in the epidermis, the outer layer of the skin.

I had established that the police should be searching its files for a white, Asian, or Hispanic male, twenty-five to forty-five years old, with a medical history that included a broken left leg, and who was missing for no more than about a year. I raised the possibility that the body it was once part of could have been inside a protected environment, such as a footlocker, that had been thrown overboard several months before the detached leg was found. Armed with this information, the police began searching through missing persons reports and running down leads on suspects who might have been responsible for the person's death. The Honolulu police would also be sending divers back out to the Toilet Bowl to see if they could find additional body parts. Meanwhile, Susan Siu, the Honolulu medical examiner's investigator, obtained medical histories on all of the missing adults from the *Ehime Maru*. None had suffered a broken leg, so we could rule out the possibility that the leg belonged to a victim of that tragedy.

Hoping to figure out what kind of shark had fed on the leg, we called on shark expert and fishery biologist John Naughton of the National Marine Fisheries Service's Oahu office. He came to the laboratory and examined the femur after I'd defleshed the leg and concluded that the tooth striations were consistent with a medium-size tiger shark, roughly eleven to twelve feet long. Tiger sharks, one of thirty shark species known to attack human beings, are scavengers that feed on anything they can get their teeth on, including dead bodies, large tortoises, and automobile license plates. They're fierce feeders with large jaw muscles capable of slicing into bone or through tortoiseshells with ease. I once read of a tiger shark regurgitating a human arm tattooed with a picture of two boxers and a rope tied around the wrist. The shark gave up the arm after being held in a Sydney, Australia, aquarium for more than a week. The murder victim was soon identified as a small-time crook who had gone missing in 1936.

In his report, Dr. Naughton wrote, "In my opinion, these cuts were made by a shark feeding on the victim. The size and depth of the cuts indicate the shark was either a tiger shark (*Galeocerdo cuvier*) or a white shark (*Carcharadon carcharias*). However, because the white shark is rare in Hawaiian waters, and the tiger shark quite common, I would strongly suspect the shark involved was a tiger shark. The distance between serrations indicates the shark was a medium size tiger shark, between 11 to 12 feet in total length."

He continued, "Therefore, it is possible that the leg was consumed by the shark at another location, and subsequently regurgitated in the area where it was recovered. The random nature of the tooth marks indicates that the victim's leg was probably fully fleshed when the shark was feeding. Being familiar with the feeding strategy of tiger sharks, and having observed them a number of times feeding on large animals, I suspect the shark bit down a number of times on the leg, shaking its head vigorously to take full advantage of its serrated, saw like teeth to remove flesh." John could not form an opinion about whether the shark killed the victim or fed on the dead body.

John Naughton's report brought visions of the movie *Jaws* to my mind. I was surprised that he even considered the possibility that the feeder was a white shark. I didn't know they existed at all off the coast of Hawaii. (I'll certainly be more careful where I swim in the future.) That said, I must point out that more people are killed every year by crocodiles, dogs, and even pigs (and not from eating bad pork) than by sharks. Still, it didn't surprise me two weeks later when I heard that a seventeen-year-old boogie boarder had his left foot bitten off by a shark while surfing near a neighboring island. I wonder if his foot will show up later.

Although finding a human leg at the bottom of the ocean is unusual enough, we found another intriguing piece of the puzzle when we took an X-ray of the femur. About three inches above the knee end of the bone was a small hole encircled with a pale ring resembling a tiny doughnut, which would appear dark to the eye if it were visible, since radiographs reverse light and dark. My first guess was that the bony defect was the remnant of a surgical implant, perhaps some sort of device to keep the left knee from bending while the fibula healed.

A few days later CIL anthropologist Greg Berg and I took the bones and X-rays to the radiology and orthopedic departments at Tripler Army Medical Center. Tripler is a bright pink hospital sitting on the side of a hill a few miles from Hickam Air Force Base and within sight of the Honolulu International Airport. Its bright color and hillside location make the hospital stand out from its surroundings like a Barbie doll in a sports bar, easily visible for miles around. There we presented the case to the doctors and asked their opinion on the leg. I wanted to know if they agreed with my interpretation of the trauma and when it occurred. We learned that the small hole in the femur was the remnant of a surgical pin used to put the person's leg in traction. The pin had been removed years before, leaving only the small doughnut-shaped scar.

The doctors' best guess was that the trauma that broke the man's fibula also dislocated the left hip socket. The traction pin would have been used to stabilize the hip and keep the femur from pulling out of the socket. But what potentially would be most important to the police trying to identify the person was that the individual had definitely gone to a doctor and, even more, had probably spent at least two weeks in bed with his leg in traction. Going to a doctor meant medical records existed out there somewhere. The stage of healing suggested that the leg had been broken many years before death, possibly even when the man was a teenager.

About a week after we brought the leg to the CIL, Detective Phil Camero of the Honolulu Police Department Missing Persons Division came to see it. I'd spoken with Phil earlier and asked if he had any photos of where the leg was found. He brought several photos for me and the phone number of the diver who had spotted the leg. The diver confirmed that he and four others were boat diving that day when he saw the leg lying under some thirty feet of water, on a rock and coral ledge, just before noon. He said that the water was calm at thirty feet and that the only movement was the current above. The calmness at thirty feet ruled out any possibility that the leg rubbing against coral caused some of the striations. He also told me that he and his friends didn't see any other body parts or clothing. I asked him what he thought when he found the leg. He replied, "I thought it might have been a cow bone. Looking closer, I saw it was a human foot."

After more than a week of combing missing persons reports, Honolulu police still came up empty-handed. They still had a short list of potential victims and weren't about to give up. But trying to put a name to a defleshed leg found in the ocean off an island that thousands of tourists visit each year is no easy task. The most promising candidate for owner of the leg was a thirty-two-year-old man who had broken his leg in 1984 while skateboarding. That would have made him about seventeen when he broke his leg, leaving plenty of time for the bone to heal completely.

Thinking that we might have the right man, the medical examiner's office contacted the hospital for his records. We were all disappointed to learn that he'd broken his right leg, not his left. Although his mother remembered his breaking his left leg, DNA from the foot with which we were working ruled him out. It wasn't her son. The case was growing colder by the minute, but the search was not over. I continued to study the leg, looking for even the smallest clue that might help narrow the search and put a name on the leg.

Friday afternoon found me running around like the proverbial chicken with its head cut off, trying to complete my report on this case while giving an interview to a film crew. It was a typical Friday—everything was happening at once and the workday was coming to a close without my having accomplished most of what I'd set out to do that day. It was a downhill battle and I was running out of steam when I received a call from Susan Siu saying she had another missing person who could belong to the leg. This time it was a twenty-eight-year-old man who had been missing since 1996. The police had passed the person's name along to Susan Siu, and she began a search for his medical records and X-rays.

She called me again when she got the man's medical records, although she had yet to receive his X-rays. "The records show that he broke his left femur in a Jet-Skiing accident in 1994 and had an intramedullary rod put in it," she told me.

I replied, "It doesn't sound like our guy because the records don't say anything about him breaking his fibula. Besides, they probably wouldn't have removed the intramedullary rod once they put it in his leg. What we know is that our guy looks as though he had a traction pin in his femur that was later taken out, but he definitely didn't have a rod in it."

"Yes, but let me read on and tell me if you hear anything that matches our guy," she said. "Hmm, they took the rod out of his leg a few months before he went missing," she said eagerly.

"Well," I said, "I think we need to compare the X-rays of this guy's femur with the X-rays of the one from Hanauma Bay to see if they're from the same guy."

Using DNA, we'd ruled out the first prospect. We would probably rely on X-rays for the second one. Yet no matter what method or evidence we would be using, we'd have to be 100 percent certain that we didn't eliminate the wrong person. There is never any room for error in including or excluding a potential victim; once we rule someone out, we're not likely to reconsider him. The crucial point for me relating to the second candidate was that he'd broken his leg too near the time of his disappearance and presumed death for the bone to have totally remodeled to the point that we couldn't see the break on X-rays. Given that he had broken his leg two years before he disappeared, I would have expected to see some evidence of the fracture. Was this the leg of the unfortunate Jet Ski enthusiast? The answer would have to wait till after the weekend. And Monday was going to be a busy day because I was scheduled to meet with Susan to examine the X-rays of the Hanauma Bay leg in the morning and then meet with an FBI special agent about another case in the afternoon.

That Monday I made the twenty-minute drive to the medical examiner's office and met with Susan Siu and Kanthi von Guenthner. Susan had picked up the X-rays and was eager to see if the Hanauma Bay leg belonged to our missing Jet Skier, who was wave jumping when he sustained a spiral fracture to the midshaft of his left femur. I chose a couple of the most illustrative X-rays of the Jet Skier and put them beside the Hanauma Bay femur on the light box. I immediately knew that we had two different people: the Jet Skier's femur had two large screws above his knee, while the leg from Hanauma Bay had had only one—and it was a pin, not a screw. In addition, the Jet Skier's femur was much larger and thicker than the one from the Toilet Bowl. Furthermore, the Jet Skier's fracture was severe and almost certainly would not have healed to the stage that we couldn't see evidence of it, even several years later. We'd struck out again.

I went out of town for a week, and when I returned I phoned Susan to see if she had any new possibilities. She was working several leads. Susan and Detective Camero, working more or less independently, were busy gathering information and records for all missing persons who fit our biological profile, not only from Hawaii, but from the coast of California and from tour ships as well. The one piece of evidence that everyone was using to separate our missing person from all others in the world was the broken left leg. Later, Susan sent me the medical records of a five-foot ten-inch white man who, at twenty, had broken his left tibia and fibula in an automobile accident.

Although having a broken fibula was consistent with our guy, the tibia from Hanauma Bay didn't show any evidence of having been broken. If it had been, the break couldn't possibly have been as severe as the one described in the report sitting in front of me. Unfortunately, we didn't have the leg of this other man; there was no way that the type of fracture described in the report could have healed so completely as to match the leg in question. So far we'd eliminated four individuals; the search continued. The police would also be asking for the records of a thirty-three-year-old white man who had gone missing the previous year, while boating some three miles off Diamond Head, a volcanic crater that sits along the southeastern coast of Oahu and is visible from most locations on the southern half of the island. It rises from the coastline like a hollowed-out rook on a chessboard, with the ocean side of its rim eroded and submerged, allowing water in and out.

Diamond Head is also visible from the air as you fly in and out, as well as from the sea. On Oahu, it is often used to give directions. Locals will tell you to "go Diamond Head," meaning you should head toward the southeast edge of the island. If someone tells you Building X is "Diamond Head of the shopping center," it means you should go past the shopping center in the direction of Diamond Head. It is also a very popular tourist spot, arguably the most famous volcanic crater in the world. It rubs shoulders with downtown Honolulu and Waikiki Beach to its immediate left and Hanauma Bay to its right, about a twenty-minute drive, or some six miles as the crow flies. Diamond Head crater still houses a military installation and civil defense unit, as well as several World War II cannons and footpaths that lead to its more than seven-hundred-foot summit. Standing along the rim offers a panoramic view of the island and blue-green ocean. Driving toward Hanauma Bay (which resembles the open jaws of a bottle opener) from the airport, one passes Waikiki Beach, Koko Head (another crater), then the Blowhole, and the tiny *From Here to Eternity* beach, site of the love scene in that 1953 motion picture. It's all quite picturesque.

I was scheduled for a month in Vietnam, so I had to put aside the matter of the leg in the Toilet Bowl. Not long after, on a two-hour Vietnam Airlines flight from Ho Chi Minh City to Hanoi, I picked up one of the English-language newspapers and was surprised to see a short article about a skull, arm, and hip being found in the belly of a tiger shark caught off the coast of Australia. The authorities were still trying to figure out if the human remains were male or female. It seems as though the tiger shark has a plentiful supply of human meals. I was now aware of four instances of human remains associated with tiger sharks.

As this is being written, the mystery of the leg in the Toilet Bowl remains unsolved, but not for lack of trying. Enough people are interested—in the Honolulu Medical Examiner's Office, the Honolulu Police Department, and the CIL—to ensure it won't be forgotten. Although I've seen bodies in bags, babies in suitcases, bones in closets, and a head in a box, this was the first time I'd seen a leg in a toilet bowl. Life never ceases to amaze me.

14. A PEARL HARBOR SAILOR

Good men must die, but death cannot kill their names.

—BOOK OF PROVERBS

When he was seventeen, Thomas Hembree—Tommy to those who loved him—persuaded his mother to sign the necessary papers so he could enlist in the U.S. Navy, joining his older brothers Walter and George in military service. A slender brunet with blue eyes and what a relative later described as "a cheeky smile," Hembree was an apprentice seaman on board the seaplane tender USS *Curtiss,* moored in berth Xray 22 in the Middle Loch in Pearl Harbor, Hawaii, off the island of Oahu. The 527-foot ship was built in New York and commissioned in November 1940. It carried 1,195 men. An early aircraft carrier of a kind first used in World War I, it had a hangar but no flight deck; the tender used cranes to lower aircraft into the sea for takeoff and recovered them when they touched down on the water.

Shortly before eight A.M. on December 7, 1941, the ship's crew was called to general quarters. Japanese bombers and fighter planes, supported by several midget submarines, were attacking the Pacific Fleet. Shortly after Hembree entered his battle station, which was in the ship's radio room, the ship took a direct hit, igniting an intense fire. Hembree's navy career, which had lasted no more than two months, came to a sudden end.

Twenty sailors on the *Curtiss* died immediately; two of them were not identified. One sailor was missing and fifty-eight were injured, thirty-three badly enough to require transfer to a hospital on land. The dead were among the 2,403 Americans, most of them service members, whose lives ended at Pearl Harbor that day. The attack sank some of America's mightiest ships, including the USS *Arizona*, USS *California*, and USS *West Virginia*. When the smoke cleared and the bodies were recovered, all but three of the *Curtiss* crew could be accounted for. Nikolas S. Ganas, Wilson A. Rice, and Tommy Hembree were declared killed in action, but their bodies were not immediately found.

Shortly before his death, Hembree had written a letter to his mother, Elizabeth Hembree, telling her how sorely he missed his Kennewick, Washington, home. Mrs. Hembree, who received the letter weeks later, thought her son had survived the Pearl Harbor attack. Then, on April 15, 1942, a letter on navy stationery arrived, informing her that her son was a casualty of the attack. Mrs. Hembree wrote back, asking for more information. The reply couldn't have been worse: except for two, all of the *Curtiss* crew members were accounted for. The bodies of the two were burned beyond recognition. Her son was one of them, but the navy couldn't say which one.

The two unidentified corpses recovered from the interior of the USS *Curtiss* had been interred in the Nuuanu Cemetery on Oahu on December 9, 1941. Six years later, in 1947, the two sets of remains marked as "Unknown X-24" and "Unknown X-25" were exhumed from Nuuanu and examined by renowned anthropologist Dr. Charles Snow. He was able to identify X-25 as Seaman Second Class Ganas. The other set of remains, X-24, which could have been one of only two possible *Curtiss* crew members—Seaman First Class Rice or Apprentice Seaman Hembree—was reburied at Nuuanu on the same day. In 1949, the navy wrote to the Hembree family asking if they wanted his remains returned to them or reburied in the National Memorial Cemetery of the Pacific, a 116-acre cemetery nestled in a volcanic crater known locally as the Punchbowl. The family chose to have him rest in the Punchbowl, so the remains of X-24, wrapped in a cream-colored wool blanket emblazoned with "US Navy," was buried in grave C-258 in the picturesque and serene crater.

Hembree's sister, June Braidwood, a beautician from Tacoma, traveled to the Punchbowl a few years after Tommy was transferred there, intending to visit his grave. A cemetery attendant told her that her brother had been buried at sea. Braidwood accepted this information as fact until 1989, when she visited and asked again. This time the cemetery worker, lacking any new information, telephoned a Honolulu man who had catalogued all 18,093 World War II fatalities buried in the Punchbowl. The man, Ray Emory, was a veteran himself. He had manned a .50-caliber machine gun on the deck of the USS *Honolulu* on Pearl Harbor Day. He knew that Hembree and a nineteen-year-old seaman first class named Wilson Albert Rice were the only *Curtiss* crew members whose remains had not been identified. When Emory and Braidwood met, Emory began an eleven-year quest to get the remains of X-24 identified. Eventually, relying on recent advances in DNA research and with the help of Hawaii's Congresswoman Patsy Mink, who died in 2002, Emory was able to get adopted legislation that allowed X-24's remains to be exhumed once again. By that time, though, June Braidwood had died, and her niece, Beth LaRosa, of Seattle, had taken up the cause. The bones of X-24 were disinterred in January 2001.

Part of the law allowing the exhumation required that a DNA sample from a relative be available before the remains were dug up. Because mitochondrial DNA was specified, and mitochondrial DNA is inherited from one's mother, the sample had to come from the offspring of one of Tommy Hembree's sisters. LaRosa was the daughter of Tommy's oldest brother, Walter, so she didn't qualify. She located her cousin Marion Price, daughter of June Bailey, the middle of the Hembree siblings and the only Hembree sister who had children. In December 2000, Price gladly furnished a blood sample from which her DNA could be extracted. During the next month, the bodies of X-24 and three other unidentified military men, one from World War II and two from the Korean War, were removed from their graves in the Punchbowl.

Price had grown up thinking her uncle, who died when she was three and whom she didn't remember, had died on the USS *Arizona*. "My mother was closer to him than the others," Price said. "When he died, my mother's life and emotions became somewhat disturbed. She had a brother who died in Pearl Harbor, and her whole life went into shambles."

About all Price remembers of World War II is a small flag with a gold star that hung in her grandmother's window, signifying that one of her children had died in the war, and the fact that at night the curtains and blinds had to be drawn shut—a wartime precaution that Price thought had to do with her uncle's death. Price says that later in life her mother was convinced that her brother Tommy was alive, and that amnesia prevented him from remembering his family and coming home. Like the rest of the elder Hembrees, June Bailey died without seeing her brother's remains identified.

As is sometimes the case in science, the results were disappointing. X-24's bones and teeth failed to yield DNA. Scientists at the Central Identification Laboratory in Hawaii and the Armed Forces DNA Identification Laboratory in Maryland were stymied. We pooled our collective talents trying to figure out what had destroyed the DNA or was preventing it from being sequenced. The body had been interred inside a waterproof steel casket and buried six feet deep in the volcanic ground. Guesses were flying like mosquitoes. Was it the volcanic soil? Was it the embalming powder that had been placed on the remains before they were buried? Was it because the remains had been fluoroscoped? No one knew the answer, and it was driving the DNA experts crazy. It just didn't make sense. But we had other options and weren't about to give up.

After giving DNA our best shot and hitting a brick wall, we turned to traditional anthropology to see if we could find something in the remains that Dr. Snow had missed. Although he was a gifted anthropologist, forensic anthropology had come a long way since his examination of the X-24 in 1949, the year I was born. After more than half a century of research, anthropologists had developed new techniques and more precise standards for determining age, race, sex, and stature from the skeleton. The pioneer scientists of Dr. Snow's generation had given us much to work with; scientific advances had given us more.

I laid out the remains on one of the lab tables and compiled a biological profile that almost exactly matched the one Snow had developed more than fifty years earlier. Based on the development of the teeth and fusion of the long bone growth caps, I judged that the individual was between sixteen and nineteen years old when he died. The skull's narrow nasal opening, absence of alveolar prognathism (a forward jutting of the midface), and the shape of the upper palate were features most often found in Caucasoids. Using the left femur I computed his stature as five feet nine inches tall. The features of his hips and skull, combined with the overall size of his arm and leg bones, left no doubt that the bones were those of a man.

The only thing that I was able to add to Snow's assessment was that the individual had a small pit in the back of his left thighbone, just above the knee. By all appearances this healed bone scar, which could have been caused by an injury or localized infection to the leg, had formed long before death. The only evidence of injury that might have occurred during the attack was a small scooped-out defect on the shaft of his left femur and a fractured hand bone. Once I'd completed my analysis, I could look at the records of our most likely candidate, X-24.

Like many World War II and Korean War records, there wasn't an abundance of information or detail. Flipping through the serviceman's record, I found that X-24 was a seventeen-year-old sailor named Thomas Hembree. I was able to eliminate Rice, the only other unidentified crewmen from the USS *Curtiss,* because he was five feet six inches, much too short for the man whose femur was lying on the table in front of me. Reading on, I found that Hembree was white, stood five feet nine and three quarters inches tall, and, to my surprise, had a two-inch scar on his left knee. The two strongest pieces linking the remains with the sailor from Kennewick, Washington, were the lesion on X-24's left femur and his height. Knowing that the best method of identification is the teeth, however, CIL dentist John Lewis began his examination.

We had already compiled a biological profile from the bones and now needed to see how it all fit with the dental evidence. John examined each of the twenty-nine teeth in X-24's dental sockets and compared his findings to the dental records of Hembree, Rice, and, just to be certain, Ganas. The results were indisputable; the combination of fillings, cavities, and extracted teeth were consistent with Hembree and totally inconsistent with Rice and Ganas. We had our man.

On November 5, 2001, sixty years after he went missing and three months after his last living sister died, we finally knew that X-24 was young Tommy Hembree, who perished on board the USS *Curtiss* in 1941. Price received notice later that month, and the family opted for a full military funeral at the Punchbowl. Coincidentally, Marine First Lieutenant Ed LaRosa, one of Hembree's great-nephews, was on active duty at Schofield Army Barracks, Oahu, when Hembree's remains were identified. In an earlier assignment to Schofield, between 1993 and 1995, LaRosa had worked as a funeral escort at the Punchbowl, but never knew that his great-uncle was buried there. This time Emory took LaRosa and his wife, Traci, to the place where Hembree had been buried and from there to the Courts of Missing, where marble tablets list the names of 18,094 service members killed in World War II. Until 1995, Thomas Hembree's first name had been misspelled "Tomas"; Ray Emory had seen to having the error corrected.

The reinterment ceremony at the Punchbowl was attended by twenty of Hembree's relatives, who flew in from Washington, Oregon, and California; a navy chaplain; a bugler who played taps; an honor guard that rendered a twenty-one-gun salute; several of us from the CIL; and a slew of reporters. Two of Hembree's nieces spoke at the ceremony, offering fond remembrances of their uncle Tommy, and more than fifteen nieces, nephews, great-nieces, great-nephews, great-great-nieces, and great-great-nephews witnessed Hembree being buried with honors.

Price said, "I think Uncle Tommy is at peace now and the family is at peace." She explained the decision to leave her uncle's remains at the Punchbowl instead of bringing them back to his hometown in Washington State. "The family, when they were alive, wanted Uncle Tommy here, and we needed to carry on their wishes."

She had high praise for Emory, who she said made the reinterment possible. "We can never repay Ray Emory for the years of effort on this journey, but [he] will forever be in our hearts," said Price.

Later, reflecting on the entire experience, she noted that while the Hembree cousins hadn't been close before Tommy's remains were identified, and some had been entirely out of touch, the identification and commitment ceremony had brought them closer together.

On the afternoon of March 5, 2002, exactly five months after being disinterred and at the request of the family, Apprentice Seaman Hembree, in his dress blues, was reburied in the same grave at the Punchbowl, using the same white navy blanket and safety pins he'd rested with for sixty years. His casket sported the same style and color as the one in which he had been buried in 1949. The difference now, however, is that Bosun's Mate First Class Guy Newton Warren of Kentucky, Private First Class Frank L. Turensek of New Jersey, Second Lieutenant Floyd R. Snyder of Illinois, and Coxswain Samuel B. Roberts Jr. of Oregon now know the name of the sailor resting beside them.

The reburial of the Hembree cousins' uncle Tommy had a special significance to me. I, too, had an Uncle Tommy, whom I loved and miss. Mine used to visit my family in Tampa in the summer when I was still too little to reach the cookie jar that stood on my grandmother's kitchen counter. I remember him well, with his large shoulders and a back slightly hunched from a life of hard work, and a beaming smile that was a bit crooked on one side.

He was my adoptive father's brother, and, like my father, Uncle Tommy served in World War II and bore the scars of war. My father's scars were visible; Uncle Tommy's were on the inside. I remember on several occasions his talking in hushed tones to Grandpa, telling what I took to be war stories. I remember him as something of a big, sad teddy bear. Although he passed away several years before Thomas Hembree's identification and reburial, I felt my uncle Tommy's presence with me when Hembree was laid to rest.

. . .

Two weeks after Thomas Hembree's second funeral, my wife, Vara, and I returned to the Punchbowl to visit his grave. We walked across the impeccably manicured cemetery lawn, reading the rows of headstones. They stretched out in every direction, seemingly extending to the horizon. Some of the names were familiar to me; most were not. Hembree's grave, now two weeks old and covered with small patches of grass struggling for survival, was in the process of changing from brown to the lush green all around as nature erased the scars of our intrusion. Soon Hembree's grave would blend into the Punchbowl lawn like those of the other 33,230 heroes resting there.

Walking through the rows that day and looking off to my right, I saw two small circles that looked like cartoon eyes perched atop one of the flush grave markers. Moving closer, I saw they were golf balls—one white, one green. They marked the graves of a father and son, united in death as in life, I guess, by their love of golf. We saw many other mementos that day. A golden floral wreath, lying on its back, had lost its fight with the strong winds that sometimes rake the Punchbowl. A green vase, faded by its many days in the Hawaiian sun, leaned precariously against one of the large, sprawling shade trees. Three beautiful flower leis carefully placed beside one another like so many Olympic rings topped the grave marker of another soldier buried there that month.

These were personal expressions of love and remembrance for heroes and loved ones who had already completed their journey to final rest—simple reminders to all who visited there that these people had once walked among us. Perhaps they sat next to us at a movie matinee one day, or let us cut in front of them at an intersection. They were beloved brothers, husbands, sons, uncles, and friends.

Although I've seen thousands of graves in my career, the one marked Thomas Hembree holds a little something special for me. After all, I not only held his bones in my hands, but I also met his family and attended his burial ceremony. Looking back at this visit to the Punchbowl, I'm still a little surprised that walking through a cemetery—whether it holds civilians or soldiers, sailors, airmen, or Marines—and reading names on grave markers could have such a dramatic impact on me. After working with bones for more than twenty years, I'm pleased to know that death still scares me, and that hearing "Taps" still moves me. I went to the Punchbowl that day because I wanted to say good-bye to another family's Tommy, and I did that. By the time I left, I'd said good-bye to my own uncle Tommy, as well.

15. OUT OF THE BLUE
TERRORISTS STRIKE ON 9/11

The true mystery of the world is the visible, not the invisible.
—OSCAR WILDE, *The Picture of Dorian Gray*

The ringing phone woke me. I looked at the clock: five A.M. Clinging to the fragments of broken sleep, I picked up the handset. Silence greeted me. A wrong number or a prank? I'll never know. Back in bed, I soon realized I was finished sleeping. Something out of the ordinary had awakened me, and something terribly sinister would keep me awake that night.

I switched on the television and saw smoke and flames billowing from the heart of New York City. Nudging my wife awake, I asked if she thought what we were seeing was reality or a movie. "Looks like it's real," she replied.

The date was Tuesday, September 11, 2001. Under a late summer sky so astoundingly blue it made the whole Northeast sparkle, terrorists had hijacked two American Airlines planes and steered them straight into the Twin Towers at the World Trade Center. We were witnessing another Pearl Harbor. It was eleven A.M. on the East Coast. Hawaii is six hours behind during daylight savings time, five hours behind the rest of the year. What we were watching had occurred two hours earlier, while Hawaii, America's westernmost state, slept in peaceful oblivion.

I phoned my boss, Tom Holland, at his home to see if anyone had called the laboratory into action. No one had—yet. With more than twenty anthropologists available, we were likely to be asked to help in the recovery and identification of the victims. I grabbed a quick shower and made my way along the already congested highway leading to the naval base at Pearl Harbor and its neighbor to the south, Hickam Air Force Base, home of the CIL.

By this time the radio stations were carrying detailed descriptions of an attack on the Pentagon. Local announcements were telling nonessential civilian personnel who worked on the military bases to stay home. Still, the mile-long stretch of highway leading to the main gate at Hickam Air Force Base, where I worked, was almost as static as a parking lot. What was normally a smooth and quick entry had become a trickle. In an instant we had moved from normal peacetime security procedures to what the military calls Force Protection Delta (FPCON Delta, in military terminology), the highest level of security, invoked when a terrorist attack has occurred or when intelligence suggests terrorist action against a specific site is likely. No one knew whether the terrorists were done for the day or had something more planned for us.

Anyone wanting access to the base had to show their military ID card and driver's license. The guard waved no one through the gate, not even those who came to work there every day and whose faces he surely recognized. Car trunks and interiors were subject to random searches; all briefcases, handbags, and packages were inspected. As we waited, we listened to our car radios for the latest scrap of information, edging our cars forward when an inch of space opened up, changing lanes and jockeying for position to get onto the base as quickly as possible. Ground that I normally covered in fifteen minutes took nearly an hour that day.

Five or six people got to the laboratory before me. I went to the main conference room to catch the news update. Although I'd seen some of the destruction on the news while at home, nothing could have prepared me for what I saw on the conference room TV set—the tape segment that showed the north tower's upper floors burning while a second plane flew into the midsection of the south tower. I could hardly believe it: smoke billowing everywhere and the sky a sea of gray smoke, as though a volcano had erupted in lower Manhattan. Huge chunks of the buildings cascaded from the towers, then they simply crumbled to dust, the south tower and then the north, the reverse of the order in which they were hit. Although the attacks lasted only an hour and twenty-five minutes from start to finish, the recovery and identification of the victims would take months. Even then I knew the pain, horror, and anger would linger for generations.

At ten A.M., Tom Holland came to my office to tell me he'd just gotten off the phone with Bill Rodriguez, the forensic anthropologist at the office of the Armed Forces Medical Examiner, part of the AFIP, at Walter Reed Hospital. He would be leading the effort to identify the victims killed at the Pentagon. Rodriguez told him that within minutes of the attack a triage location had been established at the base of the north tower, but that hundreds of rescue and first aid workers ended up trapped in rubble as the tower collapsed. One of those injured and feared dead was anthropologist Amy Zelnick, who, only a few weeks before, had visited our lab in Hawaii. (A few days later we learned that Amy had sustained a few broken bones but was alive and healing.) Tom called a meeting of the anthropologists and dentists to discuss the likelihood that we would be called on to help with the recovery and identification of victims. We compiled a list of anthropologists who were available and experienced in identifying victims of mass disasters. Three days later, the Armed Forces Institute of Pathology, the organization that would handle the Pentagon identification operation, asked the CIL for four anthropologists. We agreed to send Tom Holland, John Byrd, Andy Tyrrell, and me. (The FBI was responsible for the recovery phase at the Pentagon, but received guidance from AFIP.)

Our first challenge was getting out of Hawaii. For three days after the attack, all commercial flights in the United States were grounded and the airports were closed. The first flight our operations office could book for us was a Continental flight directly to Newark, New Jersey, on Sunday, September 16. I phoned my wife and told her the uneasy news that in two days I would be flying to the mainland. She seemed to take it in stride, saying that she was proud of me for helping. "I only wish I could help in some way," she said. She *was* helping, of course, whether she knew it or not. Vara knew I needed to make this trip, and she didn't try to keep me from doing it.

Although I'd flown hundreds of times, and the atmosphere in the terminal and on board the plane seemed normal, I was extraordinarily apprehensive. Others must have been, too: we clung to every word of the flight attendant's safety briefing, which most of us would at other times have ignored. The door closed, the airplane began moving, and the engines roared as we taxied onto the runway. Moments later, we were airborne, and it was too late to change our minds.

We covered nearly five thousand miles in slightly more than eight hours on our way to Newark. Descending through bumpy clouds, we landed, and rolled the last mile or so to the terminal. Off to the left was the New York skyline; I had my first real look at the devastation. What I saw raised a lump in my throat just as it boiled my blood. Manhattan was smoldering, its appearance forever changed, looking—in the words of Dave Rosso, editor of *American Citizens Abroad (ACA) News Report*—"as though it had lost its two front teeth."

At the Newark terminal we picked up two rental vans in case we were to be sent to different sites, and drove three hours to the Dover Port Mortuary at Dover Air Force Base in Delaware. When we opened the van door, the unmistakable smell of death assaulted us. The thick aroma of burned flesh and decomposing bodies instantly saturated my clothing and invaded my nose and mouth, overwhelming my senses. I felt as though I was back at the Body Farm.

The mortuary was a converted hangar, all steel and concrete floors, everything washable. Passing the blue-carpeted administration offices and a makeshift cafeteria, we found the work area. We donned surgical scrubs, plastic aprons, and gloves, and soon we were in the middle of a bustling reception area, among a throng of people desperately working to identify the more than two hundred victims who arrived by helicopter in batches. These were the one hundred twenty-five workers and sixty-four airline passengers who had been killed at the Pentagon.

Bill Rodriguez, dressed in a white disposable scrub suit, booties, and gloves, moved through the crowd of workers to greet us. I could see that he had put his normally quick wit and playful demeanor in storage while he attended to what had to be the most daunting job in his twenty-plus years as a forensic anthropologist. Already at work were two longtime friends and anthropology colleagues, Dr. Doug Owsley and Dr. Doug Ubelaker. They were on loan from the Smithsonian Institution, about one hundred miles to the southwest. I knew both from my days as a graduate student at the University of Tennessee. Fourteen years earlier, Owsley had brought me to the Smithsonian when he became its curator in physical anthropology. While I was at Dover I learned that one of Owsley's two daughters had been in the part of the Pentagon that got hit. A supervisor had pushed her into a corner and shielded her with his body. They both came through unhurt. How horrible it would have been if we'd had to identify her remains. It was at that point that I first wondered if anyone named Churchwell, the name I was born with, had died in the attacks that day.

I'm sure Rodriguez was unaware of his importance in my life; he was, in part, responsible for my presence in Dover. I'd met him in 1983, when I came to the University of Tennessee to study with Dr. Bill Bass. I looked upon Rodriguez as a kind of forensics guru; he and Steve Symes were Bass's right-hand men. As a thirty-four-year-old first-year graduate student, I was a rare bird in those days, ten or twelve years older than my classmates. Having no one with whom to compare myself, I got the idea that I wasn't doing well in my classes. At one point, I decided to drop out of the program and called Dr. Bass to tell him so. I also went to see Rodriguez and told him. He said, "Hang in there. Stick it out for another month, and then, if you still think you're not succeeding, you can drop out." A year later, Rodriguez, Symes, and I were sharing an office in the anthropology department. When he left Tennessee, I took his place as Dr. Bass's forensic anthropology assistant. If Rodriguez hadn't persuaded me to give it more time, you wouldn't be reading these words now. And I wouldn't be living the most interesting life I can imagine.

The mortuary was separated into specialized examination rooms, all of which were filled with blurs of activity. Investigators were in a race against time: the world watched and waited. Our Hawaii contingent had arrived near the end of the workday. Once we became familiar with the place that would be our workstation for the next week or so, we went to our hotel and prepared for the next day.

Tom, John, Andy, and I reported for work early the following morning and were soon transformed from curious observers into blood-soaked investigators. Although a large team of skilled forensic pathologists from the AFIP was doing the identifications and autopsies, our presence added experience with highly fragmented and burned bones, not to mention knowledge as to how to distinguish bone from nonbone items such as melted plastic and rubble. We made a good team—they examined each body; we focused on body parts and bones. We worked twelve-hour days, and by the time we finished our cases each day we were thoroughly exhausted.

Throughout the day bodies arrived at the mortuary's back door. A computerized tracking system assigned a number to each victim to ensure accuracy and efficiency. Then each set of remains was x-rayed, the radiologists and bomb disposal technicians hunting explosives, box cutter knives, and other weapons that might be carried by terrorists, or by security personnel on the plane or the ground.

Scanning bodies for unexploded ordnance was a lesson we had learned from the first Gulf War, during which bodies of the American soldiers sent to Dover for identification during Desert Storm sometimes contained explosive material. While we found none in the bodies we examined at the Dover mortuary this time, the precaution was necessary. A fatal explosion at the Dover Air Force Base would have been more than most Americans could bear. Examiners were also on the lookout for pieces of the airplane, especially from the cockpit, which could potentially yield DNA of the terrorists if in fact they had been in control of the plane when it crashed.

Bill Rodriguez handled triage on the corpses as they left the preliminary X-ray station. Triage originated as a battlefield tactic for sorting casualties into three groups—those who could be treated on the spot, those who needed transport to a hospital, and those for whom nothing could be done—but here it meant determining where each set of remains went first. His decision depended on each set's completeness and condition.

As I recall, the sequence went: triage, photography, fingerprints (done by the FBI), dental, X-ray, pathology, anthropology, embalming, and casketing. Whole bodies went to the pathology station, where pathologists performed autopsies. Groups of bones were x-rayed so experts could determine whether they belonged to a single person or more than one. Radiologists searched the X-rays for evidence of old fractures, or teeth with fillings, which would make identification easier and more certain. FBI fingerprint technicians inked and rolled fingers, toes, palms, and heels before the body went on to the dentistry station. Forensic photographers documented visible injuries and personal effects. At the end of the line army mortuary specialists embalmed and dressed those we identified and placed them in caskets for release to their next of kin. We forensic anthropologists moved from table to table at the pathology station, identifying body parts and bones. In mass disasters, anthropologists are most valuable in associating body parts and small pieces of bone, even ones charred by fire, with individual victims. We're the last link in the identification chain.

Over the next eight days I saw the corpses of men, women, and children, dressed either for a cross-country flight or for a day at the office. It was intensely sobering to reflect on the fact that none of them had started the day knowing it would be their last; it was comforting in a way to think that death had come so suddenly that they had no time to feel pain. I held disembodied hands and fingers still adorned with rings given in love or in recognition of success—engagement rings, wedding rings, school rings. Some cases consisted only of a tooth, a piece of scalp, or some skin, which we washed clean of soot and debris and stretched out on the table so we could search for evidence of stab wounds. The hijackers had been armed with box cutters and knives, and the pathologists needed to see if anyone had been stabbed or cut. As far as I know, we found no such evidence. Our job—whatever the completeness of the victim's body or its condition—was to identify the individual and return whatever we could to the victim's family. The work wasn't all that different from what we did every day in Hawaii with the remains of soldiers missing in action, but these weren't soldiers. And, although it looked like they had, they hadn't died on a battlefield.

In a back room dedicated to personal effects recovered from the crash site I saw children's toys that had been burned into the airplane carpet and empty lipstick containers, their contents having melted in the fire. For some reason it's always these things, these tiny reminders of our humanity and personal preferences, that serve as the visual and emotional link to the torn and tattered bodies that I handle. Many anthropologists whom I've talked with say the same—it's the toys, shoes, eyeglasses, key rings, and watches that bring everything to life.

I've shown many people the remains of their formerly missing loved ones. Perhaps it is the emotional sterility of the laboratory environment—devoid of softness and full of metal tables and chairs, microscopes, and people in lab coats moving purposefully about their work—that often renders people inexpressive at the sight of remains, even to the point of handling them without visible emotion. One man, for example, walked up to the table where his father's remains were laid out at the CIL and said, "So these are my father's remains." He picked up one of the bones and nodded his head up and down as if he recognized his father in it. We seem to get more "aahs," "oohs," and lumps in throats when people coming through the lab see handwritten letters, watches, dog tags, books, medallions, combs. Perhaps it's that we all look pretty much the same without our skin on. Watches, rings, and the like, however, express our individuality. Our selection of particular items is what sets us apart from everyone else.

Often, though, the death of a loved one hits those left behind hardest at the grave site, where friends and family assemble to see their loved one off for the last time. Seeing remains at the lab must be painful, but putting people in the ground is the final step in saying good-bye, and the point at which most of the emotional reaction typically takes place. One woman, whose dad went to war one month before she was born, saw her father for the first time in her life at our laboratory. In effect, she said hello and good-bye to her dad in the same breath.

I slowed down as I walked past the tables of personal effects, looking to see if I recognized anyone's driver's license or photograph. I didn't. On some of the ten or so evidence tables lay torn and burned fragments of newspaper—one *Washington Post* was dated September 11, 2001. Except for its burned edges and water-soaked pages, it was nearly complete. There were magazines, currency, shoelaces, shoes, and teddy bears; melted plastic, aviation electronics, and headsets; belts, charred shirtsleeves, and pants; credit cards, family photographs, bent and twisted car keys, melted cell phones, and Barbie dolls. There were personal papers and plastic medicine vials, the labels of which claimed they came from Springfield and McLean, Virginia. On one table were golf tees, an umbrella, and a red pocketknife; neatly folded stacks of charred bras and panties, neckties and socks, a checkbook and a woman's watch stopped precisely at nine forty-three, one hour and forty-three minutes after takeoff. The second hand was frozen in time at the precise moment of impact. We would return to family members as quickly as possible the personal effects that we could link to specific passengers, regardless of whether their remains had been identified. The rest would be held for six months then destroyed.

Investigators not only had to sort out airplane passengers and debris, but also office items and Pentagon workers. What was so hard to believe was that a passenger airplane had crashed during work hours, full force, into the largest military office building in the United States. There were parts of melted office telephones, paper clips, and office stationery. There were even a few old dried-out chicken bones. They were very dry and dark, unlike bones recently discarded. I can't be certain whether they were five years old or fifty, but my guess is they were the remains of a worker's lunch discarded during construction of the Pentagon in 1943, in the middle of World War II. I saw pieces of burned wood, government-issue pens still in shirt pockets, photographs in melted frames, and partially burned file folders. Two distinct environments, one stationary and one moving at more than five hundred miles an hour, had collided; the result was a mass of tangled debris, human remains, broken hearts, and agonizing memories. Two worlds, one in the air and one on the ground, had been simultaneously joined and irretrievably altered in the same instant.

We were all working twelve-hour shifts, and exhaustion was rampant. But the military and several local volunteer organizations took good care of us. There was a break room, well stocked with sodas, fruit, snacks, and even boxed lunches. We were free to take a break any time we needed one. About a hundred people were on the site most of the time, some working, some in the break room, others changing shifts. Mornings began with a meeting, mostly devoted to announcements to keep us informed on what would be coming in that day. There was usually a pep talk to help us stay focused and as comfortable as circumstances would allow. Our daily meetings ended with a prayer, led by one of the two chaplains who, throughout the day, walked around the mortuary, looking for people who needed to talk, helping us to handle the stress of what we were doing.

I'm sure people have different ways of handling the horror involved in a job like the one we were doing at Dover. Although I have spent years exposed to the remains of those for whom someone is grieving, each case is still an emotional drain. I don't think anyone can ever get so accustomed to dealing with remains that they feel nothing. Underlying my ability to handle my feelings is the knowledge that I was trained to do this, and that somewhere a family is waiting for the information I'm about to uncover. I don't have any problem removing flesh from bone to get to the truth, but I couldn't be a dentist and pull a tooth. I'd have a hard time changing a diaper, but it's not difficult to put a skull back together. I love dealing with skeletons, the part of people you never see in ordinary life.

By September 22 most of the bodies had been removed from the Pentagon, and, within a few days, the recovery process ceased. The task of identifying the bodies, however, would go on for weeks and months. Not all of the victims had fingerprints on file, nor were adequate dental records available for everyone who perished that day. Pathologists at Dover took more than eight hundred samples for DNA testing. Many of the identifications would be done using DNA from soft tissue or bone. The undertaking was immense. Sadly, some victims may never be identified.

When the smoke cleared and the identification work was completed, federal investigators, despite their best efforts, were unable to identify one young child on the plane and four people on the ground. They did, however, get DNA sequences for the five terrorists. Airport surveillance cameras had captured images of four of the five terrorists, including the al-Hazmi brothers on American Airlines flight 77, as they set off metal detectors at Dulles International Airport the day of the attack.

My contribution to helping identify the victims of the 9/11 attack is something that I'll never forget. The faces of people, their lives cut short, the smell of jet fuel in everything we touched, and the burned debris are as vivid today as they were at that time. They're burned into my consciousness just like the moment I learned President John F. Kennedy had been assassinated, and the evening phone call telling me that my adoptive mother had died. The attack on the Pentagon is one of those catastrophic events that is indelibly etched into my mind and can never be ignored, minimized, or forgotten.

After nearly a week, the names of the identified began to reach the public, and the bodies started home to the families for burial. A cross section of America died that day. My hope is that we at the mortuary and those who recovered the bodies of our fellow Americans from the Pentagon, the crash site in Pennsylvania, and the World Trade Center were able to provide family members, friends, and colleagues some small measure of closure. Despite our best efforts in Dover, however, I am still left with a feeling of disbelief, a hollow anger aimed at the terrorists, those who backed them, those who protected them. The only consolation comes in those moments when I realize I share those feelings with the rest of America.

16. RIPLEY WOULD BE PROUD

Appearances are deceptive.
—*Aesop's Fables*

It was another one of those crazy Friday mornings during which nothing was going right when I got a call from FBI Special Agent John Krebs of the Honolulu office asking for assistance. Although some people are embarrassed about the skeletons in their closet, Carl Patterson (not his real name) wasn't one of them. Patterson was in the navy and living on Oahu when he purchased three human skulls on eBay, the popular online auction site. Although purchasing human remains is usually not against the law, buying those known or suspected to be of Native American origin is prohibited. The skulls Patterson bought were advertised as Native American, originating in North Carolina. An agency that tracks items sold on eBay had notified the Bureau of Indian Affairs (BIA) of the sale. The BIA called the FBI, and that's when I got involved.

Special Agent Krebs wanted me to examine the skulls and tell him if they were in fact Native American remains. If they were, Patterson could choose to turn them over to the FBI or face charges of violating the Native American Graves Protection Act (NAGPRA). If the skulls were illegally sold, the FBI would try to trace them back through eBay to the person who sold them. The goal was to find the ultimate source of the remains: what state, what tribe, and what burial ground. Native Americans consider their burial grounds sacred space; digging up Indian remains is a desecration, whether the act is done knowingly or in ignorance.

Krebs's call gave me flashbacks to my days at the Smithsonian Institution, where I was involved in examining Native American remains and trying to detect from which tribe they came. Tribal affiliation is an important aspect to NAGPRA because each tribe wants only their ancestors' remains so they can be reburied according to their specific customs.

Carl Patterson met us at the front door and led us into a small town house that was sparsely but tastefully decorated. On his dining room table were two complete skulls and a third that was incomplete. Within seconds I knew that the remains would be going back to the Bureau of Indian Affairs for burial. Their shape and heavily worn teeth left no doubt that they were Native American.

Carl cooperated fully with the FBI. He seemed genuinely dismayed that he'd broken the law by buying American Indian skulls and obviously happy to get them out of his house. Several times he nervously asked if he needed to get an attorney and what he should do to protect himself if he bought remains in the future. I told him he should purchase bones from biological supply houses or reputable stores, such as Maxilla & Mandible in New York City, and avoid private dealers on the Internet. For one not trained in forensic anthropology, it's difficult if not impossible to figure out the origin of human remains. They could be stolen from a university or medical school anatomical collection, an old cemetery anywhere in the world, or a Native American burial ground in the United States. It's also possible that remains bought on the open market could be those of a murder victim.

After Krebs and the agent who accompanied him asked Patterson a few questions and packed up the three skulls, they asked if he had any other remains he'd like me to look at while I was there. "You've got an expert here," one of the special agents reminded him. "Why don't you let him look at them now?" Patterson replied, "The rest of the remains are okay. There's just a few bones, and they're not American Indian. But I guess I could let you look at what I've got since you're here." He cautioned us to be quiet going up the stairs because his wife was asleep in the next room. When I entered the small bedroom, I realized how much Patterson had understated his collection.

In one corner stood a complete skeleton in a wood-and-glass case. "I'm told this was a member of a man's secret lodge," Patterson told me. I moved closer to get a better look at two large rings on the bony fingers. "Hmm," I said. "This is an elderly woman." She had classic female pubic bones where the hips come together in the front, a large sciatic notch on both sides, and small cranial features. I had no doubt about her sex. The quality of the wood-and-glass case made me think it came from a medical school museum. The skeleton had all the hallmarks of an anatomical specimen put together around the turn of the century and used either to teach medical students or to adorn a doctor's office. The bedroom featured several large swords and lances and a bookcase with a skull sitting on a textbook. But nothing could have prepared me for what I saw when Patterson opened the closet door.

The shelves were covered with human skulls, mummy parts, beaded necklaces and headbands, war lances, animal bones, and even a small Philippine log burial—part of a tree trunk had been hollowed out and stuffed with two human heads. I was personally stunned and professionally elated. This man owned several items the Smithsonian Institution would have loved to add to its collection. In fact, his assemblage would have made Robert Ripley of *Ripley's Believe It or Not!* drool. Entering Patterson's closet was like stepping into the den of a successful safari hunter. However, this hunter had found all these not in the Serengeti, but on the Internet. His collection of the hundred or so pieces of human memorabilia had probably cost more than a hundred thousand dollars. But what was most amazing to me was that he didn't have just run-of-the-mill human skulls; he had some of the most unusual I'd ever seen.

He must have had twenty human skulls from around the world, many with small tags of the sort you see in antiques shops telling where they were from, who collected them, and when. Many were from the turn of the twentieth century. There were a couple of withered and mummified Egyptian hands blackened from the embalming process. They were probably two thousand to four thousand years old and appeared much like the ones I had examined at the Smithsonian. I saw a mummified baby girl that, judging from its condition, came from an area of the American Southwest, or maybe Central or South America, where arid conditions favor mummification. My guess was it came from a desert burial or cave in Peru. Had it been buried in moist soil, it surely would have decomposed and become skeletonized long ago.

Patterson showed me what appeared to be a shrunken human head taken by the Jivaro headhunters in Ecuador. The Jivaro shrank the heads of enemies killed in battle until the Ecuadorean government banned the practice in the late twentieth century. Genuine shrunken heads are about as rare as hen's teeth; Patterson said he'd paid forty-five hundred dollars for this one. It had all of the features that I'd come to know as authentic. The mouth was stitched shut to keep the spirits from coming out. The nose was upturned and packed with black pitch. The facial and head hair were present. I could even see beard stubble suggesting the man hadn't shaved during the week before he died. It was the practice of the headhunters to remove the skull before shrinking the head, since bone won't shrink when the head is boiled. They would decapitate the enemy where he fell, peel back the scalp and head hair in one piece, and discard the skull in the forest. They then would shrink what was left in an elaborate process that reduced it to the size of a baseball. Jivaro warriors took these trophies, believing they imparted the prowess and strength of their fallen enemies.

I saw also a human right foot, its bones wired together as though it, too, had served medical students in the early twentieth century. Most interesting about the foot was a legend written on the underside: "Dr. Scholl, Chicago, Illinois." I later did an Internet search and learned that Dr. William M. Scholl was in Chicago in the early 1900s. This medical curiosity must have belonged to the famous Dr. Scholl, who died in 1968, and whose company's products are sold to this day. Despite my interest in bones of the human foot, I'd never run across anything like it.

Among the items that intrigued me most were two carved human skulls from Borneo, a skull that seemed to resemble that of a vampire, and a man's head with the mouth sewed tightly shut by means of the kind of stitching used on baseballs. Embalmers use the same stitch to close the chest and stomach cavity after an autopsy. The Borneo skulls were blackened, either by having been smoked over a fire or painted with a substance resembling tar. They appearanced to belong to people who had died a hundred to a hundred and fifty years ago. Looking closely, however, I realized that one was real and one was made of wood and animal bone, and crudely done at that. It didn't take me long to realize the teeth were from a dog, not a human being. The real skull had probably been used as a template to carve the phony one. Both were incised with crudely drawn human and animal figures on just about every surface. Many tribes, including those on Borneo, Easter Island, Tasmania, and Fiji, practiced carving on skulls with a knife or a sharp stone. Carl admitted to having inserted two alligator teeth into the upper sockets of another skull to make it look like a vampire. He thought it looked "cool."

Yet another skull, accompanied by an old photograph of what Patterson referred to as "natives," was said to be of a victim killed by Philippine headhunters in the 1920s. Closer inspection, however, again belied the story accompanying it. The misshapen skull hadn't come from someone whose head was bound as a child, but from a person with a congenital defect called craniostenosis, which causes the bones of the skull to fuse at too early an age. The result was that the skull changed shape to adapt to the growing brain during childhood. Clearly, again Carl had purchased something with a bogus story behind it.

One of the most interesting and intriguing items in Carl's closet was a human skull labeled "Butter Cup." He kept it in a wooden box lined with red velvet, along with a handwritten letter explaining the history of the skull and how it got its name. My skepticism was on high alert when I read it. The letter came in an envelope bearing this notation: "This skull was given to the S.F. College of Mortuary Science by Bill Stirlen on November 7, 1980. This letter to the College explains about the skull and should be kept with 'Butter Cup' for the information it provides."

Inside, on notepaper inscribed "From the Desk of William H. Stirlen," was the following text:

This item was the skull of an escaped professional convict from Joliet, Illinois Federal prison—sometime during the period of 1927–1928.

Shortly after escape from Joliet, was recaptured in the tri city area of Davenport, Iowa, Rock Island & Moline Illinois on the Mississippi river. During the holding time before transfer back to Joliet—this person complained of a severe tooth problem. During the visit to the dentist—the convict overpowered the guard, & the dentist, escaped to the river where he manned a motor launch—heading south. In the area of Muscatine, Iowa he abandoned the boat—allowing it under motor power to continue down the river—while the convict debarked on one of the river islands.

It is not known how long he was on the island, but during the time the Mississippi river rose above normal & completely submerged most of the islands.

Sometime later hunters found his body on the island, almost completely deteriorated—an apparent drowning victim.

For identification the remains were taken to Fairbanks Funeral Home where the body was buried in a welfare plot, but the skull was kept for positive identification, as there was no knowledge that this person would be the escaped convict.

After positive identification—Fairbanks Funeral Home had the skull. At this point in time Robert, son of Roy Fairbanks, in 1929 was to attend Cincinnati College of Embalming—took the skull with him for anatomical study. After his college returned the skull & was closeted until I came on the scene May 1—1936, at the time I entered the Funeral Service industry.

The fall semester of 1937—off to Cincinnati College of Embalming—

goes our illustrious educational convict, to be of assistance to others nearby—during our studies.

Prior to his second trip to Ohio—he was christened under the name of "Butter Cup" for the future—proposed giving him to your Mortuary College anatomical studies.

Even with this record as a professional convict—it is uncanny how he became more helpful to humanity after death rather than before his demise.

Respectfully submitted—

Bill Stirlen

My goal in examining the skull was to see if there was anything about it to support the story in Mr. Stirlen's letter. Carefully cradling the skull and lifting it out of its wooden box, I immediately knew it was a man—a white man, to be exact. Judging from the degree of suture closure and condition of his teeth, he was probably in middle age when he died. I probably could have narrowed his age a bit if I'd had more time, but I was already straying far from the purpose of my visit. Yet I just couldn't ignore the skull. I planned later to try to identify this man through prison and court records from Joliet, Illinois, and to see if I could find anything about a prison escape in the Joliet newspapers for 1927 or 1928. I turned the skull slowly in every direction, looking for anything that might help me tell where it came from, who it was, and how he had died. Someone had stripped the skull of all flesh and hair and cleaned it thoroughly, perhaps with bleach, to get rid of the smell. It showed signs of having been much handled over the years. So far everything about the skull matched the letter. Still, I wanted proof that this was the skull of a convict, as the letter claimed. Above all, my scientific training has taught me to be skeptical.

Moving closer to the large sliding glass patio doors and the bright light of a sunny day, I rotated the skull, looking for evidence of fracture. If Butter Cup had lived the kind of rough life that leads to prison, I expected to see some broken bones. Within seconds I answered my own question. His nasal bones were twisted and mangled, just as they would be from a blow to the nose delivered from his right side. The blow had splintered the fragile nasal bones, dislodging them permanently to the left. Although the bones had healed, they'd done so in an unusual fashion. No doubt in life this man had a crooked nose from fighting. It was clear that no doctor had set the bones. They had healed naturally—exactly what I would expect of a hardened criminal, someone who lived on the run. However, that wasn't all: the bridge of bone known as the left zygomatic arch, which runs from in front of the left ear to the cheekbone, had been broken and healed, also without the aid of a doctor. This man had sustained several severe blows to the head, one of which broke his left cheekbone and the other his nose. Either he wasn't a very good fighter, or someone got in some lucky punches.

At that point I remembered this was supposed to be the skull of a convict who sought dental care because of a toothache. The toothache part of the story was actually the easiest part to prove; I could see the hole caused by a gigantic abscess in the upper right side of his mouth. The tooth would have soon fallen out if he had lived much longer. So here was perhaps the most compelling piece of evidence that the skull was in fact that of a convict who sought dental treatment and escaped.

The last piece of the puzzle was to find something supporting Mr. Stirlen's statement that the skull had been in the hands of mortuary students and funeral homes from 1938 to 1980, when it was donated to the San Francisco School of Mortuary. Proving that it had been in a funeral home, and not a medical school or biological supply house, turned out to be easy. I was turning the skull side to side when I noticed that the mandible, the lower jaw, was wired in place not with standard surgical wire or wire from a hardware store, but with the kind of wire embalmers attach to an injector needle to staple the mouth shut during the embalming process. The metal needle looks like a ribbed rivet. It is driven into the bony parts of the mouth with a specialized rivet gun. Once embedded in bone, the needles can't be pulled out. A needle and wire are driven into the bone at the base of the nose and another is placed between the incisor teeth in the lower jaw. The embalmer then positions the mouth the way he wants the family to see it at the viewing, and twists the two wires together to keep the mouth closed. Morticians often use a bit of superglue to keep body fluids from oozing through the lips. With Butter Cup, two injector needles wired the lower jaw to the skull. Injector needles are not commonly stocked in medical schools, biological supply houses, or, for that matter, morgues. However, every funeral home carries them.

Finally, I was satisfied that Butter Cup was the man Mr. Stirlen said he was, a convict with a toothache who escaped from Joliet Federal Prison in 1927 or 1928. I now had no reason to doubt the rest of the letter's account: that the man had drowned off one of the small Mississippi islands and that his head was removed before his body was buried in a pauper's cemetery. This story bears an uncanny resemblance to that of the first man executed at Joliet, on July 27, 1856. The inmate killed a deputy warden during an escape attempt and was later hanged for the murder. The man had refused to give his real name, but officials thought it was George Chase.

"I don't think I'm guilty," the *Suburban Chicago News* quoted him the day after he was executed.

Like Butter Cup, George Chase's head was removed during an autopsy, and his headless body was buried in a pauper's grave. The main difference between the two is that Butter Cup made it all the way to Hawaii. As Mr. Stirlen said in his letter, Butter Cup served mankind more after death than before. I only hope that someday we learn his real name. I'm sure he would have liked that.

Two fascinating hours later, I'd examined just about every bone, mummy, and artifact in Carl Patterson's bedroom and closet. Although I didn't tell him and he never asked, I'd judged that only a few of the things he purchased were genuine. For the rest, the stories that accompanied the objects didn't match what I saw. Although his passion for collecting ancient and curious human body parts may sound macabre, it's no different from how every museum in the world got its start. Robert Ripley sent people around the world looking for the odd and unusual. Carl did essentially the same thing, except that he used the Internet and his museum is a closet in Hawaii.

I spent the better part of three months running down leads on the Internet and at several libraries, and even made a couple of phone calls to the man who handles Joliet's prison records trying to find out who Butter Cup really was. I was hoping to find a list or register of escapees, but in a phone conversation I learned the government doesn't have one—at least for Joliet. In fact, the only way to find out who escaped from Joliet in a particular year is to know the escapee's name and then refer to his prison record, filed according to the day he was put behind bars. Knowing when Butter Cup escaped, I soon learned, was about as useless as knowing what he had for breakfast. There's simply no way of connecting that information to his file.

My only hope of learning Butter Cup's real name was to search the one newspaper that followed escapes and captures at Joliet, the *Chicago Daily Tribune* for 1927 and 1928. I was hoping to find some mention, as Stirlen's letter stated, of an escaped convict, a flood, and the Mississippi River. I was able to eliminate some escapees right off the bat because they were either too young or the wrong race. One by one I pulled up the fading front pages and scanned each word before moving on to the next day. At times I found myself immersed in a time when Calvin Coolidge was president, Charlie Chaplin was comedy king, Ford's first Model A rolled off the assembly line, newspapers sold for seven cents, and headlines everywhere told of a young man named Charles Lindbergh.

Three months and several headaches later, I was able to narrow the list of possibilities down to a few convicts, including one involved in the murder of an assistant warden. The prime suspect was a convict named Charles Shader, who, along with six others in 1927, had escaped from Joliet right in the middle of Chicago's worst flood. Once again the pieces were all coming together, and I, like the Chicago police, was moving closer to "catching" this elusive convict. Closer, that is, until I pulled up the hazy print for 1928 and read that Shader had been recaptured and hanged on October 9. I was disappointed to find that all of the escapees in 1927 and 1928 had been recaptured, killed in shootouts with the cops, or, like Shader—the last man hanged in Illinois—executed at Joliet gallows. The identity of "Butter Cup," it seemed, had vanished like the wind. But I wasn't ready to give up. In fact, I was more determined than ever to keep on searching records looking for that one piece of evidence that might reveal his true identity.

I moved one step closer to knowing Butter Cup's name two years later, in 2005, when I reread Stirlen's letter to see if I'd missed anything. While reading the letter I realized that the great Mississippi flood had occurred in 1926 and, quite literally, spilled over into 1927—but not into 1928. Based on these dates, my guess was that Butter Cup must have escaped in the fall or winter of 1926 or spring of 1927—not 1928, as Stirlen's letter stated. According to historical accounts, the Mississippi River began rising in August 1926, reached flood levels in Cairo, Illinois, on January 1, 1927, and by April 1927, had flooded seven states, including Illinois.

The Great Flood of 1927 lasted 153 days, killed more than a thousand people (including the man whose identity I now sought) and displaced nearly a million people from their homes and farmlands. Armed with this new information, I began searching prison records and Chicago newspapers, and I contacted the people at the Illinois State Archives to see if they could help me figure out who had escaped from Joliet twice—once from the prison itself and a second time on his way back to Joliet in 1926 or 1927. As you recall, Butter Cup had been recaptured after escaping from Joliet, then had pulled his "tooth trick" and escaped on his way back to Joliet. So, technically, he hadn't made his final escape from Joliet, but on his way there. I was hoping to find something in the Chicago papers describing just such an incident.

The next thing I did was phone Bob Caldwell in the microfilm center at the Illinois Department of Corrections to see if he knew of any escapee lists for Joliet or some way to get at Butter Cup's real name. He told me that if an escapee such as Butter Cup is never discharged, he would have what they call an open file, and that this file might have been sent on to Stateville Penitentiary when Joliet closed in 2002. As best I could tell, Butter Cup had escaped from Joliet, had been recaptured, had escaped again en route to prison, and then had been identified when his body was found after the 1927 flood. But I still needed to know his name to find out the circumstances of his incarceration, escape, and subsequent death. I also learned from Bob that there were only four Illinois institutions open in the 1920s: Joliet, Pontiac, Menard, and Stateville. Joliet, it seems, was the reception and classification facility for all offenders from the Chicago area.

Once received at Joliet, they might be transferred elsewhere based on security risk, crime, and the like.

I guess you're hoping to read that all my research unraveled the mystery of Butter Cup: who he was, what he did, and when he died. But it didn't. I haven't given up trying, though, and I certainly haven't given up hope of learning this man's identity. He, like the rest of us, was given a name at birth, and he deserves to take that name with him to his grave. The mystery of Butter Cup is one that I simply can't put to rest.

By the time we finished examining everything, I felt as though Carl had given us the opportunity of a lifetime. We'd seen some things that few others had, even in the Smithsonian or in any of Ripley's many museums. Although Carl had been sold some spurious items during his five years as a collector, he loved his artifacts. And as far as I know, he still loves to sit and look at them. I hope he's more careful about what he buys in the future, or his retirement fund won't be sufficient to get him through his golden years. But perhaps the memories and mysteries will.

17. A SHOT IN THE DARK
THE DEATH OF PRIVATE HORNER

*Every great mistake has a halfway moment, a split second
when it can be recalled and perhaps remedied.*
—PEARL S. BUCK, *What America Means to Me*

Under orders to push eastward along the Moselle River near the town of
Millery, in southern France, the young men of the 317th Infantry Regiment's
H Company knew nothing of the German soldiers dug in on the hilltop
overlooking their position. For twenty-one-year-old Private Robert B.
Horner, World War II was about to end. At about four A.M. on September 18, 1944, with troops from two SS Panzer divisions lurking above, an
American guard accidentally shot Horner, having mistaken him in the
darkness for the enemy. A single bullet entered his shoulder and opened a
wound that would not stop bleeding. Horner went into shock. When light
came, he was carried to a field aid station and given a blood transfusion,
which didn't help. Soon the West Virginia native, who had grown up in
Coraopolis, Pennsylvania, was dead.

In one of those unfortunate and inevitable errors so common in the
chaos of battle, someone in his company declared Horner missing in action. It seems word had not reached the company that he'd died at the aid
station; all they knew was that when the fighting was over, Horner was
missing. Years later his sister, Mary Atchison, of Benton, Illinois, still

could not erase the memory of the car that pulled into the family drive-way to deliver the telegram that began, "We regret to inform you . . ." Robert was missing in action. His loss fulfilled a prediction he had made two years earlier when Mary, one of his seven siblings and a year older than he was, had driven him to the train station in Pittsburgh at the end of a leave at the family home. When Robert said good-bye, he told his sister he didn't expect to come home alive. A year and a day later, his status was changed to killed in action, following standard practice during World War II.

Nearly fifty-seven years later, on April 27, 2001, a Frenchman named Michael Matheu was digging in his garden when he came upon a World War II American-style metal helmet. Inside the helmet was what seemed to be skeletal remains. Matheu stopped digging and called the police; together, Matheu and the police excavated the site. The next day, French police notified the U.S. Army Mortuary in Landstuhl, Germany, which sent a representative to collect the remains and other items found during the excavation. Fourteen months later, late in the evening of June 5, 2002, the remains arrived at the Central Identification Laboratory in Hawaii.

Matheu and the police officers had done a surprisingly professional job of recovering the remains. They even found some of the smaller bones that many would have overlooked—the fingers, the toes, and the tiny hyoid bone in the neck. The bones, buried in a country and soil famous for its wine, were in an excellent state of preservation. The only negative effects of burial were that some thin roots had grown along the shafts of the bones and created a mahogany discoloration reflecting the color of the soil around them. Some fragments resembled wood more than they did bone. I'm always amazed at how much better preserved are remains from Europe, compared with those from Southeast Asia. The cold European winters and mildly acidic soils are simply kinder to buried bone.

Among the objects found with the remains were two dog tags bearing the legend "HORNER ROBERT B." We have no way to know who buried Horner, but the fact that he was buried with both dog tags suggests that someone other than an American soldier put his body into the ground. To this day, American soldiers are issued two identical dog tags so that one can be buried with them and the other removed and sent up the chain of command, to furnish a record of death.

Opening the box, I laid out the jumble of remains on an examination table and began putting them in anatomical order. The first thing to catch my eye was that the skull was shattered into more than a hundred pieces. I got my first glimpse of what I would be dealing with when I glanced over at the cardboard box of military-issue equipment on the next table and saw several holes in his helmet. My first thought was that he'd been shot in the head several times. I counted three entrance wounds and at least one large exit hole, maybe two. I later found a fourth entrance hole. Whatever had entered and exited the steel helmet had caused the edges of the holes to peel back, resembling flower petals. Although I didn't know if bullets, grenade fragments, or artillery rounds had caused the holes, I knew that his helmet hadn't been enough to protect him.

But there was more. Laying out the bones of the spine, arms, left hand, left hip, right scapula, sacrum, legs, and left foot, I found more broken bones and evidence of severe trauma. His injuries were so bad that most of his bones from the waist down had been shattered—incredibly, even two of his fingers were in splinters. Not having read the background on the case, I could only guess that he must have taken the full brunt of an explosion and flying shrapnel at close range. His wounds and the pattern of bone fractures didn't have the typical appearance of gunshot wounds, so I suspected that something other than bullets had killed him. But the truth of what killed Private Horner would have to await discovery until I finished piecing together the bones.

I spent the next four days hunched over the table reconstructing the bones. Using masking tape to hold the fragments in place before gluing them, I painstakingly compared every piece of bone larger than a fingernail to see if any of the edges matched up. If they did, I glued them together and then compared them again to see if they fit yet another bone.

This went on until I rebuilt most of the skeleton. The hardest part was the skull, shattered as it was. The largest fragment was about the size of a credit card, the smallest was dust. Most pieces were no bigger than postage stamps. Once I assembled as many pieces as I could, and temporarily held them in place with masking tape, I took apart the skull, piece by piece, then glued it back together. I used the tape first because I wanted to be sure that the bone fragments hadn't become warped while lying in the ground. Without taking care, it's easy to end up with a lopsided skull with mismatched edges. This time, most of the bones fit back together perfectly.

I could not put the fragile bones of the face together because they'd been shattered into thousands of tiny fragments, as they often are in the events of motor vehicle accidents and gunshot wounds. Other than being able to refit the two nasal bones, which resemble a ski slope jutting out from between the eyes, I simply couldn't reconstruct the rest of the face. Giving it my best shot and nearly a week's work, I could rebuild most of the cranial vault, but not its base. Most surprising, however, was that nearly every one of the dead man's skull bones had been fractured. It was the kind of trauma we see in someone who dies in a plane crash or falls from a twenty-story building, not from a gunshot wound to the shoulder. Something else had happened to this man. I was going to find out what.

I finished gluing the skull back together on a Sunday. My wife was visiting her family in Thailand, so I had plenty of time on my hands, and I could do little else but anticipate working on this case. This was one of those cases where I just couldn't wait to get to work every morning. The lab was nearly empty on weekends so there weren't any distractions—no phone calls, no meetings, no interruptions. The puzzle was coming together nicely. By Sunday I was ready to see if I could match up the holes in the skull with those in the helmet. I placed the helmet on its back in a small box of granulated lava—plentiful in Hawaii—to keep it from rolling off the examination table. Placing the head in the helmet in about the same position it would have been in when the soldier was wearing it, I found the fit wasn't so good at first. But within about a minute the old lightbulb went on. Turning the skull slightly to my left, I found that the size and location of two entrance wounds in the left side of his head matched perfectly with two holes in the helmet. I had it! The days of matching and gluing hundreds of broken bones had paid off. I now had a rather good picture of what might have killed this soldier.

We don't often get helmets and such pieces of military equipment because people usually take them from battlefields as souvenirs or, if they are buried in damp soil, they rust and typically fall to pieces in thirty or forty years. This was one of the few times in my career that I could compare a piece of protective equipment to a bullet hole or shrapnel wound in bone. The evidence before me seemed to suggest that he'd sustained at least two injuries to the left side of his head. Judging from the pattern of fractures, the first bullet or piece of shrapnel entered above and in front of his left ear, and the second one entered behind and above the same ear. By studying the fracture lines, I could tell that he received the wound in front of his ear before the one behind it. Scientists have learned over the years that a fracture doesn't cross an existing fracture; fracture lines serve as "dead ends" to subsequent fractures. It was clear to me that either of the injuries could have been fatal.

Using thin wooden dowels to track the trajectory through the helmet and skull, I found that whatever had caused the two large holes near the top of the helmet had entered and exited without ever striking bone. This potentially made sense as his thin helmet liner would have served to cool him while suspending the steel "pot" an inch or so from his scalp. Looking inside the helmet I saw that a piece of the thin liner was wedged against its inner surface, held firmly in place by the jagged, flower petal—like edges formed when the shrapnel tore through it. The entire back half of the liner lay in several hundred pieces from the shock wave that passed through it. My guess is that he sustained the shrapnel injuries to his head when a mortar or artillery round went off near him.

A few minutes later I went into the autopsy suite, where the rest of his uniform equipment was stored. Archaeologist Dr. Greg Fox and forensic anthropology assistant Kiyomi Parrish had already begun the painstaking process of identifying and analyzing the material evidence. Anything that isn't a bone or tooth falls into this category, and many details of this case would unfold through my colleagues' analysis. The artifacts were still inside the plastic bags just as we had received them from the mortuary in Germany. He had been buried in his uniform and equipment, including a tattered green raincoat sticking to the back of his rusty helmet. His rifle and sidearm were missing. On one corner of the table lay two size-eight leather boots. An X-ray of the right one revealed nails ringing its rubber sole like a white picket fence. Although the leather was fragile and easily torn, the soles were in good shape, despite having been buried nearly six decades. They were preserved well enough for me to see the waffle-style tread and worn heels. Private Horner had put quite a bit of mileage on those Goodrich combat boots. Two inch-long pieces of shrapnel embedded in the heel of the left boot and torn sole spoke volumes about the fierce battle that shattered Private First Class Horner's body and, possibly, took his life.

Off to my left was a broken plastic cigarette case. Next to it was a six-inch-long green toothbrush with "Park Avenue" stamped into the handle. Nothing fancy, purely functional. It was still covered with the same brown dirt as his boots and bones. These were some of the personal effects that his sister Bertha of Washington, Pennsylvania, had so desperately requested from the War Department a few years after her brother's death. Also found with this young soldier were a rusty spoon handle, a P-38 can opener that more resembled a clump of rust than a tool, a few unfired bullets from his M1 carbine rifle, broken and unbroken buttons, the base of a U.S. Mk II "pineapple" grenade, and a 1943 Deutsches Reich pfennig. The dime-size zinc coin was adorned with a swastika and eagle. A rusty army M3 fighting knife was lying on top of another plastic bag, waiting its turn at analysis. The knife looked as though it had seen little use other than opening C-ration cans (C-rats) containing such delights as cheese spread and crackers. Accompanying the body were seven empty

C-rats cans and an equal number of can opener keys, resembling rusty watch springs.

Was Private Horner carrying these when he was killed, or had someone else tossed them in with his body? The most likely explanation is that he was buried in an area of fighting previously occupied by American soldiers and their meals. Last were some empty foil packets of Nescafé coffee, Nestlé's hot chocolate, and "Lemon juice powder synthetic," made by Miles Laboratories in Elkhart, Indiana. My guess is that this synthetic lemon juice was as bad-tasting as the navy's "bug juice," which I'd endured aboard ship. Maybe it was even made by the same company.

Once I'd reconstructed the skeleton, I was ready to compile a biological profile before comparing my findings with his military records—a "blind" analysis. The features of his skull were classic Caucasian: he had a high vault, narrow nasal opening, prominent nasal bones and nasal spine, and a narrow palate. I measured one of his arm bones, plugged the length measurement into a mathematical formula, and found he was about five feet seven inches tall. His pubic bones were a series of ridges and valleys, and many of the growth caps in the bones of his arms, legs, and hips had not fully united. His bone and tooth development suggested he was between seventeen and twenty years old when he died. A subsequent check of his medical records revealed that Private Horner was a white male who was nineteen when he died, a month short of his twentieth birthday. His recorded height was five feet seven and a half inches. Seeking a positive identification, I called on CIL dentist Dr. Ken Dunn. "Kenny D.," as we call him, is not only a skilled forensic dentist, but also an accomplished black-and-white photographer. Tall and with chiseled features, he's the kind of guy who makes a seventeen-hour flight from Hawaii to Vietnam a pleasure. Dr. Dunn confirmed Horner's identity based on several dental fillings and surgically extracted teeth recorded in his records. Horner, like so many other soldiers during World War II, didn't have any dental X-rays.

The biggest challenge for me in this case was interpreting Private Horner's wounds. I wanted to see if there was any skeletal evidence to support the medic's report that Horner had been shot in the shoulder. If I didn't find signs of trauma to the shoulder bones, the medic's statement would still be included in the scientific director's report to the family. Charting all of the broken bones on a skeletal diagram to see if I could see any particular pattern of breakage, I found damage to his left scapula; a large piece of eggshell-thin bone was missing. This was evidence, but not proof. The bone in that part of the scapula is so thin that it rarely reflects the size or shape of the object passing through it, and a bullet that hits there almost never leaves beveling, the telltale sign of a projectile. The only possible evidence of the bullet fired by the American sentry was through the thin body of the scapula. Two of the scapula fragments were old and discolored, suggesting they were broken long before the skeleton was excavated in 2001. If he had been shot in the scapula, as I suspected, there wasn't a bullet embedded in the bone. I wondered if it went entirely through his body.

I also meant to determine what had shattered his body below the waist. The left side of his body had been injured more than his right, and the fractures were more consistent with trauma from an explosion or multiple shrapnel wounds than from bullets. Horner probably sustained the worst of his injuries at the field aid station after he died. Surely he wouldn't have been treated for blood loss if he was already torn apart by mortar or artillery rounds exploding near him. Perhaps he was lying with his hands by his sides. That would account for the shattered lower body and two fingers. A CIL ordnance specialist identified one of the projectile fragments recovered with his remains as the nose fuse from a 7.5 centimeter projectile fired from a German light mountain infantry gun. This gun on wheels was a favored weapon of mountain troops. It weighed nine hundred pounds and could hurl a twelve-pound shell more than two miles. Although the Americans were pinned down and received hours of deadly mortar and artillery rounds, the only report of injury to Private Horner was a gunshot wound to his shoulder. I'm surprised that no one in his company or at the aid station reported seeing him shelled.

A few days later, while sorting through the small mound of uniform buttons, C-rats, shrapnel, and other military equipment, Greg Fox found what at first we believed was the most important piece of the entire puzzle: an American .30-caliber bullet that had apparently been fired. The bullet, bright green with oxidation, had a deep crease along one side, suggesting that it had struck something in flight—in this case, Private Horner. We thought it might have been creased when it hit the young soldier's body or something he was wearing—a button, metal buckle, or the like. Our enthusiasm was short lived when we noticed that the bullet didn't have any rifling grooves on it. Here, the *absence* of evidence gave us the answer: the lack of rifle grooves made clear that the bullet hadn't been fired from a gun. This bullet, like Private Horner's body, was probably the random recipient of a piece of shrapnel.

We never did find the bullet that killed Private Horner. Not recovering the bullet, however, didn't disprove the account of his having been shot in the shoulder. This raises an often-confusing concept that all forensics specialists have to deal with at one time or another: the absence of evidence is not evidence of absence. We know he was shot because the soldier who treated his injury filed a report, but the bullet wasn't recovered. It may have passed through Horner's body. An example of the "evidence of absence" would be if witnesses saw Private Horner alive and well the day after the battle. In many medical/legal cases, the absence of evidence proves little, if anything.

One of the most perplexing questions of this case is why he was buried in his helmet. Medics working to save his life almost certainly would have removed it when treating him. Of course they may have left his helmet on if artillery rounds were exploding all around them. If Americans buried him, why didn't someone on the burial detail record the exact location of his grave so it could be found later and his remains repatriated to home soil? And why had they not removed at least one of his dog tags as proof of his death, and sent the record up the chain of command? I personally don't think Americans buried Horner, but exactly what happened to his body after he died is a mystery. It may have been overlooked or misplaced when the Americans pulled out of the area. I think someone came along after the battle and buried him. One way we could have answered the question of who buried Private Horner was if one of our CIL teams had excavated the grave themselves and documented the precise position of his body in the grave. After excavating so many burials over the years, we've learned that a person's body posture can provide significant information on whether the burial was performed by friend or foe. For example, if he was buried lying on his back with hands crossed over his stomach, that would be consistent with American burial customs, suggesting an American soldier buried him. However, if his body was found crammed into a small pit, one arm under his belly and one over his head, we could surmise that the enemy or someone who found his body long after he was dead had buried him. Although we may never know for sure, I'm still hopeful that someone who fought beside him will come forward and explain what happened to this young soldier after he was shot.

Working late one evening I put aside the science and tried to imagine what this young man from West Virginia was like. Looking at his bones I could tell that he had a prominent nose, his head was rounded, he wasn't very tall, and that he, like me, had lost a few teeth through neglect. Reading his military records, I would later learn that, although he died five years before I was born, we also shared the same first name, birth state, height, hair color, and eye color.

Private Horner, the only member of his company killed in battle that night, was laid to rest in 1944 on a lush French hillside. I think he must have been buried within a few days of his death, because the skeleton we recovered was nearly complete. If he had been left exposed, it's likely that someone would have taken his fighting knife and dog tags for souvenirs. After a few months, animals would probably have scattered his remains. There were no roads or farmhouses in the area, just rolling hills and the nearby Moselle River.

It would take the luck of a farmer and the combined efforts of authorities in three countries—France, the United States, and Germany—to bring this American soldier home after nearly three generations. He was identified on September 10, 2002—three months after having arrived on U.S. soil. I was proud to have been part of the effort, and handling his remains brought me a little closer to what it must have been like for our soldiers to fight and die in Europe. In some respects, his remains brought him back to life, even if for only a moment.

18. MURDER IN PARADISE

The arc of the moral universe is long . . . but it bends toward justice.

—THEODORE PARKER, *Ten Sermons of Religion*

The police dispatcher listened helplessly as a man shouted into his cell phone, "Help me! I'm being chased. No, Jason! Oh my God! I'm being killed! What are you doing, man? Jason! No!"

"Sir, you have to tell me where you are so I can help you," pleaded dispatcher Tracy Simao, but her urging was answered only by what sounded like muffled gunshots and then a long series of beeps. She waited for a reply, then disconnected the call.

Simao and the Kona, Hawaii, emergency dispatch service tape recorder were the only witnesses to a deadly beating. Who the victim was, she had no idea. But the tape seemed to contain the name of the assailant. Police could do nothing, however, but wait for something more to happen. Nine days later, on April 10, 2003, two things happened.

Early in the morning, the parents of a man who lived in Kailua-Kona called to report he had been missing since April 1. Later in the day, a family walking along the gravel road to Makalawena Beach, on the Big Island of Hawaii near Kona, called to say they had discovered a partly decomposed body. No identification was found near the body. An autopsy concluded that the man, Michael Taylor, forty-one, had died of severe head injuries. The coroner said the injuries were consistent with foul play—in other words, the man had been murdered.

A few days later, Kona detectives charged twenty-eight-year-old Jason Campbell with second-degree murder, which meant the killing wasn't planned. Bail was set at a quarter million dollars. Prosecutors called the killing "especially heinous" and cruel. Under Hawaii state law, that formulation meant that the suspect, if he was found guilty, would receive a life sentence without the possibility of parole. Campbell pleaded innocent and remained in police custody.

The suspect gave police a couple of differing accounts of events that led to the killing. First, he said there was a fight among several men. Later, according to court records, Campbell said he and Taylor got into a fight over drugs and money, that Taylor made a call on his cell phone, and that Campbell hit him on the head with a wrench. A detective had found a torque wrench about two tenths of a mile from the body, and a check of Taylor's cell phone records revealed that he made a call to 911 on April 1, the day his family said he went missing. What police first thought was the sound of gunshots on the dispatch center tape later proved to be the assailant striking the cell phone against the victim's ear with such force that he splintered the phone and tore into the victim's skull. Authorities later recovered the shattered phone some distance from the body. Campbell had tossed it away, trying to hide the evidence.

In my more than twenty years as a forensic anthropologist, this was one of the most brutal beatings I'd ever seen. Certainly, it was the most chilling. I got involved in the case when Detective Wayne "Keala" Young of the Kona Police Department called on April 25, 2003. Young told me that a man's decomposing body, dressed only in Speedo shorts, had been found. Judging from a trail of blood and skull fragments, it appeared that the body had been dragged about fifty feet from where the victim was killed, and partially hidden in the brush. The condition of the body, both from trauma and advanced decomposition, made it difficult to see the facial features.

The texture and color of the hair on his head, however, indicated that the body was that of a Caucasian; the genitals were those of a man. Fingerprints confirmed Taylor's identity. The massive amount of damage to the victim's head and the large injury to his left cheek led police to believe that he might have been shot to death. That's what Dr. Tony Manoukian, the medical examiner for Maui and the Big Island, thought as he went into the autopsy—that he might be dealing with gunshot wounds. Once into the autopsy, however, he found no bullets, and he determined the pattern of injury suggested blunt force trauma. That's when Young brought me into the case.

Tony Manoukian and I had collaborated on several cases and had grown comfortable working together. We had both survived the craziness of the sixties; unlike me, Tony still wore his long hair loose, halfway down his back. Although he looks more like a rock star than most people's image of a forensic pathologist, his skills and manner in the autopsy room leave no doubt of his years of experience and kind heart, not only for those he works with but also for those he works on. We received the victim's partially skeletonized head a few days later, and I began cleaning up the bones with bleach and reconstructing the skull. Dr. Manoukian wanted to know what had happened to the victim—how he died and what had been used to kill him.

I was quick to tell him not to give me any more details of the trauma or his thoughts on what might have happened. Working in the blind, or as close to it as possible, is the best way to ensure an unbiased analysis. I didn't want to know if they'd found a weapon, if someone had confessed, or anything else. I just wanted to do my analysis without any coaching and then see how my findings compared to the rest of the case. Dr. Manoukian's basic request was for me to see if I could determine how many times the victim was struck in the face and head, the sequence of the blows, and the type of implement or weapon causing the injuries. In legal terms, he was asking me to interpret the injuries and provide an opinion on the cause of death.

Judging from the type and amount of damage that was in front of me, I thought the cause of death was probably either multiple gunshots or blunt force trauma. But there was no way to tell until the skull was put back together. In the skull's broken state, I couldn't say anything about the pattern of trauma or type of implement used to kill the man. If a gunshot wound to the head causes the skull to break up into a hundred pieces, it is nearly impossible to say much about the trauma until the skull is reconstructed. To determine if a gun was involved, it is necessary to reassemble the skull and see the holes made by the bullet's entry and exit. Only then do the beveled margins and fractures encircling a gunshot wound become visible. Without that, it's just a jumble of bone fragments.

Once the skull was pieced back together with glue and tape, I set it on a soft, cotton-filled ring resembling a doughnut to keep it from rolling onto the floor. Placing it directly on the foam-covered table can damage the two delicate spikes of bones known as styloid processes located at the base of the skull—and damaging remains is every forensic anthropologist's worst nightmare. A defense attorney could make such carelessness a point of contention in a trial, calling into question the anthropologist's competence to testify. This is something you will probably never see on any of the forensics shows on television, where every crime is solved in an hour, minus commercials.

I handled the skull as gently as possible to ensure I didn't push in or snap off any of the small pieces of bone I'd glued back in place. At that stage, it was much like handling an empty eggshell that had been broken and reassembled. I didn't want to introduce any postmortem damage to an already damaged skull. It was essential to ensure that everything I was looking at was associated with the victim's death and not due to the way I handled the evidence.

Shot from a weapon, a bullet travels at enormous speed. When it strikes bone, the bullet is likely to splinter. Most often, fractures appear in the bone. In the case of a gunshot wound to the head, if the bullet doesn't break up, it is likely to be deformed—pushed into a mushroom shape—as it passes through the bone and pushes a cone of soft tissue in front of it.

An entry wound to the skull is almost always smaller than the exit wound. As the bullet leaves the skull, it pops off a ring of bone around the exit wound on the scalp side, leaving a beveled margin wider on the outside than on the inside of the skull. The bevel, resembling an inverted pyramid, points toward the entry hole, much like an arrow. Beveling is the telltale sign of an exit wound.

Gunshot wounds may also result in two types of fractures in bone: radiating and concentric fractures. Radiating fractures form first, followed by concentric fractures. To visualize a skull fracture caused by a bullet, it is helpful to think of a wagon wheel: the wheel's hub is the point of entry or exit, and the spokes are the radiating fractures that extend out from the injury. There may also be concentric fractures—semicircular fractures that connect one radiating fracture with an adjacent radiating fracture, much like a spider's web. The fracturing property of bone lies somewhere between those of cast iron and granite rock. A .45-caliber bullet leaves a gun barrel at a speed of 565 miles per hour. A fracture moves through bone at about 3,400 miles per hour. In other words, the fracture travels roughly six times faster than the bullet. Thus, a bullet entering the skull from the victim's right side may send a radiating fracture up and over to the left side of the skull so fast that the bullet passes through the exiting fracture on the left side of the skull. This is true regardless of the caliber of the bullet or the grain of gunpowder the bullet contains.

Whether the injury is caused by a bullet or blunt force, the pattern of fractures in the skull provides evidence that helps determine the sequence of injury and the kind of instrument that caused the injury. One of the factors in determining the sequence of blunt force blows or gunshot wounds is that a fracture will not cross an existing fracture line; it will run into an existing fracture line and stop—terminate, in ballistics lingo—there. An easy way to replicate fractures in a human skull without using an actual skull is to hit a hard-boiled egg against your knuckle or strike it with a piece of tableware. If you do this with several eggs and a variety of implements, you'll be able to see that the fractures appear different, depending on what hit the egg. You'll also produce an accurate replica of cranial trauma.

. . .

After several days spent cleaning, drying, and reconstructing the skull, I began to see what had happened to the victim. When I'd rebuilt the victim's skull, using masking tape and glue, I took some X-rays of it, looking for evidence of a bullet. There was none. I felt confident reporting that the victim had not been shot in the head. The next step was to photograph the skull from several angles and, using red ink so that the marks would stand out, to draw in every fracture on a skeletal diagram. Once that was done I had a good visual representation of the trauma, down to the tiniest fracture line and broken bone.

The fact that the delicate bones around the nasal opening were broken but the adjacent bones, or the frontal (forehead) bone, was not implied that the victim had been kicked, kneed, or punched in the face. Without suggesting any particular sequence of blows, I referred to this facial trauma as Blow 1. The rest of the skull, however, revealed that more than just a fist, knee, or foot had been used. Picking up the skull and turning it ever so slowly, I noticed several areas of damage in a straight line extending from the lower jaw to the left orbit (eye socket). This I called Blow 2. It seemed that something slender, but heavy, had struck the left side of his face. Turning next to the victim's lower jaw, I found that he'd received an upward blow under the right edge of his chin; this was Blow 3. The damage in this area was shaped like an elongated circle, suggesting the shape of the implement used. Other damage was evident in the left side (Blow 4) and back of the head (Blow 5). One injury at the back of the head, in fact, left the unmistakable image of a square outlined with a circle in the occipital bone that would later match with the working end of an automotive torque wrench.

In an early interrogation, the suspect had told police that some men had jumped Taylor and had fled the scene. Only later, Campbell claimed, did he notice that his torque wrench was missing from his truck. This wrench, with hairs and blood matching Taylor's, was found five days later in a lava field, after Campbell described to the police the area in which he had hidden the wrench.

By the time I finished my analysis I felt confident that Taylor had been kicked, punched, or kneed in the face, and then struck several times on the head with a slender implement heavy enough to crush bone. This was all confirmed when the killer told authorities that he got into an argument with Taylor and struck his head five or six times. Campbell also described how he dragged Taylor by the left leg into the bushes. All the while Taylor was alive and looking right at him. Incredibly, Campbell says he didn't know that Taylor had died until he was arrested.

Although I was prepared to testify in court as to the victim's trauma, I was spared the trip. Faced with the evidence, Campbell changed his plea to "no contest" in a plea bargain in which prosecutors dropped the classification of the crime as especially heinous. He was sentenced in May 2004 to life in prison with the possibility of parole. But that wasn't the end of the case for Taylor's family.

A few days before Campbell was sentenced I received a call from the victim's brother-in-law in Tennessee. He asked when we would be able to send them the skull so it could be cremated and buried along with the rest of the body, which had been cremated in Hilo the previous year. I had to wait until sentencing was complete before calling back to discuss releasing the remains. Until that point the skull was evidence; the prosecutor's office had to wait for the case to be closed before releasing the remains. If Campbell had changed his mind about the plea bargain, I might have had to use the skull in court. Once Campbell was sentenced, I called Janice Taylor, one of Taylor's sisters, in Tennessee to discuss returning the skull. I suggested that we send it to a local mortuary for cremation and that we could then send the cremains to bury with the rest of him. After a few phone calls back and forth, that's what we did. On June 30, 2004, a courier from the medical examiner's office picked up Taylor's skull and sent it on to the same mortuary in Hilo that had cremated the rest of his body the previous year.

Before our conversations ended, Janice asked me some questions that I hadn't planned on answering, at least not without giving the answers some thought. Prosecutors had intentionally not provided her with a lot of detail, thinking that she might have to testify. "How many times was he hit?" she asked. "Was his head broken up? Was there a hole in his head? What do you mean when you say [you] 'reconstructed' the skull?" A description of the trauma that I saw in this skull was not going to be easy for family members to take. It was heartbreakingly difficult for both of us, but necessary nonetheless. Although I'd worked at two funeral homes, attended hundreds of funerals, and handled hundreds of dead bodies, it just doesn't get any easier to describe something as horrific as this crime to the victim's sister. I felt badly for having to go over some of the details, but, as in many cases, those who care about the deceased person want to hear it all. They don't want their feelings spared or details withheld simply because they may get upset. Taylor's sister even listened to the police recording of the 911 call her brother had made. As gruesome as it was, it was better to hear what he had actually said than to spend the rest of her life wondering.

Sobbing gently on the other end of the line, Janice listened to all I had to say. I told her how sorry I was that this had happened and that no one in my family had ever been killed or had endured such a tragedy. What I wanted her to know was that she was no longer talking to a forensic anthropologist working her brother's case, but to another human being who could do very little to help her in her grief.

A few months later I spoke again with Janice and learned that Michael was a master diver who loved to surf. Ironically, it was Campbell who had taught him to surf, and Makalawena Beach had been one of their favorite spots. Michael had visited Hawaii about a year before his death and fell in love with it. He moved to the Big Island of Hawaii in 2002 after selling his home on the mainland, hoping to open his own dive shop. He was tending bar in Hawaii at the time of his death.

A few weeks later I got an e-mail from Janice offering to let me hear the audiotape of her brother's call to 911 that the Kona police had given her. Taking a deep breath, I accepted the offer. I'd handled thousands of human skeletons and watched such reality shows as *Cops*, *America's Most Wanted*, and *CSI*. I thought I'd seen and heard it all, but this recording would teach me that I hadn't.

Within days I received the emergency dispatch cassette in the mail, along with a handwritten card, a typed letter that Janice had read to the judge before Campbell was sentenced, and two photographs—one of Michael vacationing in Hawaii and another of him and his four siblings in the family's backyard.

I took everything home after work that day and sat down in front of our stereo in the living room. I popped the tape into the player and, much to my surprise, found myself hesitating when it came to pushing the Play button. I sat there staring at the stereo, wondering what I was about to hear and how I would react. This was reality, not the pseudo-reality of prime-time TV. I had to force myself to push the Play button, to hear Michael's voice pleading for his life as he was beaten with a torque wrench. I'd held his bones in my hands, seen his photos, heard what a wonderful brother he was. "Do I really need to do this?" I asked myself. But I knew I had to listen, despite my trepidation. I grabbed a piece of paper to write on, scooted up closer to the stereo, and pushed the button. It was difficult for me to make out all of the words on the tape, but here's what I heard:

DISPATCHER: *"Hello?"*
MICHAEL: *"Yes. I'm being chased. I'm being killed. I'm being chased on the road ... Stop, Jason!"*
"Where are you?"
"He's trying to kill me!"
"Where are you?"
"Oh my God ... Oh my God!"
"Where are you?"
"We're past the airport!"
"Which airport?"
"Off down the road ... We're at Makalawena Beach ... What are you doing, man? No! Help!"
"Hello?"
"What are you doing, man?"
"Hello? Hello? Hello?"
"Stop! No! Jason, no! Help! Help! Help!"

"Sir, you have to tell me where you are so I can help you."
"What are you doing, man? Why? Why? Why?"
[The phone beeps several times and then a sustained beeping continues.]

The call lasted less than ninety seconds. I guess the phone was smashed to pieces at that point. I spent the next half hour replaying the tape as I tried to catch Michael's every word as he struggled to get away from his attacker. At no time could I make out Campbell's voice. There were several sickening thuds that to me sounded like a baseball bat hitting a tree.

Having heard this tape, I can tell you that the brutality depicted on reality shows doesn't come close to the real thing. I awoke three times that night, Michael's screams ringing in my ears.

19. THUNDERBOLTS AND LIBERATORS

They sleep beneath the shadows of the clouds, careless alike of sunshine or storm, each in the windowless palace of rest.
—ROBERT GREEN INGERSOLL, *Memorial Day Vision*

In 2003, U.S. search teams from the army's Criminal Investigation Division (CID) and several nongovernmental organizations (NGOs), guided by information provided by Iraqi witnesses, discovered mass graves holding the remains of an estimated ten thousand people outside of Baghdad. That discovery led to a phone call from the Armed Forces Medical Examiner's office in Washington, D.C., that for me would result in a three-week trip to Hungary and Russia—a classic example of what we at the CIL call the domino effect.

The call came Tuesday, June 3, 2003. The caller was Dr. Craig Mallak, the armed forces chief medical examiner. The CIL was to furnish four of our anthropologists for a recovery-and-identification mission to Iraq—a war zone. "Make sure they're all comfortable with shooting a sidearm," Mallak said. "And by the way, they'll have to wear helmets and flak jackets." I asked what kind of protection our anthropologists would have while working in Iraq. "Do you know what Bradley fighting vehicles are?" was Mallak's reply. I did. More than twenty-one feet long, ten feet wide, and nearly ten feet tall, Bradley tanks weigh twenty-five tons. A single unit costs more than three million dollars—not the kind of vehicle you'd use for a pleasure trip.

I went to the office next to mine to check in with my boss, Dr. Tom Holland. Together we looked over the CIL mission schedule and selected four physically fit anthropologists, all men, whom we could take off other work and send to Iraq. None had signed on to work in a war zone, but we would send them nonetheless. They'd have a few days to break the news to their wives or girlfriends; pack what they would need for a six-week trip; and get a battery of vaccinations, including anthrax and smallpox. We all knew that if they were going to have any adverse reactions to the shots, those would occur while they were in transit or already in Iraq.

If you stand a stack of dominoes on end, one after the other, and tip one over, the whole orderly arrangement tumbles. Similarly, if you schedule a crew of anthropologists to a variety of assignments and then change the assignment of even one of them, the whole schedule falls apart. That's what happened when we chose the four men who would go to Iraq; I was one of the dominoes that fell off schedule as a result. One Iraq-bound anthropologist was Dr. Andy Tyrrell, a gifted scientist who had been assigned to an upcoming mission to Hungary and Russia. I was that expedition's alternate. As it happened, we had already sent my passport to Washington for a Russian visa, just in case I would be needed. Now I'd have three days to finish what I'd started at work, pack up what I'd need for three weeks, and break the news to my wife that I was again leaving for a place halfway around the world.

The mass graves with which our folks were assisting had been located by local witnesses, CID staff, and NGOs that had been searching for them since the war began. One of our CIL anthropologists oversaw the excavation of the mass graves before assisting in a temporary mortuary outside Baghdad where he met with two other CIL forensic anthropologists. They were working out of tents in the desert; this, they believed, was safer than being in Baghdad. I knew it was an important mission, but that didn't ease my anxiety for the safety of our people who were going there. I'd seen videos of militants beheading people and forcing them to sit on grenades.

This was definitely not a place I wanted to visit. Luckily for me, Andy Tyrrell, whose place I'd be taking on the trip to Hungary and Russia, was experienced in digging up mass graves; he'd done it many times and was our prime choice to do it again.

My wife, Vara, took it like a trouper when I told her I'd be leaving Friday, although for her it meant three weeks of solitary dinners and three weekends alone. It also meant putting off a Saturday shopping trip to buy materials for a kitchen renovation project we'd been planning for a long time. Vara was glad I wasn't going to Iraq; that possibility scared her. I didn't tell her I might have to go if a second round was required. After eleven years of missions, I liked traveling less and less.

My trip would involve investigating several World War II crash sites and graves near Budapest, Hungary, and in the Russian Far East. We planned on about twelve days in Hungary and ten days in Russia, on the Kurile Islands off the southern tip of Kamchatka, Russia. This was a remote, isolated region just north of Japan that, until our visit, had not allowed visitors, especially Americans. Although the sites would be relatively easy to get to, the one in the Kuriles had me a bit concerned; we were to be accompanied by a hunter whose job it would be to ward off bears. The prospect of encountering a Russian bear became the last thing on my mind each night as I fell asleep. I kept imagining our pushing our way through dense vegetation when a bear pounced on me. The hunter would swing his rifle around, but, by that time, I'd be dead or, at the least, mauled. I'd seen bear attacks on television and knew it was best to assume they could attack without apparent provocation. I remember tossing and turning all night before I left and not being able to tell my wife why. The last thing I wanted was to worry her—again.

The team would consist of only three people. Major Aaron Tipton was the team leader, the person on our team representing the U.S. military—what we call a "green suiter." The team leader is responsible for logistics, getting us to and from the site safely each day, and coordinating work with the locals. Also on the team was a navy chief petty officer out of Washington,

D.C., named Dennis Friedbauer. He worked for the Joint Commission Search Directorate (JCSD), an offshoot of the U.S. office, concerned with U.S.–Russian research dealing with personnel listed as missing in action, primarily from World War II and the cold war. Dennis was trained as a Russian linguist, is a native speaker of Hungarian, and has relatives in Hungary. He had spent a lot of time researching aircraft losses in Hungary and had compiled a list of possible counties where U.S. aircraft, associated with missing American crew members, were lost. Dennis also had established contacts with what some might call relic hunters—war buffs and World War II aircraft historians who had located several U.S. crash sites in Hungary and, in some cases, recovered human remains and identifiable aircraft wreckage. The United States had yet to locate some of these crash sites in Hungary. Our contact with several people in Hungary, including Nandor Mohos, who had found many U.S. crash sites, Dennis was an analyst and historian, not a field investigator of crash sites and graves. I was hoping he would lead us in the right direction. The three of us pooled our talents to form the investigation team.

Although illegal, scavenging aircraft crash sites and graves in Europe is a popular pastime, as it is in Vietnam. Groups of amateur historians scour the countryside with shovels and metal detectors in hand. Once they find a site, they spend their own time and sometimes substantial amounts of money to recover wreckage, remains, and other artifacts. When we visited Nandor's small house, he took us to his bedroom and showed us a .50-caliber machine gun that he'd removed from one crash site and several pillowcase-size pieces of aircraft fuselage (aircraft skin, as we call it), with tail numbers on it from U.S. crash sites. Sometimes the searchers help us find crash sites, and sometimes, when they remove the wreckage and sell it, they hurt our efforts. In this instance, without their help, we might not have found the sites.

The number and type of specialists on our teams depends on the type of mission planned. For example, if we're going to excavate an aircraft crash site, we'll take an anthropologist (a necessary position on all search-and-recovery teams, regardless of what we're going to do); a military officer who deals with the logistics of getting to and from the site, handles payments for land and crops that we disturb, coordinates with locals for workers to help dig the site, and acts as liaison with local authorities; an explosive ordnance disposal technician who deals with the bombs and explosives that we encounter on top of the ground or that we find with our pickaxes and shovels; a medic; an interpreter who speaks the local language; a communications expert who sets up and maintains radio and phone communication with the outside world; and two or three mortuary affairs specialists trained in handling of human remains. Since this mission was solely to survey four sites in a relatively safe environment, the American part of the team was whittled down to a minimum of two people from the CIL and Dennis, the interpreter, from Washington, D.C. The key members this time were the anthropologist and the interpreter, although Major Tipton's skills in map reading and experience in the jungles of Southeast Asia with other search-and-recovery teams made him a great asset. Besides being a West Point graduate, he was a world traveler and adventurer in his own right.

Aaron and I left Hawaii on different days and met at the hotel in Washington. Dennis was already in Hungary. This was to be our first mission as a team, and we would climb the inevitable learning curve as we went along, starting with our first breakfast together and the drive to the site. We were delayed in D.C., waiting for our Russian visas to be approved. Finally we decided to move on and let our visas catch up with us. We were four days behind schedule when we arrived in Hungary. Working for the U.S. government had taught me patience and flexibility. As the saying goes, part of the job is to "hurry up and wait."

We checked into the Intercontinental Hotel in Budapest and virtually passed out on our beds. We had been on the road for more than a day without sleeping. We'd had to go by way of England, with an eight-hour layover between flights at Heathrow. To add to my discomfort, I was nursing a stomach virus that I'd picked up somewhere along the way, and jet lag, which isn't normally a problem for me, was kicking my butt.

On the positive side, the view of the Danube River from my hotel room was spectacular, and the city surprised me to no end. I knew it would be old, but I never expected it to be so picturesque. Apart from the ubiquitous graffiti, it was exceptionally clean; its narrow, tree-lined streets were well maintained. What impressed me most were the ornately decorated buildings with classic Romanesque and Gothic architecture. And the food— wow! I was in heaven and happily tossed my intention to lose weight on this trip out the window.

Our first trip was a two-hour drive from the center of Budapest to a crash site outside the small village of Nemesvita. Dennis and local historian Nandor Mohos had done most of the leg work in lining up witnesses who had seen an American B-24 Liberator bomber get shot down and crash in the hillside on June 30, 1944. We climbed into our rented Alfa Romeo, armed with a road map, and made our way along the winding country roads to a small pond. The Liberator's crash had formed a large crater that later filled in with ground water. We call such craters "ponds" because they are often stocked with fish, shrimp, or the like. Our destination was on property owned by a local hunting club, and on the way we'd picked up Nandor, an engineer with Nokia, who had run down nearly half the Liberator crash sites in Hungary. Also accompanying us was László Hangodi. Like Nandor, László was a military history buff who had been collecting information and wreckage from shot-down aircraft since he was a child. László was also a teacher and professionally trained archaeologist.

Witnesses to the incident reported seeing a German Messerschmitt 109 strafing the bomber, whose pilot was trying to evade it. In the crash record is a July 3, 1944, letter from First Lieutenant Kennon Sorgenfrei, an American in another Liberator who reported seeing about fifty Messerschmitt 210s peel off in waves of eight and come in firing. Unfortunately, bombers are not built for dog fights, and Messerschmitts are. Nandor later gave me five color photographs, taken by a hiker, of the Liberator being trailed by the Messerschmitt before crashing and burning. One photo, yellowed by age, shows the bomber coming in just above the tree line as a crewman falls to earth just behind it, under a fully deployed parachute. The last photo shows a large fireball on the ground. The Messerschmitt is nowhere to be seen. Seven of the U.S. crewmen parachuted from the aircraft that day and were taken prisoner by the Germans. Some were hospitalized for their injuries and later released. One crewman with dog tags was found dead near the crash site, and another died when his parachute failed to open. We were there hoping to find the airplane and recover the remains of missing tail gunner Staff Sergeant Martin F. Troy, thirty-two, of Norwalk, Connecticut, who was believed to have gone down with the plane.

The supposed Liberator crash site was in a dense stand of willow trees. We drove ten minutes along a narrow grassy path with ruts so deep that the Alfa bottomed out several times. We soon realized that our rental car was not designed to be loaded with five people and used as a Jeep. To its credit, the car got all of us—and itself—there in one piece. We parked in a large open field and changed clothes.

Aaron and I came equipped for the walk, but changed into thicker pants to shield us against the thornbushes. We always try to anticipate the type of terrain and clothing we'll need, but sometimes have to sacrifice one thing for another. In this case it was hot as heck and jeans add to the heat, but the thornbushes and tall grasses that were about to cut our unprotected skin prompted us to don our boots, jeans, long-sleeve shirts, and hats. We'd left our four-star hotel dressed more presentably so that guests wouldn't complain. We often raise eyebrows walking through hotel lobbies dressed in muddy combat boots and clothes reeking of jet fuel, no matter how unobtrusive we try to be as we make it to our rooms. Especially in Southeast Asia, where we so often work, hotel managers sometimes ask us to change before we return to the hotel.

Approaching midday, as we headed into the tall elephant grasses, stinging nettles, and thornbushes, the sun overhead had brought the temperature into the nineties. At times we had to raise our hands over our heads like prisoners of war to avoid the razor-sharp grasses and nettles that struck at our arms and faces like so many knives. Other times we crossed our arms in front of our faces to protect them, but the grasses would snap back from the guy walking ahead. Like skillfully wielded weapons, the tall, sharp grasses reached between our arms and still managed to cut us on the hands, cheeks, ears, and neck. We try our best not to look like we've lost a battle with a morning razor, but it's usually a futile effort. We walked through the dense brush, past a pile of corncobs used to lure wild boars out of the woods where hunters wait to shoot them, and turned left at a decaying dog carcass before coming to an hourglass-shaped crash crater. Whatever had crashed there had gouged out the mud about two meters deep, twenty-five meters long, and eight meters wide. The resulting pond was stagnant, filled with mosquito larvae and algae, and surrounded by large, drooping willows. The scene reminded me more of a Florida swamp than a hunt club in Hungary.

We began taking measurements and searching the banks and soft muck for pieces of the airplane and crew. Although Nandor and László had found a few shards of what was probably human bone, we still had to make a positive identification of the airplane. While we'd hoped to find a piece of wreckage with U.S. markings, a dog tag, or remains, we found only what might be part of a World War II flak vest and a few small pieces of aircraft wreckage outside the crater. The rest was probably buried ten or fifteen feet deep in the soft mud. Finding so little at the crash site didn't surprise me since local residents had had nearly sixty years to salvage whatever was there. I have a magazine article in my mission packet showing a man pulling out a propeller from the crash crater in 1995. I had the photo with me, but the people who pulled out the propeller had sold it for scrap to an unknown individual, and it wasn't available to us. The vegetation and area had changed over the years, and we weren't able to tell exactly where the man in the picture had been standing in relation to the pond.

Taking measurements and photographs consumed about an hour. By that time we'd had all we could take of the swarming, stinging insects, and we headed back to the car. Although we hadn't found any significant wreckage, we were a little more confident that it was an American crash site that warranted an archaeological excavation. That would be the only way to answer the question of what had crashed there in 1944. My money was on a Liberator named, ironically, *Miss Fortune.*

Back at the hotel, Aaron and I wrote up our findings and recommended the site for excavation by a CIL recovery team. The answer to this mystery airplane would have to wait a few more months. Still, it felt good to know I had helped take a step toward closure for a family who had waited nearly sixty years.

I was hoping to return with a full-size team to excavate this crash site in the autumn of 2005. But because that would probably require multiple missions over several months, and I couldn't afford that much time away from the lab, I reluctantly gave the site to another CIL anthropologist and took on a shorter mission. In effect, I traded a Liberator crash site for the opportunity to excavate some possibly American graves in Hungary, Belgium, and Poland.

The following day, Dennis, Aaron, and I climbed back into the Alfa and drove southwest for an hour to the town of Szabadegyhaza to pick up a man named Ballai, who brought us to the factory where his friend, László Lamperth, worked. Lamperth looked more like a Viking out of a movie than a Hungarian machinist. He was a big man with gray hair and a thick white mustache. The factory in which he worked manufactured Everclear alcohol. After introducing ourselves and getting some details of the shoot down—a different one than we'd investigated the previous day—we drove to his small apartment to examine pieces of the aircraft he'd collected from the crash site when he was a child. His school had organized a class outing to the site; they asked the children to collect wreckage. It was certainly not the kind of class trip American children are accustomed to, but it was 1950, and the cold war was in full swing.

Although he was a factory worker living on a moderate salary, László's apartment was nicely equipped with seventies-style furniture and countless doilies. He had decorated the walls with his many hunting trophies— deer and moose antlers at the end of the hall, and a large wild boar skin in the front room. We were visiting so we could look at the aircraft wreckage and see if it had any serial numbers that would help us identify the airplane, and there were two possibilities: an American B-24 Liberator or a P-47 Thunderbolt. László believed it was a B-24. He said it had crashed into a large open field now used to grow beans, about one hundred meters from the highway and a small cemetery dating back to the 1800s. On the other hand, a P-47 Thunderbolt was shot down on April 13, 1944, near the village of Szabadegyhaza while on an escort mission from Italy to Budapest. Another American fighter pilot saw a German Messerschmitt following this Thunderbolt as it climbed down to about five thousand feet, where it disappeared. First Lieutenant Richard Malloy was lost in that crash. A 1947 investigation team recovered some debris from this P-47 from a deep crash crater in a large field, but found no human remains.

Sitting in László's living room, Aaron and I carefully examined four small pieces of twisted wreckage. I'm always amazed at how steel and aircraft aluminum can be torn like paper. Little wonder I don't see much point in wearing a seat belt when I fly, at least in terms of how it would serve me if we crashed. But I figure the cushioned seat would be gentler on my body than the aluminum of the fuselage, if I were left to bounce around the aircraft like a billiard ball. Every piece of wreckage was no bigger than a driver's license; each showed the effect of the violent crash. We photographed every fragment, placing it on grid paper to show its size, and recorded the tiny numbers and characters stamped on each piece. One piece was olive green and bore what looked to be an overlapping "RR." We guessed it was the logo of the Rolls-Royce company, which made many aircraft engines during World War II.

With Aaron driving, Dennis in the front passenger seat serving as navigator, and Mr. Ballia, László, and me scrunched into the backseat of the Alfa, we drove three kilometers to the garage where László stored not only his prized Peugeot, but also a small cardboard box of twisted metal he'd recovered from the crash site. Again Aaron and I sifted through the twisted metal looking for American markings and colors that might help identify the aircraft. All we could find were three pieces of metal—one painted a brilliant blue, one painted green and white, and one painted red. That didn't tell us anything definitive about the aircraft, but we now knew something about its appearance. It wasn't much to go on, but this information took us one step closer to identifying the aircraft and deciding whether we should recommend this crash site for excavation. It was still too early in the investigation to decide. We needed more evidence.

László led us to the bean field, a few minutes from where he lived. The heat was horrendous for someone like me, accustomed to Hawaii's moderate climate. We walked about two hundred meters into the field. No one could have guessed that an airplane had crashed in the area or that its Rolls-Royce engine was probably buried a few meters below the surface. What had once been a deep crater had long ago been filled in so the field could be cultivated. Over the years villagers had removed the largest pieces of the airplane and sold them for scrap, and all visible evidence of the terrible event had been erased.

The five of us walked the field looking for pieces of the airplane, personal effects, and human remains, but we found only a few pieces of twisted metal. When a plane crashes in a field, even one that is cultivated every year, the landowners find themselves unearthing pieces of wreckage for years to come. The presence of scrap becomes so commonplace that they often begin to consider it more of a nuisance than a salable trophy. Sometimes, however, they stumble upon dog tags, belt buckles, and bombs. We once removed eighteen hundred-pound bombs from a crash site I worked on in Vietnam. Later, Senator John Kerry visited it. I'm still amazed at how much wreckage remains behind even after a landowner clears an aircraft crash site of wreckage to cultivate it. Sometimes we recover enough debris to equal a car in size and weight; other times we're lucky if we get five or ten bucketfulls. In Southeast Asia, we often recover many thousands of small pieces of wreckage within the upper two or three feet of ground; the largest and heaviest pieces of wreckage plow deeper, and the landowners cultivating crops have no need to go that deep. If a plane crashes into the ground and forms a deep crater, the landowner may remove as much of the wreckage as possible before filling it in with dirt. Other times, they remove what they can and turn it into a pond or reservoir for watering their crops. If there's enough clay in the ground to hold the water, they may let the hole fill with rainwater over time.

We locate crash sites by doing either a visual walking survey looking for pieces of aircraft wreckage, which are usually easy to see, or going over the ground with a metal detector. In the latter case, we mark the location of each metal detector hit with brightly colored surveyor's pin flags and use wooden stakes and string to mark out an area that encompasses most of the pin flags. That's how we know where to start digging. We also look for pieces of wreckage specifically from the cockpit—canopy Plexiglas, instrumentation, ejection seat parts, parachute equipment—since we're looking for the occupants. Where we find cockpit and flight suit, we're likely to find the crew. These are also precisely the kinds of things amateur historian groups are looking for.

Clearly the aircraft had met its end at a tremendous speed and had broken into thousands of pieces. Unfortunately, we found nothing else lying about on the ground that would help us identify the aircraft. The next step was to interview a man who had witnessed the aerial fight and shoot down. He was the father of the mayor of the town of Arpad. We took László back to work and headed to the mayor's house. Turning left down a narrow tree-lined street, we saw our witness standing in his side yard waiting for us. We grabbed our notepads, introduced ourselves to Mayor József Smicsek and his wife, and began the interview. The diminutive seventy-nine-year-old man sat across from us in his favorite armchair and recounted what he had seen around noon on April 13, 1944. The incident had made such an impression on him that he even recalled the day was a Monday. As his wife stood by in the hallway, he took us back in time.

He said that several U.S. airplanes were strafing the area when German antiaircraft fire from the ground hit one of them. The plane, smoke trailing from its fuselage, peeled away from the group and came in at a low angle and altitude before nose-diving into the ground. He got to the crash site within thirty minutes and began looking for body parts and pieces of uniforms, but found none. Villagers who witnessed the incident didn't report seeing any parachutes or anyone bailing out of the plane before it crashed and burned. German soldiers searched the wreckage for days looking for bodies and anything of intelligence value.

I could tell that the war had affected Mr. Smicsek emotionally as he drifted off to another incident involving American aircrew from a downed B-24 Liberator. He said that the Germans had captured several "very handsome" young Americans and had shot one of them in the ankle as he attempted to escape. A German soldier chased after the wounded crewman and shot him in the back, killing him. Mr. Smicsek vividly described the dying man's blood freezing on his shirt. His jaw tightened as he recounted how he admonished the Germans, saying they could not injure the unarmed Americans, as they were prisoners of war. He quickly grew fond of the American prisoners and did his best to ensure their safety.

He was sitting across from me wearing an unbuttoned shirt, and I noticed a large vertical scar on his stomach. I didn't ask what had happened, but he soon told us that the Germans had taken him prisoner and badly mistreated him. His seething hatred for them slowly made its way to the surface, much the same as his determination to tell his story. This man had befriended Americans during the war and had suffered for it. My feelings for him were of sympathy and respect.

Gently, we eased Mr. Smicsek back on track, and, after only a few questions, he gave us some critical pieces of the puzzle. "What color was the airplane? Were there any markings on it?" I asked. "It was gray, and it had big numbers on it," he replied. "How many engines did the airplane have and where were they?" "One in front," he replied.

Bingo! The airplane could not have been a Liberator because they have four engines, two on each wing. A P-47 Thunderbolt, however, has one nose engine.

At that point, we could rule out the B-24 Mr. László had described, and rule in the P-47 shot down around noon on April 13, 1944. The whereabouts of the twenty-one-year-old pilot, First Lieutenant Richard K. Malloy of Dallas, Texas, are unknown; his remains have never been identified. Mr. Smicsek's memory and precise information, combined with the few pieces of wreckage at Mr. László's house, were enough to induce Major Tipton and me to recommend excavating the site in the bean field. Both of us hoped that we'd finally found a Liberator and a Thunderbolt and, more important, that two Americans were one step closer to home.

At the end of the mission we all boarded an Aeroflot A-310 and made the eight-and-a-half-hour flight to Petropavlovsk near the southern tip of the Kamchatka Peninsula. On this part of the mission we would try to find the grave of an American shot down in a B-24 in June 1945, just two months before the end of World War II.

Two Americans had parachuted from the plummeting aircraft and somehow made their way to a rubber raft floating in the ocean. Such rafts open automatically when they hit the water. The men drifted for two days before they were picked up by a Japanese ship. One man had died of his injuries the first night, and the Japanese took the second man prisoner. We had several reports that they buried the dead American in one of two Japanese cemeteries on Shimushu Island, just south of Kamchatka Peninsula. We knew it would be difficult to find the man's grave; no one knew where the American had been buried. The grave markers were wooden crosses and probably hadn't survived nearly sixty years of harsh winters. Nonetheless, we were there to investigate the case on the off chance of finding someone who had more information on the grave. Failing that, we hoped to find anything suggesting that an American was buried there. But without grave markers, we had no way of knowing where to begin digging.

The second site we were to investigate was what some analysts believed was a B-24 crash site in a rugged forest region 73 miles (120 kilometers) south of Petropavlovsk-Kamchatsky, a popular tourist area for Russians and passing cruise liners en route to Alaska. All we knew was that someone had found aircraft wreckage that might be from an American plane. A Russian pilot flying overhead in 2002 had spotted the wreckage and reported the site to Russian authorities. It was just as possible, however, that the plane was Russian or Japanese. We were there to find out. But first, with the help of a local guide, our team would have to make its way through dense underbrush to the crash site and, like the two sites in Hungary, find wreckage with serial numbers on it. The biggest difference between this site and any other I'd worked was that this one was said to be crawling with bears.

We arrived in Kamchatka on a cold, dreary day, checked into our modest hotel, and began planning our next step. The area was ringed in snow-capped mountains—picture postcard beautiful. Then the clouds rolled in, followed by more and even thicker ones. We would be flying in a Soviet Mi-8 helicopter four hours over water to and from Shimushu, and another two hours to the inland site. Obviously, we didn't want to fly into a mountainside in foggy weather, or get stuck on Shimushu if clouds suddenly rolled in. While we'd come prepared for delays, we were desperately hoping for a few clear days so we could complete the two investigations and get home. To make things even more complicated, the first four days were filled with ever-changing negotiations with the Russians. On the fifth day the sky cleared and the Russians agreed to let us fly, but I didn't get to go with the team. I had to leave early to attend the briefing of an MIA's family in Washington, D.C. Because of this appointment, the team would go to the B-24 crash site and cemetery without me.

Ordinarily, anthropologists are not part of an investigation team, as I was in this case. The role of the investigation is to collect information and locate crash sites and graves, not excavate them. I often tell people to think of a crash site or grave as a gigantic target on the ground. The investigation team's job is to locate any part of the target. The excavation team—the one that includes an anthropologist—is responsible for finding the bull's-eye, the cockpit or the grave. Put another way, the investigation team gets us to the site and the excavation team recovers the evidence. Anthropologists must be present for excavations, but not for investigations. I got to go to Russia only because I was already in Hungary.

The crash site turned out to be that of a U.S. Navy PV-1 Ventura that had smashed into the side of a hill in an uninhabited ecological preserve. Aaron told me that to get to the PV-1 crash site they had to walk hunched over for about an hour as they made their way through thornbushes and tightly woven shrubs. Aaron said it was the most difficult site he had ever visited—and remember, he'd just come from Hungary and the razor-sharp grasses. The team recommended further research on the site. Later, they would learn that the crash was an operational loss, not one shot down in battle. None of its crew, who bailed out before putting it on autopilot, was missing. They apparently had engine trouble and put the plane on autopilot before bailing out.

The bears? The Russians decided not to send a hunter with the team, but nobody saw any bears, and nobody was disappointed.

As to the Japanese cemetery on Shimushu Island, the team flew to the site and surveyed the area for American graves the day I flew out of Moscow. Other than a family that maintains a lighthouse on its northern end, the treeless island is uninhabited. The cemetery, which had a Japanese monument on it, was situated on gently rolling and lush hills along the shore and was surrounded by a concrete railing with an inner walkway. Unfortunately, the Japanese had gotten there first and exhumed the graves of their fallen comrades in 1992 and 1995, taking them back to Japan. The wooden grave markers were gone and, with them, the possibility of finding American graves. As for the second site, the team again hacked their way through the dense brush and located aircraft wreckage from a navy airplane. The next step will be to weigh the findings of both sites and go from there.

As much as I may complain about the physical discomforts of searching for crash sites and graves, I love this work. I regretted having to fly out of Kamchatka on June 25, before we finished the job. I'd traveled twenty-three time zones and thirty-three hours in the air, only to sit in a dingy hotel in the Russian Far East. But sometimes that's just how it goes.

20. THE BONE TRADERS

On what strange stuff Ambition feeds!
—ELIZA COOK, *Thomas Hood*

Late in June 2004 word came from the U.S. MIA Office in Hanoi that officials had arrested two Vietnamese citizens for dealing in human remains. Buying and selling remains in Vietnam can be a lucrative endeavor, if the police don't catch you. If they do, it could mean years of imprisonment at hard labor. Although the Vietnamese deal with such practices severely, they often have a hard time catching bone traders, as they are known. Suspects of course deny any involvement in illegal activity, claiming that they found the bones and teeth while plowing their fields, that a neighbor gave them the remains, that they believe them to be the bones of Vietnamese people, that they were planning to give the remains a proper burial. The truth is that some individuals vandalize graves under cover of darkness, in hope of turning a profit.

Many Vietnamese citizens have the mistaken belief that the United States will pay them if they turn over American remains. The reward, according to the grapevine, ranges from thousands to millions of American dollars, or to moving the finder and family to California or New York. In truth, the U.S. government doesn't pay citizens for remains. If it did, that would put a price on the head of every American traveler to Vietnam and the other countries that were entangled in the Vietnam War. Still, for some people in Southeast Asia, dealing in remains is a cottage industry, born of abject poverty and nourished by the wartime disappearance of more than two thousand American military personnel. Most of those listed as missing in action were shot down in helicopters or airplanes. Some were killed on the ground during combat; others were lured from their posts and captured. Some deserted, and the fate of the rest remains unknown. Often retrieval missions had to wait until the fighting died down, when it was safer to send in a search-and-rescue team. As we are writing this, the government is still trying to account for more than 1,800 young soldiers, sailors, airmen, and Marines who went missing in Vietnam, Laos, and Cambodia, in addition to the more than 8,100 missing men from the Korean conflict, 78,000 from World War II, and 120 from the cold war.

The search for remains is the responsibility of eighteen CIL search-and-recovery teams, armed with state-of-the-art equipment and specialized knowledge of finding fragmentary remains. It's a daunting task that takes teams of investigators to the farthest reaches of the globe—to the peaks of Tibet, the glaciers of Greenland, the valleys and rivers of Europe, the lakes of Africa, the rice fields and jungles of Southeast Asia and Papua New Guinea, and even into congested cities. Our teams go anywhere there is the slightest chance we can find our missing service members and bring them home for burial on American soil.

The first step in finding America's missing warriors is to investigate war records, documents, and photographs showing where they were last seen, what they were doing, and what might have happened to them at the time they were lost. Armed with this historical information, investigation teams scour hills, jungles, mountains, and rivers for evidence, which can come as dog tags, rings, identification cards, shreds of flight suits, pilot-related equipment such as oxygen masks and helmets, and pieces of the aircraft. We are always aware that time is working against us. Acidic soils destroy bones and teeth, villagers cart off pieces of the aircraft, and torrential rains and scorching heat move remains and destroy them. The combined forces of human beings and nature often leave only a few pieces of remains for us to recover.

Once an investigation team finds evidence of the likely location of remains, we launch a larger search-and-recovery team to excavate the site, no matter where it is or how little might be found after so many decades. Typically, a team comprises a variety of specialists—a medic, a radio operator, an explosive ordnance technician, a linguist, a photographer, a mortuary affairs expert, a military logistician (who serves as the team leader), and an anthropologist (designated as the recovery leader). Search-and-recovery teams bring with them enough equipment, food, bottled water, and camp gear to sustain themselves for a month or more in some of the most remote areas of the world as they excavate crash sites or graves, peeling back the years inch by painstaking inch. Teams are occasionally fortunate enough to stay in hotels or guesthouses. Most, however, sleep in tents, cook their own food, shower with bottled water or bathe in jungle streams, and read by a flickering lightbulb powered by a generator. Imagine how strange it must be for Vietnamese villagers watching us at work, and at rest. In comparison, they usually lead an even more spartan existence, carrying water home every day in buckets, only slightly familiar with electricity and phones. The home life of a team member is worlds away from what those who observe us could ever imagine. We leave behind not only our families, but also just about everything to which we've become accustomed—television, refrigerators, supermarkets, gas stations, and physical comfort. Base camping, as we call it, is a lonely and sometimes dangerous existence. The work is backbreaking, but totally rewarding. During my time at the CIL, I've done more than thirty missions to Southeast Asia, Europe, and Japan, and I wouldn't trade those experiences for anything— except, sometimes, an ice-cold Coke after a hard day's work in the jungle.

The bone traders in Vietnam have spent considerable time and money honing their skills. Still, try as they might they can't make Vietnamese remains look like those of a white, a black, or an Asian American. As hard as they try to outwit us, even learning from their own mistakes, we try even harder to keep them in check. Actually, it's not that difficult to stay one step ahead of them, given advancements in forensic anthropology and the expertise that CIL anthropologists have developed over the years by examining Vietnamese bones and teeth from the perspective of a scientist. I think most Vietnamese remains traders would be astonished to know that we can usually tell within minutes if the remains they have brought us are those of an indigenous Vietnamese person.

Since 1992, I've served as forensic anthropologist at more than half of the fifty-eight joint forensic reviews held in Hanoi, and ten other field reviews in Southeast Asia, Korea, Europe, and Okinawa. The typical Vietnam scenario is that someone turns in a small piece of bone or tooth along with a dog tag or dog tag rubbing on paper, along with a story that they were digging in their rice field or searching for wood in the mountains when they stumbled upon the remains. The objects, which we examine and photograph, are presented as a small sample of what the individual has uncovered. Often the piece of bone has sawed edges, suggesting that there is more where this came from. The sample is said to be a sign of good faith, proof that the rest of the skeleton—or many skeletons—will be available to us at a price. Often they say they know the remains are American "because they're so big." At that point they learn from us that the United States doesn't pay citizens for remains. After hearing that they won't be moving to San Francisco or New York, they take their alleged American remains home and try to sell them to someone else, or try again a few years later to pass them off as American remains at another forensic review. Persistence, in this case, does not pay off. However, not all people bringing in remains are bone traders, nor are they all expecting payment. Some Vietnamese turn in remains believing and hoping that they're sending home another American. They, too, may have lost a loved one in war and know the pain and anguish of loss.

Another route to the examination of remains occurs when the person who found them notifies the local police, who in turn notify district and province officials, who coordinate the next steps in the process. At some point up the leadership ladder, the Vietnamese Office for Seeking Missing Persons (VNOSMP) in Hanoi or Saigon is contacted; that office in turn contacts the U.S. MIA Office, the CIL's satellite in Hanoi. There are two options for handling suspected American remains. The preferred method is for the VNOSMP to send the remains to Hanoi, where a joint forensic review, consisting of an American anthropologist and dentist from the CIL and Vietnamese physicians from the Institute of Forensic Medicine, will examine them. The two teams work independently of each other in the small Hanoi laboratory. At the end of the review, which usually lasts two days, they sit down together at a long conference table and discuss their findings. Then they draft formal documentation to turn over with the remains to U.S. authorities. The second option is to have a smaller field review wherever the remains are being held, usually in one of the larger cities. Typically, remains brought in by Vietnamese citizens from the central and northern provinces go to Hanoi for examination while those from the southern provinces go to Saigon.

Remains selected for repatriation are put into aluminum transfer cases draped with American flags at Noi Bai Airport in Hanoi and usually flown aboard a U.S. C-141 airplane to Guam, their first stop on U.S. soil, and then on to Hawaii and the CIL for complete forensic analysis. Once they are identified, the remains are flown home to family members, where they receive proper burial, with full military honors. This final leg of the journey is what all family members yearn for and expect from their government.

Unfortunately, most of the remains presented by bone traders prove to be Vietnamese citizens. Most are elderly; some are children. Many were dug up in local cemeteries to be sold to Vietnamese citizens as American relics. Nonetheless, although we are familiar with the practice, that doesn't stop U.S. authorities from examining every case, whether it is a complete skeleton or a small piece of bone or tooth. Over the years we've seen hundreds of such specimens. The bone traders seem unaware that we can differentiate between human and animal bones, and even distinguish among those of a dog, cow, pig, or deer. So far, none of the remains I've examined that bone dealers have brought us have turned out to be American. Sometimes we even see bits of plastic, stone, wood, coral, and even metal. It's easy to dismiss the dealers as greedy villains, but it gets harder when I remind myself that extreme poverty is their main motivation. If they're lucky, they'll pass off the bones as possible American remains, but they still won't see a dime for their efforts. At best they'll receive a sincere "thank you" and a handshake, but no money or green card will come their way. And if they're out digging up local cemeteries, they might just land in jail.

Accompanied by Vietnamese translator and analyst Jim Coyle from the CIL, I arrived in Saigon, now renamed Ho Chi Minh City, Vietnam's largest city by population and area, on July 11. We were scheduled to meet with local authorities from Hanoi and the deputy chief of the Saigon police the following day. Forensic dentist Ken Dunn would catch up with us at the Caravelle Hotel in the heart of Saigon on July 13, his trip having been delayed because while he was on leave his passport had expired. We had come to Saigon to see if any of the remains in forty-two boxes confiscated by Vietnamese authorities could be those of Americans. I could probably determine if the remains came from Vietnam War crash sites or graves or from Vietnamese cemeteries, and the time since death in either case. Lastly, I could tell the Vietnamese authorities how many deceased were men, how many were women, and how many were children. Meanwhile, two Vietnamese citizens waited in jail for the results of our work. The irony was that the authorities caught one of the prisoners dealing in remains in the late 1980s. At that time, he had spent three years in jail for his activities. Here he was again, not a bit wiser from that experience, about to suffer an even harsher punishment if these remains were found to have been illegally obtained.

Staring out of my twentieth-floor hotel window on the day that I arrived, I found myself wondering what Saigon had looked like during the war. Down below, at street level, I could see the historic opera house with its arched facade and majestic outdoor balconies, and the Continental and Rex Hotels, where war correspondents and soldiers met. During rush hour many motorcycles zipped through the streets, reminding me of red blood cells pushed through human arteries by a beating heart. It was a typical Sunday in Saigon. I saw young brides and wedding parties posing for photographs on the steps of the opera house. Two blocks away was Notre

Dame, the Catholic church, with its colorful rose window and twin spires topped with crosses. Farther along were the post office and Peoples Committee building with the ubiquitous fading yellow pastel exteriors. These were the structures and sites that American troops saw in the sixties and seventies. What they didn't get to see then were the Kentucky Fried Chicken off to my right; the twenty-floor Diamond Plaza shopping center; and the Hyatt Hotel at the corner, still under construction. Saigon was changing.

At our meeting we learned that the remains were being held in Dong Nai Province, a forty-five-minute drive south from Saigon. The plan was to leave our hotel each morning at seven A.M. to beat the traffic, begin work at eight, and stop at two-thirty or three. Having to sort and lay out the skeletons of fifty people—that's more than ten thousand individual bones—in anatomical order, is not an easy task for one person. The task was going to tax my physical stamina and brain; ten skeletons are about all one person can do in a day.

But as the work drew nearer, I grew eager to get started. This would be the largest single cache of skeletons that anyone at the CIL had looked at in more than ten years. The plan was that while I laid out the bones, Dr. Dunn would examine the teeth for fillings, crowns, or root canals, looking for evidence the dental work had been done in the States. Jim's job would be to check information on the dog tags to see if any were associated with an unaccounted-for American. I expected it would take the three of us eight to ten days to complete the analysis. As it turned out, with a little training in identifying and siding bones—that is, determining whether a bone came from the left or right side of the body—Jim and Ken were a big help in laying out the remains, and we finished in half the time.

The examination took place in a long room the size of a banquet hall at one corner of the temporary holding facility of the Dong Nai security office, the equivalent to a minimum-security jail. A guardhouse stood at the entrance to the compound, which was surrounded by a seven-foot-high concrete wall that could be easily scaled. The prisoners—perhaps detainees is a more accurate term, since these people hadn't yet gone to court or been convicted—wore uniforms marked with black-and-white vertical stripes, the same as those worn by American POWs during the war. Dressed in their unique garb, they would be easy to recognize on the street if they tried to escape.

The room in which we were to work held fifteen wooden cafeteria-style tables, some of which bore children's graffiti, suggesting they had been used in a school. Many folding chairs were tucked into a corner, out of our way. We pulled four of the tables together to make a surface large enough to hold remains from two containers at a time. We laid the bones out in anatomical order and did our examination under the watchful eyes of several policemen and government officials. The brown wooden tables were about the same color as the bones, so we had to cover the tables with white sheets to make the remains easy to see when we photographed them. Three prisoners—a young man, a middle-age man, and a middle-age woman who never smiled—opened the boxes of remains for us and bagged them up each day when we were finished.

Only on the last day of our examination did I learn that the woman was the other half of the suspected remains-dealing team. Authorities had recovered all of the remains from her house in Dong Nai. I guessed she was going to have a hard time convincing people she didn't know what was going on. To my knowledge, this was her first arrest for dealing in remains, so she was looking at only a couple of years behind bars. An older man whom I would meet a few days later, however, was a repeat offender. He was facing a much harsher sentence.

The prisoners seemed to have complete freedom moving about in the exam room, and the side and front doors were always open to the outside, but the windows were covered in a latticework of steel bars. The examination ran from Tuesday through Friday, and we then had the weekend off. The Vietnamese seemed to have adopted the Western-style workweek. While we would have preferred to work the weekend and get home faster, the enforced time away from the compound gave our bodies a much-needed rest—bending over to lay out bones for hours on end is hard on the back and legs—and time to catch up on our reports.

The security force had placed the bags of remains in cardboard boxes numbered from one to forty-two. Each box held from one to four red cloth bags with white zippers. Once we laid out the contents of a bag, barefoot Ken climbed up on the table and took a bird's-eye view photo of them. We took additional photographs of anything unusual. We also made notes on the remains and compiled a biological profile of the individual's age, race, sex, trauma, evidence of disease, and any signs of storage or sawing. It took us anywhere from ten to thirty minutes to examine the contents of each bag, another five to ten minutes to write it up and for Ken to photograph it, and then a similar amount of time for the prisoners to bag up the remains and for me to explain to our panel of police and officials seated behind us what we'd found. The officials took a two-hour lunch break each day, and ended work at three so they could make it back to their office to file their reports before rush-hour traffic clogged the city streets.

Whoever had collected the remains and sorted them into what they thought were complete skeletons didn't have much knowledge of human anatomy. Most of the bags that were supposed to contain a single skeleton actually held the remains of two, three, and even four people. Evidence of more than one person might be as obvious as three right femurs and two left hip bones or as subtle as an extra tooth. In other cases, what should have been one skeleton sometimes had one hip bone from a male and the other from a female. In one case, the bone traders had mixed the remains of a six-year-old child with those of an adult man. Beyond bones and teeth, some bags contained remnants of coffin wood, one held several buttons, another an eyeglass lens, and yet another a wooden drawer pull.

On the fourth day of the exam we had a new prisoner helping us. From the Vietnamese officials we learned he was the older man arrested for collecting and trying to sell the remains we were looking at. He was small, even by Vietnamese standards, with graying hair. My guess is he was about seventy years old. I think they brought him in to witness the exam both as a lesson in humility and to show him that the remains he was dealing in were those of fellow Vietnamese, not Americans—as if he didn't know. Most of the time he sat quietly along the back wall as we moved from box to box. At one point he walked over to my table, picked up a humerus with a paper dog tag wired to it, and slowly handed it to me, saying, "Thank you." His tone and stern look seemed at odds with his words. Later that day he again walked over and, in a hushed voice nearly devoid of a Vietnamese accent, said, "Nice to meet you," before settling back in his chair. Again I was at a loss to guess the motive behind these social niceties. Both exchanges made the hair stand up on the back of my neck. From what they told us, this man was facing a minimum of seven years in jail, which at his age was probably a life sentence. I was one of the people putting him behind bars.

I think what surprised me most about the old man was that he could speak any English at all. Thinking back, I wonder how much he learned from watching us work. Our routine gave him enough time to learn some English, as I had to tell the Vietnamese officials seated in the room what we'd found so they could record it in their own notes. Of course the old man heard everything we said both in English and Vietnamese. Some of the Vietnamese officials spoke English, but to ensure that there was no miscommunication, I told the officials our findings in English while Jim stood beside me and translated what I said into Vietnamese. A trained military linguist, Jim has been translating English into Vietnamese and vice versa for decades. He can slip back and forth between the two languages without apparent effort, and he can write in both as well. Additionally, one of the younger Vietnamese officials had studied in New York and spoke English fluently. Although the officials asked the old man questions about many specimens as we worked on them, I'm not sure bringing him into the exam room was a good idea. But it was their show, and they had their own way of dealing with criminals.

We worked from eight to eleven each morning, took a two-hour lunch break, and worked again from one to three in the afternoon. Jim, Ken, and I spent one hour of our lunch break at a small restaurant just outside the compound, followed by an hour in a small room on the compound catching up on our daily reports and downloading photos onto my laptop to carry back to the CIL. Like all the other buildings on the compound, our makeshift office and break area featured bars on the windows and doors. This one, however, also contained a bust of Ho Chi Minh. Fortunately, it also held an air conditioner, which provided a pleasant respite from a sweltering exam room, which was cooled only by a couple of ceiling fans that did little more than push around hot air.

We completed our exam the following Monday and again met with the provincial deputy police chief to tell him our findings. We'd examined forty-two boxes containing seventy-six bags of remains from at least seventy-eight people. The hardest part of the exam for me was trying to figure out how many people were represented in each bag. Since almost every bag contained a skull, I chose that as the basis for determining how many people there were. Most skeletons were those of elderly men and women, as evidenced by the lightness of their bones due to osteopenia (loss of bone tissue that occurs as we age), toothless jaws, and arthritic joints. Others were children ranging in age from about six to sixteen years. Unfortunately, none of the remains had any of the characteristics we could associate with a black, white, or Asian American man.

My guess is that the bone traders had dug up Vietnamese graves, some marked and some unmarked, removed the skeletons from the ground, and carted them off to their houses, where they inadvertently combined the bones of several people, not knowing that we could tell the difference between men and women, young and old. They then put dog tag rubbings with the remains in an attempt to legitimize them. I don't think there is any way for these people to remember where they got the remains, so there is no way to return them. I doubt they made any notes or drew maps of the graves or cemeteries, so the origins of the remains are lost forever.

In all of the remains we found only one tooth with a filling. In the United States, most skeletal identifications are made based on teeth and dental records. With no dental charts, no idea of where the bone traders had dug up the remains, and no medical records to turn to, we were not able to identify even one skeleton. The families of these people might never know the grave they were visiting had been emptied by grave robbers. After our examination the remains were slated to be cremated, or, as Vietnamese say, "destroyed."

During the examination, Jim checked the names on the dog tag rubbings against a list of all missing American servicemen and found not one match. I'm sure the bone traders took the information from the plentiful supply of lost-and-found dog tags vendors sold on the streets of most cities in Vietnam.

We looked in vain for any sign among the remains that could lead us to the recovery of another American fighting man. What we saw were features common to indigenous Vietnamese—small nasal bones and round nasal openings; squared parietal bones; short, thin arm and leg bones; heavily worn teeth, many with large deposits of tartar and large cavities and, because of their curvature along the lower borders, several mandibles that rocked back and forth when placed on a flat surface. This so-called "rocker jaw" is a trait usually found in Polynesian mandibles, but we sometimes see it in people from other Asian groups. We felt profound disappointment in our inability to find evidence of Western-style dentistry, gold crowns, or root canal work; the large nasal bones with the narrow nasal opening and large nasal spines so characteristic of whites; or the nasal guttering—small grooves present at the base of the nasal opening—wide nasal openings, or facial prognathism (the forward prominence of the area surrounding the mouth) commonly seen in people of African origin.

By the end of the examination we knew we had a cross section from a Vietnamese cemetery of elderly men, women, and a few children. The bone traders had dug up the bones of at least seventy-eight people, based on the number of skulls present; the remains could have come from a hundred people or even more. There was no way for us to know the exact number without sampling each bone for DNA. Surely the people who had dug up the bones hadn't dreamed they would be caught and, worse, that the United States would send a team of experts to examine what they'd found.

Two days later we examined two more skeletons in Saigon, these found by a man who was converting a rice field to a shrimp pond. (Shrimp are a more lucrative crop than rice.) After our investigation in Dong Nai, we were skeptical that we'd have better luck finding a missing American by looking at two more skeletons. However, this case was a bit different from the others, and for two reasons. The man wasn't asking for money or relocation to the States for what he'd found. Also, there were indications that the remains might be those of two Filipino men who went missing in the area while riding a bike during the war. Although they weren't American citizens, they were there on official U.S. business and, upon their disappearance, were given a reference number just like the American MIAs. We were to examine the remains at the public security office in District 7, Saigon. It was a fifteen-minute drive from our hotel through a new housing subdivision that looked as though it had been plucked out of Hawaii, with its neatly manicured lawns, large parks, and Mediterranean-style houses. I'm sure it's the most luxurious housing development in all of Vietnam.

Arriving at the public safety office, we were led through the usual guarded gate, past heaps of stolen and recovered bicycles and motorcycles, including a Harley Davidson or two. After the usual introductions to Vietnamese authorities, we interviewed the Vietnamese man who had found the remains in June 2004. He said he'd also found a dog tag, but lost it in the river as he tried to wash it. I thought it strange that he would lose something as important as a dog tag and was skeptical about the truth of his story, but we still had to examine the remains without jumping to conclusions. We laid out the first bag, which contained a nearly complete skeleton of an Asian male. The amount of dental wear and poorly done gold-crowned teeth suggested he was Vietnamese. It wasn't the quality of dentistry that we usually see in the United States. The second set of remains was packed into a fertilizer bag. These, too, came from an adult Asian man. Also in the bag was what appeared to be a .32-caliber (7.65-millimeter) rifle bullet that the farmer found in the pelvis, although I found no obvious sign of a gunshot wound to either hip or sacrum. My interest was piqued when I saw his large mandible. The shape of the lower jaw just wasn't what I was used to seeing in Vietnam. He also had large nasal bones, a narrow nasal opening, and a small but prominent nasal spine. Although the overall shape of his skull was Asian, some features weren't consistent with those of Vietnamese remains. Ken, our dentist, examined the jaws and teeth and commented on a gold-colored "picture frame"–style crown on this man's upper right central incisor, one of his two front teeth. Surely it would have been visible when he smiled, and family members or friends might recognize it. We asked the Vietnamese people watching us in the exam room if they had ever seen a similar crown in Vietnam. No one had. We knew we were looking at something uncommon in Vietnamese dentistry. It was, however, common among other racial groups, including Filipinos, so we thought we might be on the right track.

Picking up the man's skull, I noticed that it was broken in many places, suggesting that trauma to his head caused his death. Not knowing the circumstances of the loss of the two men in the war, we erred on the side of caution and forwarded the remains to Hanoi for further analysis. Sending them on to Hanoi would also give us time to see if either man had dental records. If they did, we would probably see some annotations of their crown work.

So after examining a total of eighty skeletons over a period of nearly two weeks, we finally had a possible lead on two men. Although they were foreign nationals, not Americans, we would still follow up on the case, hoping to send two more men home from the war. I was disappointed at our failure to find even a single American, but we must examine many skeletons to find one of our MIAs. We will keep searching, as the motto of our organization says, "until they are home."

At the end of my stay in Saigon I headed back to Bangkok to meet with Dr. Porntip Rojanasunan, known to some as Dr. Death. The director of the newly established Missing Persons Centre in Thailand, she's a forensic pathologist and author of twenty-three books. Dr. Rojanasunan has not only changed the way people look at death and crime scene investigation in Thailand, she has also become a Thai celebrity and household name. I had met with the leaders of the Central Institute of Forensic Science several times and had been asked to serve as a forensic consultant, providing suggestions on the design of their new building, as well as equipment they would need to replicate what we do at the CIL. These forensic scientists considered the CIL to be the gold standard in the field and wanted to model their facilities and methods after us. Having an entire country follow the lead of our lab is quite an honor.

AUTHOR'S NOTE

Looking over my shoulder, I sometimes wonder how that boy from Appalachia, with so many things working against him, ever made it to the Smithsonian and the Central Identification Laboratory. I also realize that I never set out to be an author, a university lecturer or, least of all, a forensic scientist. But of course it didn't just happen.

This book, like its author, rose up from humble beginnings. What began as a few notes scribbled here and there, intended to while away the hours in a day in the field, became a journal with drawings, then a more polished manuscript, and finally, more than a decade later, a book.

I hope I've accomplished my goal of entertaining you with some of the most interesting cases in my career. Along the way, I've also tried to interject a bit of my own background . . . my likes, my dislikes, and what makes me tick as a person. I didn't include this personal and sometimes embarrassing information to make anyone flinch or put a tear in anyone's eye, but to show how and why one person's career and passion developed. My hope is that that's one of the things that sets this book apart from most others.

So while I've tried to give you a slice of what it's like to be a forensic anthropologist, I've also tried to lure those of you who are interested in mysteries, puzzles, and CSI to spend a few hours with me, to find out what goes into the making of a forensic scientist—a "bone detective"—and how we go about solving mysteries. The best part of it all is that these are true cases—not television, not Hollywood, not a novel. In this book, there is no need to develop sinister characters, innocent victims, or deceptive plots that unfold with incredible accuracy—the cases you've read here didn't spring from my imagination. They exist in reality . . . in your city, your town, perhaps your backyard. The protagonist is no supersleuth or genius who re-creates crime scenes and solves ancient puzzles in an hour, but a person like you, filled with curiosity, wonder, and all the normal things that make us who we are. I guess you could say this is life mimicking fiction and not the other way around.

I've often been asked why I do what I do, and the best answer I can think of is because I love it. I love the mystery, the detective work, the excitement, and the adventure. I assume you read this because you're interested in the same things; I honestly hope you found them in these pages.

ROBERT MANN, PH.D.

JUNE 2005

INDEX

ABOUT THE AUTHORS

DR. ROBERT MANN received his Ph.D. in physical anthropology from the University of Hawaii. In 1987, Dr. Mann was assistant director in pathology/assistant morgue director at the University of Tennessee Medical School in Memphis before accepting a position as an anthropologist at the Smithsonian Institution from 1988 to 1992. Dr. Mann has worked at the CIL for thirteen years. He participated in twenty-nine Joint Forensic Reviews in Hanoi, two in North Korea, one in Russia, and one in Latvia, where he examined remains suspected of being American MIAs. He has published two books on bone disease and more than ninety-five papers in the popular and scientific literature, including *American Antiquity, American Journal of Physical Anthropology, Annals of the Carnegie Museum, Forensic Science International, International Journal of Osteoarchaeology, Journal of Craniofacial Genetics and Developmental Biology, Journal of Forensic Sciences,* and *Oral Surgery, Oral Medicine and Oral Pathology.* Dr. Mann is one of only seventy-three scientists certified as a diplomate by the American Board of Forensic Anthropology.

MIRYAM EHRLICH WILLIAMSON is a former newspaper reporter and magazine writer. She is the author of a book on artificial intelligence, five books on health and longevity, and several published poems and short stories. Her work has won awards from the Associated Press and the American Medical Writers Association.